IN THE SHADOW
OF
MOUNT McKINLEY

In the shadow of Mount McKinley

IN THE SHADOW OF MOUNT McKINLEY

by William N. Beach

Illustrated by Carl Rungius

THE DERRYDALE PRESS

LANHAM AND NEW YORK

THE DERRYDALE PRESS

Published in the United States of America
by The Derrydale Press
4720 Boston Way, Lanham, Maryland 20706

Distributed by NATIONAL BOOK NETWORK, INC.

Copyright © 1992 BY THE DERRYDALE PRESS, INC.
First Derrydale paperback printing with french folds 2000

Library of Congress Cataloging-in-Publication Data

Beach, William N. (William Nicholas)
   In the shadow of mount McKinley / by William N. Beach ; foreword by
John Burnham ; introduction by Robert Sterling Yard; illustrated from paint-
ings by Carl Rungius and from photographs by the author.
      p. cm.
   ISBN 1-56833-155-X (alk. paper)
   1. McKinley, Mount, Region (Alaska)—Description and travel. 2. McKinley,
Mount, Region (Alaska)—Discovery and exploration. 3. Natural history—
Alaska—McKinley, Mount, Region. 4. Beach, William N. (William
Nicholas)—Journeys—Alaska—McKinley, Mount, Region. 5. Big game ani-
mals—Alaska—McKinley, Mount, Region. I. Title.
F912.M2 B32 2000
917.98'3—DC21   99-044075

♾™ The paper used in this publication meets the minimum requirements of
American National Standard for Information Sciences—Permanence of
Paper for Printed Library Materials, ANSI/NISO Z39.48-1992.
Manufactured in the United States of America.

DEDICATED TO

MY WIFE

WHO ACCOMPANIED ME

ON MANY OF MY WANDERINGS

IN THE WILDERNESS

PREFACE

THE pages that follow are but a chronicle of my various wanderings on the north side of the Alaskan Range within the shadows of that great mountain, McKinley. It is one of the choice sections of that marvelous garden spot of the North American continent, Alaska. A large part of this country may be reached today without undue exertion, and it is my hope that those who read these pages may become sufficiently interested to go and see the wonders and beauties that await there.

My thanks go out first to my wife who has put up with my vagaries and wanderings and has followed me on many of my wild trips. Then to Jim Steese and John Gotwals, former president and chief engineer respectively of the Alaska Road Commission, whose efforts made possible my first successful trip on the north side of the Range; and to Jim Gibson, Jim Burrows, Andy Simons and Slim Avery, soldiers of fortune and my associates who helped engineer the Mount Dall expedition.

Stephen R. Capps, of the United States Geological Survey, is entitled to the credit for my wanderings through Ptarmigan Valley and Rainy Pass, and helped check up my manuscript.

A word for Jack Lean who with smiles and good nature twice helped us work our way up the miserable Skwentna River.

I am grateful to my old friend Carl Rungius who has shown great interest in my work and has permitted me to reproduce some of his paintings, and to John Burnham who read my manuscript and made constructive suggestions thereon.

To George Godley and Marcus Daly, who were willing to follow my sketchy plans and accompany me, I extend my thoughts and thanks for their confidence in my ability to carry on.

To my many friends in Alaska who always stood ready to help, and to Robert Sterling Yard, who has advised me concerning my manuscript and its presentation, I owe a deep debt of gratitude.

May you have one grain of the pleasure in reading these pages that I had in making the journeys they chronicle.

W. N. B.

CONTENTS

LIST OF ILLUSTRATIONS

LIST OF ILLUSTRATIONS

LIST OF ILLUSTRATIONS

Facing page

LIST OF ILLUSTRATIONS

FOREWORD

By John Burnham

I HAVE *always admired Billy Beach for his sand. He is a big fellow physically, who in the struggle of the business world came out on top, but the kind of game he was in as a rule burns out a man early and unfits him for that other kind of struggle with the forces of nature required of the hunter and explorer. Here too, however, Beach has been successful. He has crossed the white, unmapped places, forded wild rivers, climbed mountains standing on edge and stood the gaff. To the frontiersman who specializes in wilderness travel Beach is a puzzle. He just cannot see how he does it. But he has to hand it to Beach for the results he accomplishes.*

The casual reader will not appreciate the difficulties Beach has overcome. He conveys too much the idea it is easy, and that his party gets over the tundra and mountains of the North much as a rider would travel the bridle paths of Central Park. Believe me, there is a great difference!

While Beach has followed the lure of the trail in many countries, including Europe and Africa, he has specialized in the big game territory of North America—Newfoundland, New Brunswick, Alberta, Wyoming, British Columbia, Yukon Territory and Alaska. In Alaska he is probably the best known sportsman of any. I can think of no other outsider who has so large an acquaintance in our Arctic empire.

In all his travels Beach has carried cameras with him, and he has made photography a major interest in his hunting trips. He has accumulated a wonderful collection of game pictures, both moving and still. Years ago he brought back from the Cassiar some of the very best moving pictures of the day of white goats, mountain sheep and other game animals of that country. The men who knew realized that a worth-while new hunter-photographer had arrived to give pleasure to those whose love is game and the far places. Since then, almost every year Beach has brought out pictures to delight his following. His work is always interesting.

Beach's present book is devoted to the high country of the Alaskan Range surrounding and including Mount McKinley, our highest mountain in North America. No other writer has seen so much of this tremendously rough and sublimely lovely region. The country described is larger than Switzerland, with higher mountains and greater glaciers, and in many respects even more startlingly scenic. It is a region about which every American should be informed. To all who have the wanderlust I commend this book.

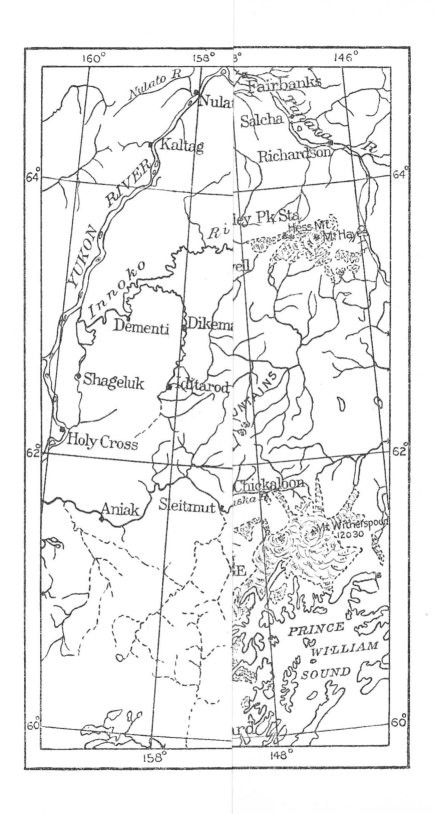

THE MOUNTAIN CLIMAX OF NORTH AMERICA

By ROBERT STERLING YARD

FOR the layman to appreciate fully this story of a big game hunter's explorations and observations in the shadow of Mount McKinley, it is desirable not only to locate the Alaskan Range with whose gigantic climax it deals, but to discover its position and relationships in the Pacific mountain system.

An important part of the area which the author crossed in his several expeditions here recounted, whose big game animals he closely observed, photographing them in motion, and here reports upon, lies partly within Mount McKinley National Park, much of which is still little known except to the geologist and the explorer. Even the maps of this untamed wilderness are still in process of making. Mount McKinley itself is 20,300 feet in altitude, and the plain north of it, upon which Mr. Beach and his parties spent much time, averages about 3,000 feet in altitude. To the observer at its foot, this gigantic mountain, most of it covered with ice and snow, is a marvelous, almost an appalling spectacle.

The Pacific mountain system, of which the McKinley group is the superb climax, consists of a belt of mountain lands fifty to two hundred miles wide, entering the United States from Mexico on the south and paralleling the Pacific in a north-westerly direction through this country and Canada into Alaska. There it curves westward and southwestward, ending in the Aleutian Islands. The McKinley group is at the northwestward bend.

The system as a whole includes very many ranges, often parallel. In the United States, the most celebrated are the sculptured granite Sierra Nevadas and the ice-peaked volcanic Cascades. Passing northwesterly into Canada, it enters Alaska by way of the glacier-edged Coast Range and straightens out toward the west into the Kenai Mountains and the Aleutian Range. A sharper, high curve paralleling this bend north of it consists of the Nutzotin Mountains and the gigantic white Alaska Range. Between the Nutzotins on the north and Chugach on the south rise two connecting mountain masses, the Wrangells on the east and Talkeetnas on the west, between which are the flat gravels of the Copper River Basin.

It is with comparatively a small area of the great Alaska Range including its loftiest summits and the lowlands north of them, that this story concerns itself.

About two hundred miles south of this double curve the Gulf of Alaska pushes northward from the Pacific coastline, paralleling crests tributary to the Gulf on the north; two estuaries of large size penetrate the mainland, furnishing access by sea to the interior. Between these, which are Prince William Sound on the east and Cook Inlet on the west rises the mountainous Kenai Peninsula through which, from Seward on Resurrection Bay, the Alaska Railroad runs northward up the Susitna River, crosses the Alaska Range through Broad Pass, and descends the vast central Yukon depression as far as Fairbanks on the Tanana River.

From the mergence of the Talkeetna River with the Susitna northward to Broad Pass, the railroad roughly parallels the great mountain climax of the Alaska Range, whose loftiest peaks, Dall, Russell, Foraker and McKinley may be glimpsed on clear days from climbing trains.

Reference to the map will show that the Susitna River and its tributaries drain the entire southern slope of the climax sector of the Alaska Range. Its principal western confluent, the Yentna River, taps several summit passes through confluents of its own. A branch, known as Happy River, of its farthest western branch, the Skwentna, has its origin in Rainy Pass. Between these two principal passes, Broad on the east and Rainy on the west, perhaps no more than 175 miles as the crow flies, rises the great climax of the Alaska Range, at whose climax point is Mount McKinley National Park.

The southern front of this central group is a battlement of ice. Attempts to climb McKinley from here have ended in ice precipices 4,000 feet high. Tremendous glaciers descending from this originate the confluents of the Susitna River.

The northern front of this group presents a serrated ridge from 7,000 to 10,000 feet high from which spring the greater peaks, Mount Dall rising to 9,000 feet, Mount Russell to 11,350 feet, Mount Foraker to 17,000 feet, and Mount McKinley to 20,300 feet. The glaciers north and south of this giant group are among the largest in inland Alaska.

That the northern front of the great range is less precipitous than the southern front is not apparent to the eye of the traveler. It is a more appalling spectacle because its base is more closely approachable and can be looked up at from a lower altitude. It is by the north face that McKinley has been climbed.

The north and west fronts drop abruptly to a plateau which in places is only 2,500 feet above sea level. Its surface, except where broken by stream valleys and glaciers, is remarkably level for miles north to the rough hills of the Kantishna country, and west, but the valleys are steep and broad.

Just as the many tributaries of the Susitna drain the south front of the great central mountain group, so do those of the Kuskokwim carry off most of the turbulent glacial waters of the north front; but the Tanana River, an impressive branch of the mighty Yukon, secures a goodly share through its tributary, the Kantishna River, the formal origin of which is Lake Minchumina. There are few lakes in central Alaska.

Mount McKinley National Park, here located, includes an area of 2,645 square miles ranging in altitudes from McKinley summit on the Park's south border to valleys nearly 18,000 feet below. The gigantic ice-fronted mountain face which constitutes its northern part yields to foothills between which glaciers of great size sweep into the flat plateaus, where streams of water succeed the ice. The lower Park country contains, besides the flat plateau, many rough hills and low mountains, and its streams are numerous and turbulent.

During the summer the glacial streams are subject to daily changes in volume, swelling largely in the afternoon with the meltings of the day. Warm sunny days bring floods toward their close. During the winter, with glaciers solidly frozen, mountain-run streams become nearly dry.

On the lower hills are countless mountain sheep, and on the grassy plains caribou in bands sometimes exceeding a thousand.

The Nenana River on the east of this region, down whose course the railroad drops from Broad Pass to the Tanana, gets almost all its waters from the Nenana and Yanert Glaciers which, curiously, lie on the mountain's high southern flank, discharging nevertheless into the northern basin.

The Nenana is a swift, powerful stream flowing between steep banks, and too deep for horses to wade. Its principal tributary from the west, the Teklanika, also originates in glaciers descending from the McKinley group. Farther west the Sushanna, Toklat and others of larger size drain also from glaciers and are subject to daily variations in volume which often trouble and puzzle summer visitors. Still farther west the Kantishna, born of glaciers but slowing into a muddy stream of moderate speed as it approaches the Tanana River, compares in volume and importance with the Nenana. Its lower reaches are navigable.

The basis of the plateau and its valleys under the grassy soil is gravel and sand brought from the mountains by glaciers and distributed by streams. The coarser materials naturally were deposited nearer the mountains. As the streams descend northward toward the Tanana these are succeeded by sands. Forests of spruce and poplar are found in the greater valleys to the north.

West of the Kantishna Basin, all streams draining the Alaska Range on its north and west sides discharge into the great Kuskokwim.

This is the region principally covered in Mr. Beach's several journeys herein described. Tracing these geographic features on the accompanying map will facilitate the comprehension and enjoyment of the story.

The region as a whole constitutes the highlands of Alaska, but it is a small part indeed of the great whole, which covers, from its eastern to its western limits, an area as extended, east and west, as that between the Georgia and California coasts, and north and south, between the Canada border and the Gulf of Mexico. The area of Alaska equals one fifth of the United States. Imagine Massachusetts, Rhode Island, Connecticut, New York, New Jersey, Pennsylvania, Delaware, Maryland, Ohio, Indiana, Illinois, Missouri, Iowa, Michigan, Wisconsin and Minnesota combined! It will take all these to equal Alaska.

The part that we touch in this remarkable story is comparatively small, but it is the Land of Adventure. From the glaciers of the Gulf of Alaska, source of icebergs, to those pouring down from the slopes of McKinley, from the broad plateaus of the Kantishna country with its roving thousands of caribou, to the icy summits of North America's loftiest mountain, is a country which challenges the oft return of those who love great spaces, vast spectacles and wild animals in astounding numbers.

It was to see, study and motion-picture "big game" which Mr. Beach thinks was the reason for his four laborious journeys to this all-but-unknown difficult wilderness; but the readers of his book will disagree with him. It was the passion for exploring the unknown, conquering the unconquerable, that underlay all his big game pursuings from their beginning, many years ago, in the eastern mountains. He was an Adventurer always, and adventure, not the bag, was his real reward.

Our great national park of the future, Mount McKinley, possesses an extraordinarily numerous population of wild animals of large size, especially caribou and mountain sheep, which have been conserved in time to preserve them without startling diminution for a future which will exhibit few elsewhere. The University of California has studied them in the park itself, and similar scientific expeditions will increase in number and results with the decades. Mr. Beach's chapter on his pursuit, in all parts of the country where they are found, of the same game animals which he found in the McKinley country, and his differentiations of their varieties and habits under varying geographic conditions, make an interesting and valuable contribution to knowledge.

The experiences of the Beach parties will be valuable, also, to those whom the growing fame of Mount McKinley National Park tempt there under the impression that the great mountain and famous wild animal exhibit are comfortably accessible to visitors unprepared and unequipped to rough it. It will require many times the government appropriations available in the year of this writing, 1931, well used for some years, to warrant official invitation to the Park to all comers.

The author's experience with big game animals as a whole

affords still further proofs, should any be necessary, of the destructive way of Civilization with a new country. His recent experience of shooting in Scotland where, after centuries more of it than we have had here, there is more big game comfortably available far nearer home than there is even at immense distances here, suggests a policy that America will do well to consider.

Ketchikan

A beautiful scenic paradise,
Richardson Highway

CHAPTER II

STORY OF THE EXPEDITION OF 1922

O N a cold day in January, 1919, George Godley and I were seated before a large open fireplace in Belmore Browne's studio in one of the Oranges in New Jersey. The snow was crunching and crackling outside, while within the soft glow of the fire helped carry our imagination to that far off country, Alaska, as our host unfolded to us his experiences on that great adventure, "The Conquest of Mount McKinley."

It is needless to say that we fell victims to the fascination of his recital and, as we started back to the city, acknowledged ourselves converts and began planning at once, not for the summit of the great mountain, but for the mighty wilderness from which it rises. Immediately we secured all possible information on the country and the means of getting there. The Governor of Alaska, at that time Thomas L. Riggs, in due course came to New York and we elicited his help in framing up the trip; but even this did not suffice. Several other channels of information were also followed through to disappointment. Our Mount McKinley trip, like all smoke, went into the air. After all our efforts we came to the conclusion that this was a trip most difficult to plan, and even more so to carry out successfully. It was quite a surprise to find how little was really known about the great central uplift of the Alaskan Range in which McKinley is located; and even less about the country on the north side of the range, notwithstanding that much of it had been made a national park in 1917.

In years gone by Indians trading skins on the Yukon told of the mountain all covered with ice which they called "Denali" (the great) and of his wife (Mount Foraker) and children (the various smaller peaks). Very little mention had been made of this huge ice mountain by the early explorers of this North country, though here and there a large ice peak is spoken of as rising high above the range. Finally, in 1889, Frank Densmore made an extensive prospecting trip to the north side of the range and described the large mountain in more or less detail. For several years it was known as "Densmore's Mountain." In 1896, W. A. Dickey made a general exploration of this country and was so greatly impressed by the great mass of ice and its majestic grandeur that he decided it should be named after President McKinley, and since that time it has retained this name. Dickey estimated the height at 20,000 feet, which was afterwards determined to be within 300 feet of the correct height.

It was not long before a keen interest was shown by several parties in attempting to climb McKinley. The Lloyd party, consisting of five sourdoughs, Tom Lloyd, Charles McGonogill, William Taylor, Peter Anderson and Bob Horne, made an attempt, and it is conceded and thoroughly believed by all Alaskans that Taylor and Anderson reached the top of the

South peak, which is not quite as high as the North peak, and planted a flagpole on which they raised the American flag.

Then there was Dr. Cook's famous fake climb which has been thoroughly shown up. The Hershel-Parker-Browne party, after two unsuccessful attempts, finally, on their third trial, came within a few hundred feet of the extreme height of the North peak. Weather conditions impossible to overcome were the main factor in their failing to reach the absolute top of the mountain on their last try. In the following year the Archdeacon Stuck party was successful in making the climb, and were fortunate in that marvelous weather gave them every opportunity to make careful observations and determinations as to altitude, which was settled upon as 20,300 feet.

With all this romance current, and marvelous tales besides of the enormous quantities of game that had been seen by various persons all along the northern slopes of the Alaskan Range, can you blame two men, weak-minded and readily fascinated by new country, for yielding to the desire to explore our great country's last frontier?

As I have said, our first planning of the trip resulted in failure, and so we packed away our thoughts until a more propitious opportunity might offer. In the winter of 1921 Colonel James G. Steese, President of the Alaska Road Commission, visiting New York, happened in one afternoon for a call before his return to Washington. Naturally, the Mount McKinley country was mentioned, and he suggested that I should come to his room at the Astor and meet Major John C. Gotwals, his assistant, who, he said, on a reconnaissance during the previous summer, had made the very trip I was talking about. Over to the Astor I went, and finally in came the Major and plunged, after cordial greetings, into an outline of his adventure. Then followed the question of the possibility of my being able to make it, which the Major met with assurances that there were no difficulties in the way that he could see. He even suggested that he might be able to let me have the government pack outfit which he had used on his trip, together with Guy Burch, the packer who had been with him.

The Major returned North within a few days and I did not have an opportunity to go further into details with him. Shortly after his return to Juneau I received a letter to the effect that they could arrange to let me have the government outfit on a proper rental basis as they were not likely to have any use for the horses from August to October, and that Guy Burch would go along. Telegrams then began to fly about— to Bill Slimpert, guide, and Walter Eng, Chinaman cook, both of whom had been out with me on a former trip. Then came the question of a companion. George Godley, who had been on several trips with me, was out of reach on the Alaskan Peninsula after brown bear. I came in touch with several other friends, but my desire was to reach George as I knew what I could expect from him, and I realized that the chances were that possibly we would not find the greatest Alaskan wilderness a bed of roses. Wires to various points in the North, after several days' delay, brought back an answer. As I expected, he was willing to throw in with any wild scheme I might have in mind, and would meet me in Vancouver.

I had arranged to ship eight horses from Seattle to Mc-Kinley Park Station (Riley Creek), the point from which we planned to start for the range; but I received a wire from the Major advising me not to ship them as we could make better arrangements in Alaska. On Wednesday, July 26th, my wife, a friend of ours, and the writer arrived at Vancouver via the Trans-Canada of the Canadian Pacific Railroad, and shortly afterwards George put in an appearance, making our party complete. We sailed that evening on board the *Princess Louise* for Juneau, Alaska. The three days passed quite rapidly as the weather was fine and the ship most comfortable.

On board were Lord Byng and his family who were on their way to the Yukon. Studying this democratic gentleman of old England was most interesting. At Ketchikan the town turned out to give him a royal welcome; a large automobile was at the wharf to take him up to a reception; likewise a band. The General piled his family into the automobile, but personally dived into the crowd and walked through the town, showing keen interest in the throng crowding around the occupants of the automobile. Little did they suspect that the great General of Vimy was one of them.

We debarked at Juneau where we had three days to wait for the steamer *Northwestern* of the Alaskan Line on which we were to proceed still further north. Our stay there passed, if anything, too rapidly as we had many old acquaintances to look up and renew, amongst them our old friend Billy Taylor, one of Juneau's famous citizens.

On the evening of August 1st we set out for Cordova on the steamer *Northwestern*. The trip across the Gulf was most pleasant, the weather clear and calm. We had on board General Richardson, formerly head of the Alaska Road Commission and now stationed in Washington. Major Gotwals was with him and hoped to join us after he had completed a tour of inspection. Messrs. Knickerbocker and Bunch, officers of the Alaskan Steamship Company, with their families, were also on board on an inspection tour of their northern properties. The sun had been our constant companion since leaving New York, but as we neared the entrance to Cordova Harbor rain began to fall, and continued steadily.

General Richardson and Major Gotwals remained on board as they were to start over the trail from Valdez, while we intended going to Chitina over the Copper River Railroad, and from there take the trail to Fairbanks. Owing to the heavy rain we decided to wait overnight at Cordova. It was fortunate we did, for the next morning we started by train up the Copper River with the clouds broken up and the sun coming through.

The trip up the Copper River was most interesting, as magnificent snow-covered mountains towered on both sides, with the Copper River boiling through canyons every little while, and then opening out over immense sections of the country. At the Miles and Childs Glaciers we left the train and with motion picture cameras tramped over the rough glacier cobbles until we reached an advantageous spot from which we shot numerous pictures.

Toward afternoon we pulled into Chitina and were met at the station by Oscar Breedman, the proprietor of the Hotel Chitina and the most prominent citizen of that town. After the usual greetings we were handed a telegram from Major Gotwals at Valdez, informing us that Van Kirk, the outfitter, from whom we were to receive additional horses had decided that if we wanted his horses we would have to buy them, and at a price out of all reason. George and I discussed the question from all angles and decided we would have to get in touch with the Major before deciding. Breedman had all arrangements made for our trip across the Richardson Highway to Fairbanks, and rather hesitatingly said that he had Billy Frame to drive, and advised our going in a Ford.

"Of course," said Oscar, "you may have my car (a seven passenger Kissel), but my advice is to go in the Ford."

We met Billy Frame and after a short talk left the matter to him. The Ford was the choice and at once we began to pack up. The load consisted of two cases (twenty gallons) of gasoline, two motion picture outfits, extra springs and tires, various spare parts, and baggage for five people reduced to a minimum. While these details were being looked after we were playing with a couple of grizzly bear cubs that belonged to Oscar Breedman. They were so fine a pair of pets that I felt they should be secured for the New York Zoological Park, and after a short negotiation purchased them to be shipped upon my coming out. I am glad to say they are now enjoying good health there.

We christened our charge "Elizabeth" as, five in all, we closely stowed ourselves aboard, and with a soothing push on the pedal by Billy Frame, our caravansary started on its perilous way at five-thirty. It seemed advisable to get under way even at that hour as it did not get dark until late, and we felt that though we only made Lower Tonsina, where Jake Nefsted ran a comfortable roadhouse, at least we were on our way. The trip, somewhat over thirty miles, was through a beautiful scenic paradise with Mount Wrangell, Mount Drum and Mount Sanford in the distance on the right, and the Copper River Valley always ahead or to the side. We found the road in fair condition, and arrived only too soon at the roadhouse. Our stay at Lower Tonsina was made pleasant and comfortable by good meals and good beds, so that five-thirty came only too quickly the next morning. Billy stepped hard on Elizabeth's accelerator and we slowly drew out on the trail with a "Bon Voyage" from Jake Nefsted.

The scenery became more inspiring and absorbing as each twist and turn of the road was negotiated. We passed several roadhouses, some deserted, and reached Willow Creek, the junction point with the main road from Valdez to Fairbanks, after passing a government construction crew consisting of motor truck, tractor and horse truck. Upon reaching Copper Center, where there is a telegraph station, we tried to locate the Richardson-Gotwals party, but there was no word from them.

We were quickly on our way again, and after traveling some eight miles passed the Tazlina Roadhouse and crossed the Tazlina River over a splendid bridge, one of the longest on the trip. Following along the Copper River we finally came to the Gulkana River, which we crossed on a bridge, and shortly drew up at Mrs. Griffith's Gulkana Roadhouse for lunch. This was the most elaborate and best-fitted roadhouse that we saw, and Mrs. Griffith, besides being a most kindly woman, gave us one of the best meals on the trip. Gulkana is one of the trading posts and there was quite an Indian settlement nearby. We saw quantities of fur, including several large grizzly skins. Our regrets were that we were not able to put in two or three days at this spot, but we had many miles yet to make before starting into the mountains; and so after a most sumptuous repast we piled into Elizabeth and were again on our way, headed north.

From Gulkana we started the long steady northward rise up the Copper Valley towards the pass into the great basin of the Yukon. We were making good time and the road, though in spots rough, nevertheless was not bad. We passed the Sourdough Roadhouse in the early afternoon and from that point through Hogan we had some pretty rough going; but Elizabeth took her medicine in a most ladylike manner, and we came through without mishap.

Towards evening we came to Meier's Roadhouse, mile 172, and put up there for the night. We found that Mrs. Griffith had telephoned of our coming, so Mrs. Meier made ice cream and fresh cake to top off a fine dinner. It was certainly pleasing to see how cordially we were welcomed at all our stops. The food was excellent, and a comfortable, clean bed helped us rest up for the trials of another day. Taking numerous moving pictures of the country greatly hampered our speed, but nevertheless we kept ahead of our schedule. We had located Major Gotwals and though we expected he would overtake us we seemed to hold our position. The evening passed to the strains of the phonograph, opera and jazz, mixed with an occasional tale by Mine Host,

Meier. An early start the next morning saw us still climbing, and sixteen miles further on we reached Paxson's Roadhouse and Telegraph Station. We here learned that General Richardson and Major Gotwals had passed the night at Gulkana.

At Paxson's we had reached the summit of the pass between the Copper River Basin on the south and the long slope northward into the Yukon basin. At Summit Lake, Isabelle Pass and Bell Glacier could be seen in the distance. The scenery had been increasingly gorgeous for several days. Now every mile seemed to surpass its predecessor, and when, just across the summit, we reached the beginning of the north-flowing Delta River and had our first view of the heart of the Alaskan Range, we realized that even the finest we had seen before could not compare with what was now unfolding.

Six miles beyond the summit we came to McCallum's Telegraph Station, and as a tire conveniently blew out at this spot we had time to visit the operator and secure the news of the day. We found that, though the Major had gained slightly on us, his stops at the road construction camps were sufficient to keep him from overhauling us before arrival at Fairbanks.

Following down the valley of the Delta River we came into the roadhouse at Rapids in good time for lunch. The weather was quite warm and the flies were out in force to the great discomfort of some of the members of the party. We were told that this was a wonderful spot to start on a hunt; that sheep, caribou and bear could be readily secured almost in the backyard, while moose were only a little less conveniently located. After our refreshing repast we were off

Paxson's, Richardson Highway

Summit Lake with Bell Glacier in the distance,
Richardson Highway

again and still traveled through the most wonderful scenery imagination could picture.

The Alaskan Range was constantly changing with the sun and seemed to stand out more majestic and inspiring than when first it came to our eyes. Some thirty miles further on we started to climb a high hill surrounded by beautiful grass-covered country with an abundance of the fine Alaskan wild flowers. After a long pull we came to the top of what is called "Donnelly's Dome." On the down grade an open culvert produced a sharp crack. "The front spring has gone," was Billy Frame's only comment. Before we realized what had happened Billy was at work and by actual timing had the new spring in place and ourselves again under way in thirty-five minutes. Shortly after six o'clock we pulled into McCarty where a ferry crosses the Tanana River into which the Delta here empties. I had been anxious for some time to meet John Hajdukovich, the proprietor of the McCarty Roadhouse, and so we decided to have supper. We then crossed the Tanana River and pushed on some twenty miles further to Richardson where we spent the night.

As we descended the mountain side into Richardson, the Alaskan Range turned a deep mother of pearl, diffused with a pink glow, as the sun gradually dipped below the horizon. If the picture could have been actually reproduced it would have been scoffed at as unreal. As we were absorbed in that magnificent setting there came to us those words of Robert Service:

"I've watched the big husky sun wallow
In crimson and gold, and grow dim."

We drew up before the roadhouse at nine-thirty, all under the spell of that fascinating northland in its glorious setting.

It was shortly after five next morning when we were out gazing again at the snowclad Alaskan Range. Could we capture that wonderful early morning view? The motion picture camera was unloaded and many feet of film exposed in the hope that success would be ours, but, sad to relate, the mountains did not show up; only the nearby views such as the gardens and the town of Richardson came out quite clearly.

It was with some misgivings that we departed from our genial host, J. W. McCluskey, for we understood that the worst section of road lay between Richardson and Fairbanks; in fact we had been under way but a short time before discovering a specially rough and rutty section. Knowing that Major Gotwals would be interested in a reproduction of the disappearing mud holes, we set up the camera and proceeded to reel off Elizabeth's capers. As a climax she plunged into a deep hole, gave a few balks, and settled. George came brilliantly to the rescue, and with his added man-power our faithful beast of burden gave a violent lurch, much to the discomfort of the inmates, and bounced out, proceeding thereafter peacefully over a more even way, for the bad section we had been expecting had recently been turned into a splendid boulevard over which we bowled at a thirty-mile clip, entering the main street of Fairbanks in some style, and drawing up in front of the Nordale Hotel at half-past twelve.

After registering and being assigned comfortable rooms, George and I started out to find Bill Slimpert, one of our guides whom we had last heard from at the Pioneer Hotel.

The day was a typical scorching tropical sunbaker, and the fluid was flowing quite freely from our pores. Glancing at a thermometer we were not at all benefitted by noticing the mercury at something over 98°. "So this is Alaska, the land of ice and snow," came to our thoughts.

We found Bill comfortably camped in an armchair at the Pioneer Hotel with Jim Gibson, another one of our explorers. Well, it took him about three seconds to begin his tale of woe. Our outfit had dwindled to four Government horses and one of these had been badly kicked by his buddy. Van Kirk, the man who had offered to furnish us with the additional horses, had decided that he intended retiring from such an unsavory business as operating a pack outfit, but would sell out to deserving parties. That meant us, and the price asked was many times the value of his highly efficient, well-equipped beasts. We realized that it was our move next, especially as our friend declared that he had many offers for his outfit.

We appealed to several owners of horseflesh in Fairbanks and neighboring towns only to discover a shortage and strong climbing market. It went against the grain to be held up by this Northern pirate, and a severe mental combat was going on within us; but at all times we realized that unless we climbed down and decided to take our medicine our trip would fall through. We awaited the arrival of the Major, and, after easing our minds in a conference with him, decided to go as cheerfully as possible to the slaughter.

We made many friends in Fairbanks whose kindness and thoughtfulness will ever linger in our minds as one of the pleasant events of our journey.

Climbing aboard the gas car on the morning of August 9th at the Government Railroad Station, we bade good-bye to Fairbanks and were off for Nenana. The trip was quite uneventful except for several stops to shoo off the right of way bunches of partridges that seemed intent on self-destruction.

Arriving at the Tanana River we transferred to a large gas boat that was to take us to Nenana, the bridge across the Tanana being then under construction. At Nenana we were met by Mike Cooney, the proprietor and owner of Cooney's Hotel, the St. Regis of the city. Mike had been busy trying to help us out in securing horses but had not been over successful, though his endeavors were earnest, and his condemnation of the action of those who were holding us up was both strong and emphatic. We had met Carl White at Fairbanks, and when he heard our predicament he offered to loan us some horses he had; but for their being on his ranch unshod, which would have meant several days delay, we would have taken up his kind offer. The afternoon was well occupied in ordering additional provisions and wandering helplessly about the streets of Nenana in a sort of dogged hope that we might, in some dark corner, stumble across a hidden pack outfit. Needless to say, our search availed us naught.

The next morning Mr. Hansen, the Superintendent of the railroad, offered to run us on to Mount McKinley Park Station in his speeder, a Ford automobile mounted on car wheels, and we accepted the offer, though down in our hearts we were sure he would balk when he saw the outfit. Shortly after nine o'clock on a bright sunshiny morning we pulled up to the speeder and loaded thereon, besides our five selves,

two moving picture outfits, several small duffle bags and a
case (ten gallons) of gasoline for emergencies; this, in addition to Superintendent Hansen at the wheel with his dog
comfortably settled in the front. It seemed to me to be a
fairly good-sized load, but our genial host informed us that
the speeder was only partly filled. Some distance down the
road we picked up the doctor and he journeyed with us to
Healey where a patient awaited his arrival. It was amazing
how smoothly this adjusted Ford slipped over the rails; at
times the speedometer showed forty to fifty miles without
any vibration. Evidently it could cover the ground with
greater speed and less effort than the standard equipment.

The road passes through a beautiful stretch of country
north of McKinley National Park, with mountains and wonderful streams all about. Following a winding course, we
entered a marvelous canyon (Sheep Canyon), and as the
scenery became so entrancing the speeder was halted and the
camera put into commission. Tunnels, snow sheds, sharp turns
alongside of mountain slides that still were gradually moving
the tracks out towards the edge of the great drop into the
river far below, were some of the spectacles unfolded to our
view. We could hardly realize when Mr. Hansen told us we
were coming into Healey, which is one of the great coal
centers of Alaska, that our trip was about over and that
Mount McKinley Park Station was but a few miles beyond.

Shortly after one o'clock we drew up before an old freight
car that had been made into a station, and on the top of the
car we could plainly see a large sign which read "Mount
McKinley Park Station." After a short stop the speeder

carried us down the track about a quarter of a mile and deposited us directly in front of Morris Moreno's Mount McKinley Park Hotel. Half-page advertisements in the various Alaskan papers had prepared us to expect a somewhat more elaborate structure, though we could see that the electric lights which the advertising had emphasized were a reality. After packing our outfit to the hotel we looked up Guy Burch, the government packer who was in charge of the horses. We found the "boys" comfortably located in Lynch's Roadhouse, already abandoned. We met Mr. Henry Karstens, then Park Superintendent; also Dan Kennedy and Mr. P. Van Kirk, the gentleman who proposed to sell us his highly valuable pack train.

Walter, our cook, conveyed the gratifying news that he had lunch prepared for us. I rounded up the women and invited Mr. Hansen and the doctor to join us. Our first real business after eating was to carry on negotiations with Mr. Van Kirk. It took only a few seconds to realize that trading was not his vocation, but one far more sinister. It required little imagination to see him in some former existence halting a wayside traveler, the lower part of his face concealed with the dark cloth and the old-fashioned firearm levelled directly at his victim. Recognizing that he was living up to tenets born in him, I realized that argument would be of no avail and agreed to his murderous price, in fear and trembling at what George would call me when I broke the news to him. At any rate the trip was now assured, though owing to insufficient horses it would be necessary to relay our outfit and to take turns riding as we were shy three saddle horses.

On the edge of the great wilderness which we were now at last about to enter, let us call up in review the men who were to help along our adventurous hunt for moving pictures of wild life and scenics in a country that had never before been shot by a motion picture camera.

First came Guy Burch, who had been in the employ of the Alaska Road Commission for many years. He was an old man of the trail and one of the best handlers of horses I have ever known. Guy had been with Major Gotwals when locating a high-line trail to the Kantishna, and was the only one of us who had any idea of what was ahead of us. He had been brought up to consider the horse before anybody or anything else. He brushed down and curried our horses religiously. He had been too many years in the government service to take chances. His temper never failed, even in the face of conditions that sorely tried it. As we had over two thousand pounds of oats to pack, which meant a relay, we decided to secure an additional packer.

Guy was fortunately able to induce Ed Woods to join us, who, in his cowboy youth, was a friend of Roosevelt and at one time a successful miner, Mayor of Valdez and owner of many fine horses. He had lost his considerable fortune, future mining prospects failed, and Valdez fell away to nothing. Ed had forgotten more about horses than most horsemen of to-day can claim to know. He proved an excellent addition to our party and, when we succeeded in getting him to talk, which was seldom, he told us many interesting tales of his early days on the Range when he rode with Roosevelt.

Bill Simpert had also fallen from affluence won during the

gold rush. An excellent machinist, he could always have a job from the copper company to help get a grubstake for his yearly prospecting. I had known him before as a splendid man on the trail. On this trip he came under the head of guide, and was one of the nurses of the motion camera. Bill was always ready with a free-flowing line of hot air and wild tales that amused us when gathered about the small stove, with the wind, well laden with fine snow flakes, howling outside.

Next came Jim Gibson, a great husky, red-headed product of a Montana ranch, who had prospected, trapped, hunted and wandered. He had been a teamster and sub-contractor, for many years employed by the Alaska Commission. Jim was untiring and never once put his leg across a horse. When we tried to get him to ride he would mumble something about having pity on the poor dumb brute. As time went by he began to lose weight, and by the time we returned to Riley Creek I am sure I am conservative in saying that he had left at least twenty pounds on the trail. He was with us as guide and really acted in that capacity to Godley.

Walter Eng, the China boy cook of our trip on the White River of a few years past, completed the party.

Of course George Godley and I came under the head of useless dunnage, but, for all of that, we had to do our parts.

As I looked over our man-power inventory it certainly seemed to me greater than was necessary. We had been warned, however, of the rigors of the trip, and, as there were several hundred miles to be traveled, I concluded that possibly it was wise. After Pirate Van Kirk had turned over his

The heart of the Alaskan Range,
Richardson Highway

Lynch's Roadhouse, Riley Creek

fully-equipped pack train, Guy inspected equipment and reported it in lamentable condition, with all the horses needing shoeing. Things began to hum as a blacksmith, hurriedly summoned from Healey, started work in Mr. Karsten's blacksmith shop. We were anxious to be off on the trail the next day, so everyone fell to in order to accomplish the seemingly impossible.

It was here that Mrs. Beach and her friend left us on their return journey. We saw them off on the Government Flyer from Mount McKinley Park Station in the wee hours of August 11th.

Up to this time the weather had been wonderful; excepting our day in Cordova, the sun had shone splendidly with hardly a cloud to change the monotony. With the leaving of my wife our sunshine literally departed, and for forty odd days we had the most miserable weather that I had ever experienced. That night we put up in Mr. Karsten's office, which was handy to the outfit. An air of bustle was evident in the morning and, though there were three horses to be shod, Guy determined to let them go until he returned for the relay.

The first day of a wilderness journey is always one of misery, and our start was no exception. We began with balancing up packs and adjusting them to suit the horses, and though no one loafed it was almost noon before we started from Lynch's Roadhouse and traveled up Riley Creek, until we came to the lately marked trail to Savage River, our first objective. We had not gone over half a mile before one of the packs shifted, owing to the restlessness of the horse, and

before that was straightened and tightened the other horses
had scattered with packs flying in every direction. It took just
one hour to repack, and at last we made our real start, with a
mild rain to help freshen our spirits.

For a time we traveled the new marked trail and as it
began to soften Guy turned to the creek. Over boulders and
sand bars we followed Riley Creek until, near the summit,
we crossed the Tundra, which gave but little, and proceeded
down over and along creeks. Towards late afternoon we
halted for Guy to get his bearings, believing there was a short
cut over a high ridge that would save us many miles. Locating
his route we began to climb a steep grade, and upon reaching
the summit we dropped down the other side through a fair
amount of timber, and suddenly came to a clearing where
there was a refuge tent and a high cache.

Guy informed us that this was the end of our first day's
journey, and though we had had our troubles in starting, and
sufficient delays on the trail to try our dispositions, we nevertheless regretted the necessity of camping as the scenery held
us deeply absorbed. At Savage River we found a large signboard telling us the number of miles we had traveled, and
pointing towards the next refuge with the miles likewise
marked down. After seeing several of these signs we came
to the conclusion that the mileage had been determined by
the temperament and condition of the man that had put them
down. Woe to the musher who sets his endurance on the mileage of those signboards! At one time I walked four miles
by the board in twenty minutes, and another two miles took
us some four hours.

We fixed up a comfortable camp in a short time and sat down to enjoy the evening. In the government tent we found a man who had mushed in from the Station with the idea that he could get some hunting, and, though he was tired and low in spirits, it was nothing compared to his feelings when we told him that he was within the National Park and could not hunt.

Guy and Ed turned back to the Station next day to make the relay while George, Bill, Jim and I started for the mountains where we had been told that sheep and caribou roamed in quantities. Well loaded with the motion picture outfit and many feet of film, we followed up Savage River, passing an old cabin of Harry Luckey's from which he had hunted sheep for the market in the days before the coming of the Park. Many old sheep heads and quantities of skins lay scattered about, all evidences of the early-day slaughter.

On up the stream we continued until the mountains rose high on either side, and we were considering what our next move was to be when Jim located a bunch of caribou on the hills across the stream. We forded the river and at once began the climb, which was quite steep but not rough. As we reached the higher country and could secure a better view, we began to locate caribou on all sides. One large bunch of bulls became our objective and we set off at once to stalk them. George and I climbed a high ridge above them and despatched Jim and Bill to come out below and try to drive them towards us.

Our plans worked out to perfection, as the bulls, when Jim showed up, came directly towards us. George was operating the camera and everything went well until the first roll had been exhausted. He hurriedly put in a fresh magazine, while the caribou were coming closer and closer, until they were within a few yards. Then he rose up to shoot the picture and as luck would have it the machine jambed. Upon examination we discovered that the film had not been properly threaded, but by this time our caribou had departed for parts unknown. This was the only trouble of any sort we had with this camera on the entire trip.

The rest of the day was taken up in stalking and filming one bunch of caribou after another. We saw two small rams a short distance off, and in the far distance, toward the head of the Sanctuary River, the mountains were covered with white dots—the *Ovis dalli* sheep. In the late afternoon, after all the film had been exposed, we turned back towards camp well satisfied with a successful day of hunting with the motion picture camera, and with full knowledge of the abundance of the wild animals that roamed these mountains. When we stopped to think that we were but a comparatively few miles from the railroad and that this was a section where meat hunting had been carried on for many years, we wondered what the country we were headed for would be like.

Our camp that evening held a group of wildly enthusiastic men, all anxious for Guy to return so as to be on our way for the large mysterious country about the great McKinley.

Toward dusk two men with two pack horses appeared. The larger one turned out to be Jack Price who held options on Copper Mountain, and the other was a Jap who was to cook for Price's camp. Price spent the evening with us, praising the greatness of Copper Mountain, and reminded us of our promise to visit him and look over his properties.

Our third morning was far from propitious, as a steady rain was falling which kept us in camp. Price pulled out early with his Jap and pack horses. We wished him good luck and promised to visit him. We began to worry as to whether or not Guy would start back, and as the day wore on some of Mr. Murie's outfit arrived and we were assured by them that they were certain Guy did not plan to return until the next day. Mr. Murie was in charge of the Biological Survey party and was planning to construct a large corral toward the head of the Savage River, with the intention of being able to drive in a quantity of caribou, which were to be used to mix in with the reindeer in the hopes of improving the latter.

Having resigned ourselves to another day at Savage you can imagine our delight when Guy and Ed appeared with the outfit heavily loaded with the last of the stuff. On their way back Ed, who was bringing up the rear, heard the barking of dogs, and about the same time saw a young caribou break from the woods with two huskies close behind. The caribou came directly to the horses and mixed with them. He was so thoroughly played out that the boys stopped the horses and Ed went to the caribou and picked him up. The poor animal was about done and was thoroughly afraid of the dogs which the boys had run off by this time. After a short delay they started up the pack outfit and the caribou followed along. When they had gone some distance the caribou seemed to have recovered; soon, with nerve restored, he trekked off into the woods again.

We were packed up bright and early on our fourth day, and with a fairly clear sky we left Savage River, heading north towards Igloo Creek. Climbing steadily over a soft, spongy ground we worked up to the top of the divide where we had a fleeting glimpse of the top of Mount McKinley. We had been told so many conflicting stories as to when our first sight of McKinley would take place that we could scarcely believe our eyes. It was but a glimpse of the top, for that was all that could be seen, and it stood out clear and glistening. We had tried diligently while at Savage River to get just a peek of McKinley, but our efforts were of no avail. I have been assured that there is some particular spot on one of the high ridges about Savage where the top of McKinley may be seen, but we had to take it on hearsay.

Making splendid time, we hardly realized that we had passed over the height of land before we came upon a well-constructed cabin located on the banks of the Sanctuary River. We stopped here but a few minutes to gaze about, and then on our way. Upon reaching the Sanctuary two large bull caribou came trotting towards us. They came within a few yards, stopped, looked us over, then trotted off, though several times they hesitated and partially started back, only to be off again. Our cameras were safely packed out of the way. Leaving the Sanctuary River we began to climb again and upon reaching the top we followed a well-defined valley between high peaks.

The monotony of the travel was constantly broken by curious caribou. Finally sheep began to appear, and they, too, showed interest in this new species of animal—man.

About this time we began to stray from our course, and after a few hours we came down to a gravel river bar that seemed totally strange to Guy. "It should be the Teklanika," he remarked, "but if it is, it has changed greatly since last year." Our maps assured us that it must be the Teklanika and we decided that we had come out a few miles too far up. After traveling between two and three miles downstream (it seemed many miles further), we discovered a tent and the government signboard which told us that we were four miles from Igloo Creek.

It was at this point that I decided to try out my walking ability, and with a goodbye struck off in the direction of Igloo Creek. We experienced considerable soft ground, and I was just as well pleased that I was on foot. You can imagine my surprise when shortly after working up a gradual slope and coming down on the other side into a fine bunch of timber, I suddenly came upon a government refuge tent, and there back of it was the signboard "Igloo Creek" plainly marked out. Out came my watch to find that it was exactly twenty minutes from that last sign. Some mushing! Four miles in twenty minutes, according to the Road Commission! But with all of that we were not disappointed in reaching our objective ahead of schedule.

Towards evening we had a caller from the west, a Mr. Wood, an engineer who had been working with the Land Survey party in setting out the boundary line of Mount McKinley Park. From him we learned that Mr. P. Van Kirk, who had sold his outfit to us had been under contract with the Park Survey party to pack in grub to them, and that, not having heard anything from Van Kirk, grub was getting low and the party breaking up.

Guy and Ed made an early start back to Savage the next morning; our friend Wood was in luck as he rode one of the horses—a twenty-mile lift does much to lighten one's burden, especially as a fairly heavy pack was thrown on one of the horses. Mr. Wood having described some of his experiences with the great bands of sheep that he had seen, we delayed but a short time before hiking to the high hills towards the head of Igloo Creek. We were not surprised at seeing sheep on every side as we progressed upstream, for there were also many in sight from our camp.

To tell in detail of each experience in filming the sheep would be almost impossible as those hills were just one great kaleidoscope of sheep. We would crawl towards the nearest bunch, stick the camera up, and shoot. Sometimes the movie stars would sidle off quietly but suspiciously; other times they would stand for our benefit, and then go on about their business of feeding, or just lie down and bask in the sun. Mixed in with the sheep, to break the monotony, would be a band of caribou and several shots were taken at them. Dame Fortune certainly smiled upon us that day, as the sun shone brightly and the wild creatures posed so much to our liking that by three o'clock our film was exhausted. On reaching camp, George at once cut off a short strip of film and developed it so that we might get an idea of our results. When the test film was held up to the light, some sheep could clearly be seen on a steep side hill, and the glory of the day was complete.

A glimpse of the top of Mount McKinley

*A well constructed cabin on the banks
of the Sanctuary River*

We were off again the next morning intent on locating some rams, for all the sheep we had seen and filmed the day before were ewes and lambs. Jim and Bill Slim said we would have to hit for the ice fields at the head of Igloo before rams could be located, but as this was more than a day's mush, George and I felt that they must be wrong. We worked hard all day but did not locate any rams, and though a few feet of film had been exposed we were far from content when we pulled into camp. Sheep in large quantities we had seen, and also many bands of caribou. In fact the more ground we covered the more animals we ran into. Shortly after our return to camp visitors dropped in, the Game Warden, Jim Burrows, with Marshall Buckley and Prosecuting Attorney Collins, who were on their way home after investigating the peculiar death of a prospector in the Kantishna district. We insisted that they put up with us, and we all enjoyed a most pleasant evening. Guy and Ed arrived with the outfit about the time dinner was ready; it was quite apparent they preferred being on time for meals.

During the evening's talk we were informed that we hadn't reached the sheep country yet, and that when we arrived at the bar of the McKinley River we would see caribou in bands of several hundred. George remarked that he had been in sections before where great caribou bands roamed, but it was always just the year before. Attorney Collins remarked the next morning as their party was about to pull out, "My wife told me if I didn't lose twenty pounds on this trip she wouldn't own me on my return to Fairbanks. Was getting along fine until we blew in on you fellows last night. Been living for the past ten days on a few old bones of a caribou that Jim here killed over on the Kantishna some time last year, but after the feed of white man's grub I've put on here, I guess I might just as well keep going until I reach the outside."

With "See you again soon" we both pulled out from Igloo; they headed for the great metropolis of Fairbanks, while we set our course towards the bleak wastes of McKinley.

Traveling up Igloo Creek I began to count sheep and had recorded something over seventy when the rain came down; not a hazy Scotch mist, but rain that pelted like hailstones. We were in for it, so on we went, and after passing through a steep canyon we saw a large sign of the Road Commission pointing up the mountain side, and on it "Sable Pass." Of course there was no trail as the sign, we later discovered, had only been placed there a couple of days earlier. We picked our way up a steep marshy side hill, while sheep on all sides looked down on us; in fact a few came closer to investigate. The horses mired slightly but soon the rain let up. Reaching the top we saw opening out before us, a beautiful, grassy meadow just reeking with water; in fact much of the snow from the past winter remained and was now melting rapidly. By this time my count, which necessarily skipped many sheep, had climbed up over the two hundred mark, and as I looked ahead I began to wonder whether I could remember how the count would go after the high numbers had been reached.

We splashed and floundered along, here crossing a stream, then stumbling back again, and many times flushing ptarmigan from their cover. We had planned to make the main Toklat, but as the rain delayed us and made traveling a misery, particularly for the horses, we decided to camp at the next government station on the East Fork of the Toklat.

In some way I forgot to continue my count of the sheep, but at that I had gone over three hundred; so you can see from this short trip of twelve miles that there are a few sheep left, and as all were ewes with one or two lambs each, it would seem that they are on a fair road to increase.

Arriving at the East Fork another complication confronted us. We were now well above timber line and the only wood was a few willows; but as coal outcropped and large pieces were lying in the creek we gathered a few sizeable lumps and in a short time the stoves were roaring with coal fires. After camp was in order we began looking over the country. Towards the west we could see the flags marking the trail, newly laid, and far in the distance, towards Polychrome Pass, the mountain side seemed to be covered with fresh snow. On closer observation the large white mass appeared to change and it dawned on us that it was an unbelievable bunch or congregation of bunches of sheep; there must have been hundreds, if not thousands. I know this will be difficult to visualize, especially to those who are accustomed to seeing but a few scattered animals in a month's trip.

George and I have covered many miles of the north country, but never in our travels, in fact in all of our travels put together, had we seen so much game as in these two weeks within the boundaries of McKinley Park!

Guy said at dinner that he thought they could make Igloo and back in a day, which sounded encouraging. The grain we were carrying for horse feed was the cause of delaying our travel, but each day the horses were doing their best to lighten the load, and we were cacheing a bag of oats at various spots where we intended stopping upon our return.

For our day at the East Fork the weather cleared bright and warm, and after a few scenic shots with the movie I decided to take a ramble towards the head of Igloo Creek. George agreed with Jim and Bill that a day's loaf about camp would help to clean up many odds and ends that had been hanging over their consciences. My conscience being clear, I picked up a pair of field glasses and was off to the high grades. After climbing a steep grassy slope I came upon a far-reaching plain well covered with moss and water. In the distance towards the southeast were the rugged mountains and huge glaciers from which start Igloo Creek, while directly south the East Fork branched off into the mountain fastness from which it springs. I carefully scanned the rugged ridges close up to the ice in the hope of locating rams, but without success. I stumbled across a few old bear signs which brought to mind that I was wandering aimlessly about with scant protection from a Brownie. Coupled with the thought of bear was the fact that I was beginning to feel the need of nourishment, and I turned back on an old caribou trail, following it until I reached the bank of the East Fork, down which I returned to camp. I had had a marvelous morning taking in those magnificent rugged ridges and the many glaciers glistening in the wonderful northern sunlight.

Everyone had a day off in camp and seemed to be enjoying it. In the early afternoon Guy and Ed pulled in, having made the trip comfortably and without undue excitement.

When we set out the next morning towards Polychrome Pass, where we had seen the mountainside of sheep the day before, we were all agog for now we were entering the real country of the Dall sheep. The pass was quite smooth traveling but the entire country seemed to be covered with about two to three inches of water. The ground appeared fairly firm and the horses were able to navigate freely. Our first disappointment came that day; our large mountainside of sheep had disappeared, and though we saw sheep I doubt if there were over a hundred. Following down a rough boulder-strewn stream bed, we finally reached the main fork of the Toklat. In the distance we could see the trail flags blowing in the breeze, and we went on to cross a wide cobble-stone river bar. On reaching the far side we discovered that we were at the Toklat camp and found a fire still going in the stove of the refuge tent. We were rapidly overhauling the men of the Road Commission.

As I gazed south from our camp I could see the main Toklat fork out into three or four small streams. Somehow it seemed familiar, and suddenly it came to me, that this was the greatest ram pasture in the North, in fact in the whole world. I remembered Charles Sheldon, in his home in Washington several years before, describing this home of the big white sheep. Getting out my glasses I threw them on a bunch of white specks and, after a careful study, was satisfied that they were all rams. As I was about to tell George, he called, "Come and help me get a big bull caribou on the river bar." Stumbling over rocks that I am sure were invented only to try a man's patience we finally came to a spot that looked good for the picture; whereupon George started the camera and ground out a nice lot of pictures of the old-timer.

George, Bill Slim, Jim and I were off to the high peaks early the next day and it was not long before we realized that it was to be a day of confusion. Several bunches of rams having been located, it was quite evident that a difference of opinion was bound to arise as to which bunch was the largest, and therefore to be honored by becoming movie stars. They all looked good to me, so, by diplomatically asserting myself, it was finally decided to stalk a fine looking bunch of seven. Before we had come within camera distance of our quarry we lost interest as we saw to the south a huge draw that was literally dotted with fine rams. Jim Gibson had the bulk of the movie outfit and as Jim is six feet three, raw-boned and red-headed, you can bet that camera went wherever the rams did. The camera was a new type motor-driven machine that George had brought with him, and results to date had been most satisfactory.

The real test was now to come. The chance for a close-up picture of rams *(Ovis dalli)* seemed almost too good to be real. We worked gradually up to the large draw, keeping well out of sight, though it's fair to say that the sheep had not shown any signs of uneasiness in cases where we had been seen. The first bunch filmed were almost lost as George ran to get a chance at them and was only successful in catching a glimpse of an old fellow going over the skyline. The next attempt was successful, and many feet were run off of a fine bunch of large rams. Several other gatherings were filmed and they behaved like veritable stars of the film.

The film was about exhausted and George was in the act of transferring some exposed film from a magazine and re-filling with fresh. The camera was lying on the ground and we were waiting and watching George. Three rams came around a point of rock, one with a fair-sized head, the others small. They stopped, looked at us, and then deliberately walked directly towards us. There was no sign of alarm, just quiet, idle curiosity.

George told me to shoot, so grabbing the camera I started running off the remaining film. The rams pretended to feed, and at the same time kept coming nearer and nearer. I exhausted the film, some of it at not over thirty feet. The rams looked us over most carefully, then suddenly showed signs of alarm and the next minute they were off at a rapid trot. I sneaked after them and peered over some rocks, to find they had stopped a short distance below and were placidly feeding again.

I have often wondered what they had in mind, and my only sane conclusion is that they were traveling towards some objective and we happened to be in their line of travel. I am sure they wanted to pass us, and intended to do so until something caused their alarm and they trotted back. I have often seen similar actions by animals that had never seen man before, particularly in a section where very little hunting had been done.

It was late when we reached camp, and though the day had been quite strenuous it was all forgotten in the thoughts of the records we had secured of those wonderful runners of the high peaks.

We found that Guy had returned with the relay from the East Fork, and after a lengthy discussion as to plans it was decided that we would cache all surplus supplies at Jack Price's cabin on Copper Mountain and from there push on to Mount Dall, where, on the Kuskokwim flats, we hoped to photograph the great gathering herds of caribou before they started on their annual migration to the eastward. The weather looked rather dubious in the morning but we decided to keep moving unless drowned out. Following the extreme West Fork of the Toklat we finally crossed over the divide and came in to Stony Creek. The sheep were still with us, there being many scattered over the side hills. At Stony Creek we overtook the Road Commission and it gave us great pleasure to meet Sam Sanderson and his two husky helpers.

We were bent on obtaining information about the lower section of the range, that great country of which so little is known and which we had been told abounded in game, beyond the western limits of McKinley Park. Sam Sanderson had been down a piece and said it was a cinch to travel there, as the high ground was hard and that old McKinley was a beacon that would always lead you home. Someone had told us there was a man named Ellis over on Moose Creek who knew the country, but we had not been able to verify this. We had now been on the trail for over two weeks and not a sign of McKinley except for the scant glimpse as we topped the divide coming into Sanctuary River. Jack Price had promised a fine view of the range and the great mountain from his place on Copper Mountain.

It is easy to picture our enthusiasm as we realized, upon

*We followed on to cross a wide
cobblestone river bar*

Motion picture enlargements

There was no sign of alarm, just quiet, idle curiosity.

coming up over the divide from Stony, and gingerly down on the East Fork of the McKinley River, that over there was Copper Mountain from where we were to drink our fill of the greatest nectar of the far North, Denali, the Great One, our own Mount McKinley. Also we were coming into nearer views of McKinley National Park's tremendous spectacle of glaciers, one of the most fascinating of its many fascinating features. The entire north side of the Alaskan Range in the vicinity of Mount McKinley abounds with marvelous glaciers.

One of the first to be encountered, and by far the most important, is the Muldrow Glacier which heads up in the high reaches of McKinley and tumbles down its eastern shoulder. This is an enormous volume of broken and tilted ice, which gives the aspirants to conquering McKinley many troublous times. In the early days before the railroad, the dog team and mushers would cross Muldrow on its lower edge. I believe that the Browne-Parker expedition on their last climb reached the north slope in this way. This huge ice mass turns to the north and separates the East Fork of the McKinley River from the West Fork. The West Fork has its source in the Muldrow. The lower part of the Muldrow appears nothing more or less than a mud bank as the ice is covered thickly with a dark brown muck. The East Fork of the McKinley passes through a canyon and joins the West Fork a short distance below the mouth of the canyon forming the main McKinley river.

One of an adventurous turn of mind and versed in glacier navigation could have some wonderful exploring on this great ice mass. It is perfectly feasible to cross the north end of the

Muldrow, come into the headwaters of the Clearwater River, and a short distance further to the west arrive at the head of the Muddy River. Here we seem to be at the base of Mount McKinley, with what looks like a mild little glacier, then known as Peters Glacier, in the foreground. I believe for some reason this name has been changed to Hanna, but always in my mind it will remain as a recognition to Peters.

To run ahead of my story for a moment: later on I was camped at the head of Muddy and decided I would like to say that I had actually been on McKinley, and had touched its great sides. McKinley stands out at this point, straight up in the air, and it seemed so close that it was a great temptation. I am not an expert on ice traveling, and have a great respect for glaciers. I can only say that I traveled the greater part of the day without apparently lessening the distance, and finally turned back as fog and darkness began to come down. Yet, I am sure there is no great difficulty in accomplishing what I attempted, especially if one is familiar with glacier travel.

Hanna, or Peters as I continue to call it, is another glacier that would keep an enthusiastic glacier-lover busy all summer in just touching the high spots. I have always felt that some day an inn should be built at this spot, where the tourist could get a thrill that would never be forgotten. I can close my eyes and in a few seconds that wonderful mountain comes back, with Peters Glacier in the foreground, as it appeared one morning after a two-foot fall of snow. A stiff north wind had cleared the sky, and McKinley was a marble statue with a heavy fog of snow curling off to the south from the summit. Peters Glacier covered with the fresh snow seemed like a bunch of low snow ridges, easy to glide over, and not the protector that it is for the magnificent McKinley.

Resuming our journey on the East Fork of the McKinley River we clearly made out the tents on Copper Mountain, and but for the fact that our solitary mule took it upon himself to become mired several times by wandering off into swamp holes, and that we blindly passed the direct trail, we would have reached Price's at a reasonable hour in the afternoon. As it was, we were all tired and swearing over going so many miles out of our way to visit Price as we wandered westward.

We were given a hearty welcome. It was like meeting lifelong friends after a long separation. One of our first questions concerned the best location for views of the great McKinley. "Oh," said Price, "the range is generally in clouds; last year some fellows waited two weeks to get McKinley clear and then left in disgust."

This seemed most encouraging as we had had hardly a clear day since we had been on our trip!

"The sun may be shining brightly but McKinley will be in clouds," was another cheerful remark from our friend.

The more I questioned the more skeptical I became as to whether Price himself, had ever seen McKinley clear, though he had spent many months on his Copper Mountain. We met several prospectors camped nearby; in fact we had to borrow some poles from one of them to put up our tents. They all were hazy about the western end of the range, so that we felt that every effort should be made to reach Mr. Ellis of Moose Creek.

We put in two days on Copper Mountain. The first saw us

off eighteen miles to a caribou lick where coal was mined for use on Copper Mountain. This spot has no wood of any sort within twenty-five miles, and the few willows that once were there had been cropped close by the numerous prospectors who had wandered those hills during the past year in quest of the elusive high grade. From the preliminary development this discovery bids fair to be a great pay producer.

On this day a heavy wind sprang up and continued until night. As we climbed the ridge across from Copper Mountain we saw for the first time the western end of the lofty central part of the Alaskan Range which concerned us—the part named Rugged Mountains by the early geographers. It was banked in clouds but what little we saw was sufficient to make us take deep breaths. The clouds were shifting rapidly and it would look as if the range were going to clear in a few minutes, only to close up again. McKinley stood out partially enveloped; sometimes the top glistened above a heavy cloud bank with a halo of blue sky and sunshine. The motion picture outfit was out and we took some two hundred feet before we finally concluded that there was no chance of the clouds rolling by. Our trip to the Lick was unsuccessful as to caribou, though we did pack back some two hundred pounds of coal to help replace the fuel we had consumed.

Upon our return to Copper Mountain we saw our tents in a state of complete collapse and Walter greatly upset. We tried to put them up again but it did not take long to realize that it was a useless effort as the wind was howling a mile a minute. Jack Price quickly came to the rescue and offered the use of his cabin and stove for cooking, which relieved our immediate difficulty. We were trying to plan some sleeping quarters, as the sky looked like rain, when Jim Gibson remarked, "I long ago found that in this country you should never attempt to plan out anything until the moment it has to be done; maybe it will let up and we can put up the tents."

Comforted with these philosophical words we returned to the cabin and entered into a long heart-to-heart talk with the owner thereof. About nine o'clock the wind died out and in a few minutes everything was shipshape again.

"Think of the amount of mental and physical effort saved by following my words of wisdom," was Jim's only comment.

We spent the next day going over the mountain with Price, and in looking over the sheep ranges. Everything points to a wonderful mineral deposit on this mountain, and when transportation gets into the country we may look for a new mining center that may open the eyes of the wise ones. We noticed that the sheep had taken to the inaccessible part of the mountains and had entirely lost that wonderful innocence and confidence in man that their relatives to the eastward had displayed.

We repacked and cut down on all surplus supplies, leaving everything at Copper Mountain but the necessities for a month's trip. We had now done with our relaying and were off for a spurt to Mount Dall. The weather was cloudy and inauspicious as we left Copper Mountain, and after we crossed the east branch of the McKinley, worked up a steep draw and pulled out on a wet mushy looking flat, the rain broke. When I say it rained, I mean it came down like a cloudburst; raincoats were but blotting paper to this soaking downpour. We were wet when we tried to ride, and when we walked it was worse.

Then, for variety, one of the horses became ornery, and that helped sharpen up tongues and tempers. After passing a Mr. Hamilton with his wife and young daughter and two mules on their way out from Kantishna, things seemed to quiet down and at one time it looked as if the clouds were about to break.

At this point Guy suggested that we strike out for the high ridge and keep down the range as that would be our shortest route, but we concluded it would be better to keep on down the McKinley River until we reached the Survey camp and at least explain to Mr. Abbey our innocence in the mix-up over his grub. The weather began to improve, and as we plugged doggedly along the clouds broke and the sun came out. Presently in the distance we could see Old Glory floating on the breeze from an improvised flagpole in front of the Survey tent.

We were rather enthusiastically greeted by the few remaining members of this valiant band of the United States General Land Office, but I am afraid their enthusiasm was more or less assumed when they discovered it was not P. Van Kirk's pack train with a load of grub. We explained our position in regard to the horse transaction and assured those present that we would gladly let them have anything they were in need of. They were a fine lot of young men and led by a most interesting engineer, Woodbury Abbey. Poor "Wood" as they call him, had certainly been handed plenty of misery and was putting up a game fight.

That evening about seven o'clock the range cleared and

McKinley stood out clear as a bell. It was our first real view of the mountain and the range. Our desire was just to drink it in, but the motion camera must do its share, so we cranked off many feet with varying exposures until it became too dark even for that.

During the evening it was decided that George, Guy and I would go to Eureka in the morning in the hopes of connecting with Mr. Ellis, and if possible persuade him to join us on our trip westward. Leaving camp early in the morning we traveled for the first few miles through a fine stand of timber, and as we came to the end of it we passed quite an elaborate log cabin where resided one Alick Mitchell, the Scotch bard of the Kantishna. As we were in somewhat of a hurry we passed without stopping, an insult that took some explaining later. We then came out upon a great swampy barren which is well patronized by the friendly caribou. As Alick Mitchell said in describing these barrens, "Thank God they're outside of the Park."

Striking out for the highest part of this huge tundra we soon saw, nestling amongst the high mountains and at the foot of converging ranges, a beautiful lake, by name "Wonder Lake." It is indeed entitled to that name, for from Polly's Roadhouse at the extreme north end of the lake the most wonderful view of the Alaskan Range and Mount McKinley can be had. It is the sort of picture that changes with each second, as does the reflection in the lake, and holds you spellbound and unconscious of your immediate surroundings,— just glad that you are alive and there to see this most wonderful creation.

We reached Polly's Roadhouse somewhat sooner than we expected. If by chance you should one day travel this trail I know that your tracks will lead to Polly's Roadhouse. It's a well-built log cabin and inside furnished with elaborate combinations of caribou horns that are used for seats, candle sticks, shelves and the like. Polly, from whom this stopping place takes its name, is known in real life as Mrs. Paula Anderson; but that being complicated for the simple and rough folks of the North, someone christened her Polly, and Polly she is to one and all. We paid our respects and departed, but only after having promised that we would return for lunch. Pushing on, we passed an old cabin of Joe Quigley's and several others possibly belonging to men who at one time had washed the creeks. We finally came to the settlement of Eureka and successfully located Dr. Sutherland's cabin. We were fortunate to find the doctor at home but were disappointed to hear that Mr. Ellis and his son had gone off hunting that morning. After going over the placer operation with Dr. Sutherland, we made our adieus to young Mrs. Ellis and the other members of their party and assured the doctor we would look for him in New York the coming winter.

Retracing our steps, we reached Wonder Lake somewhat late for our luncheon date but this made no difference to our hostess. Fresh trout and ptarmigan with various jams and vegetables, and a fine mess of blueberries was a feed befitting royalty, and it was well enjoyed by three roughnecks. I almost forgot about the cake and chocolate candy; but no wonder, as George did away with most of it, leaving Guy and me but a memory of what might have been. On the way from Kan-

Polly's Roadhouse, Wonder Lake

*The northwest gate to McKinley
National Park*

tishna I had knocked over a nice bunch of ptarmigan which we presented to Polly with our respects. As we were about to depart, Polly, with due formality, presented to each of us a gold nugget scarf pin, stating in her presentation speech that she personally had washed out these particular nuggets from her grubstake. After such a luncheon and honors cast upon us, it was a slow and dull push back to our own camp.

A call on Alick Mitchell revealed marked frigidity. Try as we would to explain our passing by in the morning without stopping, our efforts seemed to have no effect, at least for the time being. Arriving at camp we found everything in shape for a move in the morning. We had a serious conference with the government survey engineers in order to locate as closely as possible the extreme western boundary of Mount McKinley Park. We expected to reach Mount Dall, but hoped to hunt sheep as soon as the boundary had been crossed. At McKinley River bar where we were camped, the line ran only a short distance from us, possibly a mile. In going to Wonder Lake we passed through the northwest gateway which was marked by two posts, securely fastened in the ground, with many inscriptions added to the general survey data.

On the morning of August 23rd we broke camp and started on our trip down the range. For ten days we pushed westward over wild areas with the great Alaskan Range and Mount McKinley towering above us on our left. As we passed down the range it was quite evident that sheep and caribou were less plentiful, for, although we found both at almost every spot we camped, they were not in the quantities we had seen to the east. At Muddy, we met two prospectors who had just located and staked important silver deposits. On our way beyond Muddy we came across fresh tracks of two men; who they could have been was beyond us, though possibly Mr. Ellis and his son might have wandered off their usual haunts in the search of meat for their mining camp. At Birch we found the writing on a tree of the "Goin Kid," going west in the morning and east in the evening; it was discouraging for travelers in that great waste. We also passed deserted trapper cabins, and though we were on the lookout for one in particular I am afraid we were too near the timberline, as we were unable to locate it.

Foraker now loomed high, but still we could hardly believe that McKinley towered only a couple of thousand feet above Foraker. The further from McKinley we went, the higher it seemed to reach above the other great mountains in the range. We became somewhat confused over Mount Russell as many peaks seemed to stand out, while it was our understanding that Russell could be readily located. In the distance were other high peaks, and far off Mount Dall the objective of our journey.

On the second day from Muddy we reached the Foraker River, and here there is a veritable galaxy of glaciers. The east Foraker heads up in the westward of McKinley, but the main Foraker has its source from vast glaciers on the western front of Mount Foraker. Here again are huge masses of ice greatly broken, and just waiting for the ice expert to explore their twists and turns. Incidentally, Mount Foraker, though only two thousand feet lower than McKinley, has never been climbed. What an opportunity for a mountain climber who has the inclination and a knowledge of ice! We had no time to put in at Foraker but I can assure you it must have some fatal fascination. I will tell you the incident so you may judge for yourself.

We had made camp at the forks of the Foraker River after a hard day, not stopping for lunch, and our appetites were keen. The dinner was ready but for the meat, the frying pan was sizzling, and our cook went out to cut off some mutton steaks. We waited and waited; finally I began to grumble, but the others seemed resigned, and were very quiet. At last I piled out of the grub tent to find what the trouble was. There stood our cook with his hands behind his back with the knife in them, staring at what I must admit was an awe inspiring sight. Foraker in an afterglow, with the stars just starting to glisten. It was all very fine but I was too hungry to appreciate anything but a luscious sheep steak. I let out a howl, "What's the matter; get busy and get the grub." The cook came to, and slowly turning, proceeded to cut off the mutton steaks.

Whether we had lingered too long on our fascinating journey, or whether fate decreed that we had seen and enjoyed enough for one trip, the fact remains that August 29th abruptly ended our journey, short of its planned climax at the foot of Mount Dall.

That night a heavy snowstorm set in which continued all the next day and well into the following night. Our spirits fell in direct ratio as the snow deepened. We were down to the last bag of oats for the horses, and, as I have mentioned before, ours were not accustomed to hustle for themselves.

We put in three days in the neighborhood of Foraker and Russell and, as the snow continued, and grub as well as horse feed was rapidly disappearing, we decided, in a most serious conference, that our journey must end prematurely here. There was nothing to do but to return to McKinley bar where there was an abundance of horse feed and where we had left a grub cache.

The sheep were again beginning to appear in larger quantities in the vicinity of Foraker and Russell but not in any way to compare with Igloo, Polychrome or the head of the Toklat. We regretted exceedingly that we did not have clear weather so that we might have had an opportunity to study and photograph the extreme western end of the range. We were forced to be satisfied with a few pictures taken with snow in the air, and, though the results are far from satisfactory, at least they bring back to us those days of disappointment passed under the shadows of Foraker and Russell.

Our return to McKinley River bar was just one continuous grind through snow two feet deep, with horses nearly gone, and the tempers of all at the breaking point. The last day George's saddle horse had to be led. At one time we were afraid we would have to leave him, but stumbling along we finally landed him back near our old camp on McKinley River. On this day Guy and Ed Wood separated from us as they feared the horses' inability to cross the swamp through which we were short-cutting, and were forced to bring the outfit several miles along the range before they could find firm ground toward the river.

As our group approached the river bank a huge band of

caribou, several hundred, passed above us and headed up into the mountains. Unfortunately the motion picture outfits were with the pack train so we contented ourselves with several shots with a 3A Kodak.

Upon reaching our old camp ground we found Bill Shannon and his wife located there, so we moved a few hundred yards upstream to within a short distance of the survey camps. For five days we stayed at McKinley River to give our horses an opportunity to rest and fatten up as the feed was both excellent and abundant. George and I went out beyond the park boundaries in the hope of seeing caribou, but Dame Fortune played us false. One night George brought in two caribou and a black bear secured on the Kantishna hills. The entire carcasses of the three animals were packed into camp and distributed amongst our neighbors as everyone was short of meat except ourselves.

One evening Alick Mitchell made us a visit, and after many further explanations we were able to smooth down his ruffled feelings, a concoction of home-brewed wine assisting us to some extent. We finally became fast friends, and it will be many a day before I forget the delicious blueberry pie that Alick presented to us one evening; unfortunately the pie was either too small or there were too many to eat it.

Our horses having regained their one-time plumpness we broke camp and started for the railroad. The trip was comparatively easy. The horses were again able to perform their duties for, as we reached each camp, the oats cached on our way in were a welcome find.

Again at Copper Mountain we met Jack Price and Grant.

At Toklat several visitors passed us on their way, amongst them Woodbury Abbey and Game Warden Jim Burrows. We visited Charles Sheldon's cabin of time gone by, which we found very nearly obliterated by the river overflow. At Igloo we met Joe Clark who was prospecting in that locality and had just staked a large gold claim.

Each day's journey back seemed longer than it had to us going out, due probably to disappointment at having failed to penetrate the far western end of the range, and, on the Kuskokwim Flats, secure motion pictures of the immense caribou bands there reported. However, there was satisfaction in our partial success, and, with the experience and knowledge of this trip, we felt certain that, another time, we could push on to Rainy Pass and from there to Anchorage.

Without any particular excitement beyond the usual every-day tribulations of one who travels with a pack outfit, we reached McKinley Park Station on September 14th and discovered that the steamer *Northwestern* was to sail from Seward on the 16th, which gave us just time to pack up and make the connection.

Colonel Mears passed through on his way to Anchorage the afternoon of our arrival, and kindly invited us to join him, but unfortunately we had work to do. On September 16th we bade farewell to all our friends at McKinley Park Station, and to our companions of the trip, Jim Gibson and Guy Burch, as we boarded the through express for Seward. At Anchorage the next day we met Colonel Mears again and he kindly held the train for us until we were able to visit Sydney Laurence, the great artist of this North Country, and also to get a glimpse of Anchorage. The Colonel placed a special car on the train for our use, a flat car without shock absorbers, on which the motion picture cameras were set up. From Anchorage until dark we clung on to that flat car, grinding madly at each new scenic wonder as it unfolded its beauty from the dim distance.

There is not much more to tell of this adventure. We made the *Northwestern* and spent many days at many canneries. At times in the evening, while taking a few rounds on deck before turning in, I could not help thinking how interesting this ship would be if only she could talk. Many years ago (in those days the United States transport *Orizaba*) her decks rang to "A Hot Time in the Old Town To-night" as the Roughriders headed towards Cuba.

Before ending this narrative let me say a few words for those who may contemplate taking the same journey. If bent on hunting, don't. The National Park boundaries enclose so vast a territory that it is almost impossible in one summer to get beyond it where shooting is legal. If purely for the pleasure of touring the great Mount McKinley Park, be prepared for the roughest of travel and be ready to go nearly one hundred miles from Mount McKinley Park Station before seeing the top of the great mountain. There are no accommodations on the journey (this was written in 1922)* and if travel is made with horses the horse feed must be packed out ahead of the trip, or relayed, which means hard work

* The McKinley Park Transportation Company now (1931) have comfortable camps where tourists may stop at several points, and there is talk of an inn being built in the near future opposite Copper Mountain, now renamed Mt. Eielson.

and delay of many days. Some day there will be automobile roads, with here and there up-to-date hotels, but I am afraid it is a long time ahead.

Today, scattered about fifteen miles apart, are the government nine-by-ten refuge tents which are palaces to the old sourdough with his heavy-laden sled and tired dogs; but I fear they would not prove such to the American tourist. It is one of the greatest wonderlands I have ever traveled, scenically the top of the world, and literally overrun with sheep and caribou, while in the timber I understand that moose are also plentiful. We were not in the timber to any extent so I can only repeat what I was told. There were many signs of bear, but I saw none; the season may have been responsible for this as the prospectors all said they were quite numerous in the spring.

Possibly in years to come the country beyond the Park will be populated with the game from the Park overflow, but, judging from the quantities of sheep seen on our trip in the restricted sections from Savage to Stony Creek, and the enormous section to the westward which is but sparsely inhabited, it would seem that the chance for an overflow to the unrestricted country is small. Alaska has some of the greatest game sections of the North, but before the territory benefits from this great natural resource it will be necessary to study the methods of its Canadian brothers, who not only make every effort to attract hunters but endeavor to serve them in such a manner as to win them back in other years. The problem is not to sell a single bill of goods but to secure continuing customers.

Again at Copper Mountain

Looking south from Chitina

Our dream of McKinley had been realized, and though many disappointments paved our way, nevertheless it was a great trip, and as I look back I feel that the realization was even greater than the years of anticipation.

With acknowledgements to Colonel Steese and Major Gotwals, to their guides and packers Guy Burch, Ed Woods and Jim Gibson whom we were so fortunate to have with us, to our old sourdough Bill Slimpert, not forgetting our China boy, Walter, each and all of whom were responsible for making this trip possible, I bring the tale of my first journey in this section to an end.

CHAPTER III.

ALONG THE NORTH SIDE OF THE ALASKAN RANGE TO MOUNT DALL

STORY OF THE EXPEDITION OF 1925

THAT mystery country north and south of the Alaskan Range and west of Mount McKinley National Park, in whose pastures the great Kuskokwim River has its many sources, had for years a great fascination for me. Mount Dall, smallest and farthest west of the great Denali family, at whose foot I had been told all the caribou had their yearly convention before starting on migration, is the pivotal point of this vast country. Further west is the Dillinger country and Rainy Pass. I had heard much of this vast mountain range from many people who, eventually, I discovered had never been there.

Our failure to reach Mount Dall in 1922 perhaps emphasized desire, for I never ceased to dream of the wonderful scenery and the record sheep and moose that must surely reside there, not to mention the huge bear and countless thousands of caribou. Besides, one can never be sure what may turn up in an unexplored section of Alaska. On the other hand, Guy Burch, our packer on the first trip, assured me there could not possibly be sufficient feed for horses, and that a trip into that difficult country undoubtedly would mean the loss of part or all of our outfit. The abandoned pack saddles and harness which we had found in a tree on the previous trip was a gentle reminder of what might happen.

But the more I yielded to discouragement the more decided I became to attempt it. One evening in 1924, seated by a camp fire at the head of the Robertson River, I happened to broach the subject to Jim Gibson, who likewise had been with us on our 1922 trip. Jim was my first ray of sunshine.

"There's nothing so hard about that trip," he said; "we could make it easy enough. But why go to a God-forsaken country like that?"

It was not until the winter that a final decision was reached, and then only after many wires to and from Jim Gibson, which finally resulted in his "I'll go with you and get it over."

Immediately we began to gather whatever data on the country were available, and were greatly surprised to find that a number of people claimed to know it thoroughly and offered to go along. Fortunately we did not fall for their kind offers.

Jim put in most of the winter acquiring an outfit and interviewing the two or three men whom he knew had been in the vicinity of Mount Dall. As the plans developed we decided that it would be necessary to send an advance party down the range to the vicinity of Mount Dall with a load of provisions to cache for our use later on, and thus do away with relaying. We also planned to cache oats and hay for the horses and dried salmon for dog feed at stated intervals, so that an early snow would not be likely to halt our trip. I decided that a dog team was a safe insurance and should be part of our outfit.

Marcus Daly, my associate on this expedition, is a mining engineer and son of the first Marcus Daly who discovered and developed the Anaconda Copper mine, one of the greatest and most successful mining enterprises of the old days. Mr. Daly is a very keen sportsman and has been interested in hunting in various parts of the world, having been in Africa and almost all the different sections of this country, Canada and Alaska. Through an unfortunate mix-up he was unable to go North at the same time I did, and this delayed the expedition and kept us from reaching Rainy Pass which was our real objective. Mr. Daly caught up with me at the head of the Tonzona, coming down the range with Jim Burrows, in seven days, an almost unheard of trip as it was very close to two hundred miles from the railroad to our camp.

Mrs. Beach was a member of the expedition also. She has been on numerous trips with me in various parts of Canada and Alaska.

Jim Gibson was head packer on this trip. He has already been described as a member of our previous expedition.

Jim Burrows was assistant to Gibson. He was formerly Game Warden for the Kantishna under appointment first from Governor Riggs, and after that from Governor Bone. Burrows had come into the country as a prospector, had developed into the proprietor of a music and gambling hall, drifted from place to place as the various strikes were made, and, I imagine, as a last resort got the appointment as Game Warden of the Kantishna. He and Gibson did not get along very well on the trip. There was more or less wrangling between them, and it kept me quite busy straightening them out. The trouble, I think, was largely due to the fact that Burrows was not in any too good physical condition. He knew a good part of the country, however, and I was under the impression from what he told me that he knew all of the country down to the Tonzona. This we discovered was not the case. It was Burrows who turned back and met Daly and brought him down the range in his record dash.

Andy Simons, who was the real guide of the expedition, is the well-known Kenai Peninsula guide. He has been in great demand for years and is one of the best hunting guides I have ever been out with. He has a very attractive personality and a wonderfully even disposition, never gets ruffled, always takes things as they come, and is untiring. He is a great stalker of game, using his head where other people use their legs. He is now General Manager of the Alaska Guides Incorporated, and is looked upon as the outstanding Alaskan guide. He came on the trip with me largely to see a new country, and gave me a lot of data on the Rainy Pass country which he had entered with Captain Hubback, who was collecting North American mammal specimens for the British Museum. Andy was invaluable, seeming always to fill in the gaps and shortcomings of the others.

Slim Avery was also competent and efficient. He had formerly been a cowpuncher in Wyoming and had drifted into Alaska about fifteen years earlier, where he had prospected, trapped and traveled generally through the country and had been making a success. He was proud of the fact that he had never worked for anybody since he had been in the country, except two days when he helped out the government on railroad construction. I believe he took charge of its pack outfit until a new head packer was secured. Besides Avery's knowledge of horses, which was far beyond the ordinary, he was a dog musher and had done a good deal of mushing in the winter carrying mail and supplies. He had traveled the range and prospected up to within a short distance of the West Fork of the Foraker at a time when only one or two men had penetrated further than that point.

I brought Avery along in case we lost the outfit and had to pack out in the snow. The dog mushers there use their sleds, equipped with steel runners, over the tundra in summer, making pretty nearly as good time as on the snow, although the dogs are not able to haul as heavy a load. Three or four hundred pounds is about the maximum that a seven or nine dog team will haul in this way. Avery had seven dogs with him. He was about six feet three in height, and we called him Skyline Slim as he always traveled the skyline.

Albert Littlewood was our cook. He was a well educated Englishman with a delightful personality, who had been in the employ of the Alaska Road Commission for a great many years as cook. Just how he had come into the country and into the position he occupied, the Lord only knows. He was a dreamer, highly temperamental, and enjoyed scenery and generally things beautiful. He gave us a good deal of concern on the trip as he was constantly becoming lost in rapture at every new twist and turn of the mountains. He was a splendid cook but got pretty well stirred up under such constant travel.

As it drew near the time for our departure Daly was delayed by business affairs for a couple of weeks, which necessitated plans being made to meet him at the later date and hustle him on to connect with our main party. Mrs. Beach and myself started on July 21st via Chicago and from there via the Great Northern, for Seattle, where we arrived four days later after an interesting trip through the Rockies in the Glacier National Park region. At Seattle we stopped over night at the new Olympic Hotel, and the next morning sailed again for the North on board the good ship *Alaska,* with Captain Nord in command.

We had a delightful trip westward with clear weather until the morning we reached Cordova. The *Alaska* tied up at Shepherd's Cannery some distance from town, and as we were bent on making time we loaded our duffle on a gas boat and, saying good-bye to steamer friends, departed. At the Cordova dock we found a speeder (a Ford on car wheels) awaiting us, to which we lost no time in transferring our belongings, and were under way within a few minutes after arrival. We had been joined by Carl Morris, the well known Nome ditch contractor, who was on his way to Fairbanks to figure on some work for the United States Smelting and Refining Company.

Our trip up the Copper River comes under the head of noninteresting as the rain fell in a steady downpour so that the curtains were closed and very little could be seen of that wonderful scenery through which the Copper River and Northwestern Railroad thread their way.

Stopping at one of the section stations for orders, we were brought to life by word that one of the bridges was in bad shape from the severe rain, with the possibility of its going out. Finally word was received for us to proceed, so we got

Motion picture enlargements

Sheep were everywhere

The new Road Commission cabin on the Savage

off quickly and continued safely across the damaged bridge (it went out that night), everything going finely until within six miles of Chitina, when we came to a landslide that completely covered the track with rocks, trees and dirt for a hundred yards or more. There was nothing to do but back up for nearly two miles to a construction camp where we telephoned to Chitina for a section gang to come out to the slide. It took two hours for the Chitina men to arrive, and they decided it would be impossible to clear the tracks without power equipment. We were informed that if we would walk around the slide the section car would take us on to Chitina. Arriving there at half-past nine after a rather uncomfortable ride, we found rooms and baths at Oscar Breedman's Chitina Hotel. It took little time to put on dry clothes and put down a well earned dinner.

The next afternoon we started in a Dodge car, with Tom Gibson as driver, for Fairbanks. Our first night we stopped at Kinney Lake Roadhouse, a most attractive place, splendidly run by Mrs. Griffith. The second night was spent with friend Meier at his roadhouse, and the third afternoon we came to my old camping ground, McCarty. We spent the night at Rika Wallen's Roadhouse and had a regular reception with John Hajdukovich, Melo and several others of our old friends. John was very busy getting ready for some friends of mine from Boston who were going hunting with him. We could have made Fairbanks that night but just had to visit and talk over old times. Rika must take us over her additions and tell of her preparations for the tourist traffic she was planning to handle. She had certainly improved conditions immensely and will have one of the most attractive stopping places on the trail. The fourth day we reached Fairbanks, after a fairly fast run, in time for lunch.

Our trip had been most interesting, with just enough excitement to keep us keyed up. At Gunnysack Creek we found the bridge washed out, and in attempting to ford the stream discovered a bed of quicksand; but with time and patience we backed out and tried another crossing lower down which was successful. This put us off our schedule, so in attempting to make up some of the lost time by running fast we hit a culvert rather harder than we intended and knocked off one of our wheels. No serious damage resulted though more time was lost replacing it. We were thankful enough not to care.

Two days in Fairbanks visiting old friends passed only too rapidly. A talk over the wire with Gibson at McKinley Park Station informed us that everything was in readiness for our hop off. Our friends from the steamer arrived at Fairbanks the night before we left, enthusiastic over what they had seen and keenly looking forward to their trip over the Richardson Trail to Chitina.

We left Fairbanks at eight o'clock on August 5th by the Government Railroad, arriving at McKinley Park Station at two in the afternoon. Jim Gibson hustled us into waiting automobiles, saying that we would drive at once to Savage River over the new road. We stopped at Morris Moreno's Hotel, and then off to our camp. In an hour and a half we were at the new road commission cabin on the Savage with our own camp just below. To think that it had taken us four days on our former trip merely to relay our outfit to Savage River!

We spent that night in the road commission cabin, the men kindly turning over half of it for our use. In conversation with Jim that evening he told me that he and Jim Burrows had packed a load of provisions to the Tonzona River and cached them in a cabin belonging to Bob Ellis, and that they had oats and hay at Clearwater, and oats only to the Chedotlothna River; also that dried salmon had been left in all the caches so that our dogs would not go hungry. The country, he said, was a game paradise with caribou everywhere. We had, as closely as we could figure, one hundred miles to travel before we would pass through and beyond McKinley National Park, and close to two hundred miles to Mount Dall.

Thus far on our trip we had been blessed with marvelous weather; except for the day at Cordova and up the Copper River the sun had shone steadily. We realized that this was too good to last and expected the average amount of rain. Little did we know what was in store for us.

The morning after our arrival at Savage we spent in packing and, as usual, the first day did not go as quickly as those that followed. We did not have a very hard day before us as we aimed only to make Igloo Creek, fifteen miles by the government signs, but less than twelve according to our calculations. By ten o'clock we were ready to start with seven horses packed and four saddled, which meant that we were short two saddle horses. This was remedied by taking turns riding. Just as we were about to go, a heavy thundershower broke and we decided to wait until it had passed, which resulted in our getting under way at twelve-thirty. The traveling was fine and we made fast time.

I forgot to mention that we had along with us a half-wild huskie dog that had joined the outfit on its way to the Tonzona earlier in the season. Jim Gibson had named her Jenny McKinley as she was found on Peters Glacier at the foot of Mount McKinley. Jenny considered herself a very important part of the outfit and kept guard over us while on the trail by chasing all game away, and at camp woe to the rabbit or gopher that dared to assail our leather. We reached Igloo rather late, but, of course, far from dark, and after a hearty meal were all ready to turn in.

The next day we passed in taking pictures and putting the finishing touches to the outfit as we were planning to make hard drives each day until we reached the cache on the Tonzona. There were showers most of the day so that the pictures did not turn out as hoped for. Then, following a fair start, we traveled up Igloo Creek going over Sable Pass and on down to the East Fork of the Toklat. I was walking, and far ahead of the outfit. As usual sheep were everywhere with a few scattered caribou, and as I was coming down to the East Fork I saw a good-sized timber wolf hurrying along above me, and a little further on, another. Being in the Park of course no firearms were out. I would have given a good deal to have taken a crack at those marauders. The few prospectors that are left in that country told me that wolves are appearing in alarming numbers. Woe to the sheep and caribou if they are allowed to remain unmolested. On my previous trip this section was alive with ptarmigan, but much to my surprise I saw but one bunch of five as I came to the refuge tent.

I lighted a fire in the tent stove and then sat down to wait for the outfit. It was an hour and a half before it arrived. After adjusting some of the packs we pushed on, crossing the East Fork and then up and over Polychrome Pass, down into the main Toklat, where we camped.

The sheep were as plentiful as on the previous trip though the largest band contained only two hundred and thirty-eight by actual count. This was somewhat less than the large band we saw before on Polychrome.

We remained a day at the Toklat in the hopes of getting movies of some of the large bunches of rams that live on those ridges, but were unsuccessful. We saw many rams but they were all scattered in twos and threes with none of the old big fellows amongst them. Somewhere back in the high rough places the old rams must have been in seclusion, for there were no signs of any hunting having taken place. On my way back to camp I did secure some close-up pictures of caribou on the river beds, but the prize of them all would not let us close enough to get a first-class picture of his grand head. We counted over fifty points and I am satisfied it would have run ten to fifteen more. It was the largest caribou head I have ever seen and I have looked at many fine ones.

We had finished dinner that evening and were lazily going over the outfit for an early-morning start when off across the river we saw horses, and upon getting the glasses counted four riders and two packs. In due time Harry Luckey, one of the guides for the McKinley Park Transportation Company, arrived accompanied by three tourists who were bent on seeing Mount McKinley. We brought the new arrivals in and gave them of our frugal repast. The evening passed rapidly as we took particular pains to relate all of our wildest bear stories. Two of the tourists, a young married couple, were greatly impressed. Harry Luckey was at his best, and that is going some.

Next day as we went through Highway Pass we had a splendid view of Mount McKinley, and in the early afternoon we reached Ed Gern's cache and camp at the foot of Copper Mountain on the bar of the East Fork of the McKinley River. We saw many caribou during the day and as we came down on the McKinley several reindeer were in sight. The day's trip had been short and as we made camp we could see the top of Mount McKinley glistening in the brilliant sunshine. Towards late afternoon Mr. Grant, who is living at Copper Mountain, made us a call with his dogs. He told us that he had killed two reindeer, and if we cared for one of them he would gladly give it to us. We certainly did care for it, and Gibson departed with a horse to pack it down from Copper Mountain. It was our first meat in a week, and gave an added zest to that night's meal.

We had now reached the country where McKinley was our constant companion. After leaving Ed Gern's cache we pulled up the north ridge, and traveling over several miles of soft tundra, dropped down again to the East Fork of McKinley. For several miles we kept on downstream, passing the Muldrow Glacier, and finally arriving at the main fork where the West Fork comes in from Muldrow.

This was the appointed day and place where we were to meet our dog musher, Slim Avery, and his team of racing huskies. Joe Quigley, prominent mining man of the Kantishna, passed us, reporting Slim at the refuge tent up the trail. It was about noon when we reached the forks and found him. We crossed the East Fork and located a fine camping ground a short distance down on the West Fork. While Albert started in on lunch we were busy with Slim and the dogs. Everything was in ship shape, with the camp surrounded by a howling lot of huskies, before lunch was ready.

The Alaskan Range stood out as if it were carved from marble, not a cloud in the sky. It was one of the most perfect views I have ever had of McKinley and its neighbors. Needless to say the cameras, both stills and motion, were worked overtime. We sat devouring McKinley until 'way after bed time, but even in our bags we could not keep from taking in the marvelous play of light on that massive ice mountain.

From this camp we made the head of Clearwater, and stopped the next night at Slim Carlson's cabin, which we reached in a downpour. It rained all night and was still at it in the morning, hard as ever. We concluded that evening it would be wiser to send Jim Burrows back so as to be sure to connect with Daly. Towards noon the rain let up and we decided to pull out and make Muddy, if no further. We bid Jim Burrows au revoir, with instructions to hustle back with Daly and meet us at Mount Dall. As we followed downstream towards a low pass we intended to cross, I am sure Burrows was most skeptical as to when and where he would meet us. He admitted later on that he was quite sure it was good-bye and not au revoir. Our afternoon's trip brought us to Muddy River, about four miles below the Peters Glacier; we found it badly swollen from the storm, and as we were delayed so long in making a crossing we camped on the west bank, with no signs of horse feed. The range was banked low in clouds affording no chance of seeing McKinley.

It is on the Muddy River alongside of, or near Peters Glacier that some day I hope to see a log cabin, reached by auto road from the Station. The mountain climber could be indefinitely occupied in exploring this vast region, and the tourist would receive a thrill never to be forgotten, while a hunter after caribou could drop down to the mouth of Muddy, which is outside of the Park, and be certain of encountering the late September caribou migration. The present road if extended to Muddy would not be over a hundred miles, which could readily be made by motor in a day. From here Mount Dall and the Dillinger, which is outside of the Park, could be reached in five to six days with pack horses, and one would then be in a virgin game country alive with sheep, moose, caribou and some bear.

To come back from my digression, we left Muddy rather late (as our horses had wandered far afield) and kept up high at almost the base of the range, to find the traveling fairly good; though there were some soft places, they were not sufficient to mire any of the horses. We crossed several streams, Granite, Dry, and Slippery, and finally reached the East Fork of Birch which we also crossed, and finding a mountainside of luscious horse feed, we stopped at once and made camp.

Although Gibson and Burrows had made a trip to the Tonzona early in the season we were not following in their tracks, for one always feels in an unknown country that there is some better way to go than the way you have taken, and so it was

Crossing the Middle Foraker

Photo by Andy Simons

Mount Foraker

with us; we were constantly trying to find better traveling, and were not always successful. Our camp at Birch was in a fine stand of timber with grass waist-high as far as eyes could see, but the horses were not satisfied with such easy picking and rambled far, as is their nature.

Leaving our camp on the east Birch we had one of our longest and hardest days. From an early start we traveled steadily, circling a ridge of low mountains that extend down from Mount Foraker. We began now to see signs of moose, and of course our constant companions, the caribou, were with us, still headed westward and in diminishing numbers. We passed three prospectors on their way to the railroad, and Gibson went up to see them. (We were traveling about a half mile lower than they.) Upon Gibson's return he said the prospectors had been two streams below or to the west of the Tonzona, and had seen quantities of sheep, moose and caribou. When we reached the East Fork of the Foraker which, odd to relate, heads up in the base of McKinley, it was low, so we had little difficulty in crossing. After supper, Slim went out to locate the horses. Upon his return he told us he could not find them but that there was a small grizzly on the river bar a short distance below camp. We were still in the Park, and as I wasn't particularly curious to investigate even a small grizzly without a gun, he was left to himself.

Our dogs were living on dried salmon which we had cached earlier in the year, and some odds and ends of reindeer that Red Grant had given us. The salmon did not go very well with the huskies, and Slim was anxious to push on so that we would be beyond the Park line and get fresh meat.

For several days the weather had been threatening, but as we started next morning it seemed no worse than usual. We crossed the middle Foraker early and though the river was high nothing serious happened. I had the motion picture camera up and ground out the crossing of the horses and also the dogs. As the outfit was coming out on the west bank I saw one of the pack horses crowd Mrs. Beach, and for a second I was afraid something was going to happen, but fortunately the pack hit the rump of her horse and slid to one side, missing her by inches.

This was another long, tedious day's hike through a bleak and uninteresting section of country, with few if any animals visible. My recollection is that we saw only five caribou. We traveled too high and when we came out on the main Foraker we were forced to follow a long ridge until we found a spot where we could get down to the river, which was high and very swift, the black, murky water literally boiling as it rushed from the two glaciers that headed into the face of Mount Foraker. A long time was used up in making the crossing and between the good judgment of Jim Gibson and a Divine Providence that watched over us we finally landed on the west side.

But this was only half of it, for we kept on traveling. Five o'clock came and still the cotton woods for which we were looking were far off. The dogs were showing signs of wear, the horses were dragging back and endeavoring to feed, while Andy and I who had walked almost the entire trip were at a point where the cotton woods could not arrive too soon. To make matters worse the clouds lowered and the rain started. It was about dark when we reached those much-heralded cotton woods, only to discover that the main attraction of this particular spot was a basin at the head of the stream with an abundant supply of horse feed. As for our camp, we pitched tents on an overflow bar of the river among some cotton trees.

"It's a rough and ready camp," Gibson remarked, "and only one day from the real Park boundary."

I wasn't particularly pleased with the weather outlook, for as I looked toward Rainy Pass it seemed as if all the clouds I had ever seen in the Inland Passage had been consolidated and were being pushed our way. Gibson insisted we were on the very edge of the "Land of Perpetual Sunshine" and that all would be well on the morrow. Let me remark that we were a long time on that edge; a constant downpour kept us in that cotton woods camp for five days.

On the second day Stephen R. Capps of the United States Geological Survey, arrived from Mount Dall, and just about saved our lives, as he had some sheep meat, of which he gave us a shoulder. I never saw a piece of meat so tenderly handled. Every scrap was saved and cooked in corn meal for the dogs. All our corn meal and rice went the same way. The supply of fish had been almost consumed, and the dogs were far from satisfied. On one particularly rainy day I sat in Capps' tent talking over various areas yet unexplored and touched on the Rainy Pass country for which we were headed. Capps remarked that that was a region he believed would be most interesting and there was little, if any, information on it. It developed that what he had in mind was the country south and west of Rainy Pass which he was certain we would be unable to reach on this trip. Andy Simons had touched on the borders of this country several years ago when he took Captain Hubback up to the headwaters of the Skwentna.

On the sixth day we pulled out, and lost no time in leaving those cotton woods. In the morning we were bothered with soft ground and one of the horses went down but was extricated without damage. We crossed several small streams and finally in the distance we could see the Chedotlothna which heads up towards Mount Russell and is approximately the western boundary of McKinley National Park. And there on the river bar outside of the Park were many scattered caribou! That evening the dogs had food aplenty, while we likewise enjoyed fresh caribou steaks.

Breaking camp next morning we crossed the Chedotlothna River only after considerable manoeuvering as it was the largest river that we had met. We then climbed in easy stages up the dividing ridge to the Tonzona watershed. Unfortunately we kept too high up and towards afternoon, after passing the camp of the prospectors, Giles and Knudson, we became involved in the worst mess of boulders I have ever experienced with horses. It meant slow travel and careful handling, but after nearly two hours of this we finally came out on a long level bench which we followed until we reached Cathedral Creek (so named by Capps) where our cache had been made in a log cabin belonging to Bob Ellis.

Earlier in the day we had completely lost Slim and the dogs, so when we saw smoke a long way off we concluded it must be he. We were about to make an answering smoke when we located another which was very nearly in the line of our travel. Upon reaching the latter smoke we decided that it had been made by Slim as we saw tracks of dogs and a sled nearby. This completely puzzled us, especially as the smoke in the distance had become larger, and after a careful study with our glasses we were certain that we could make out two men. As nothing further happened we continued on our way and as before stated, we arrived on the banks of Cathedral Creek but about a thousand or fifteen hundred feet above it. There we located a fairly good game trail that led down the side of the mountain with only a few spots that gave us any trouble, and by half-past six we found ourselves at Ellis' cabin where we camped. No sign of Slim and the dogs, and, as we were now far beyond the region of his wanderings, we began to worry about the smokes we had seen and wonder if they could possibly have been Slim's signals that he was in trouble. We finally decided that as Slim had taken care of himself in many wild and uncharted countries for the greater part of his life, he would be able to do so in this instance.

We had finished dinner and were all set for the night when we heard Slim's voice yelling at the dogs. We began at once to hello at him and it was not long before he and the dogs appeared, accompanied by two Indians. It seems that upon seeing the smoke, Slim naturally thought we were responsible for it and answered with the smoke we had found, at once starting off for the other smoke. Upon arriving at the spot he determined it had been made by Indians. He then pulled on and dropped down the side of the mountain to the bar of the Tonzona River, determined to follow up the first stream to its head, as he figured that was where our cache had been made. He was going along, still wondering about the smokes, as he was certain there wasn't a soul within several hundred miles of us, when two Indians appeared, greeted him, and then proceeded to follow him. Thus they arrived at camp, and without ado the Indians came into the cook tent, sat down by the stove and removed their wet moccasins.

They had but little to say but we finally wormed out of them that they were camped on the Slo fork of the Kuskokwim River about a hundred miles off, and had come to look over this country for hunting next fall. We further learned that they were to meet another Indian, which accounted for their smoke, and when they saw Slim's answer they were sure he was their friend. We took them at their word, though no doubt they were lying. After a good night's sleep, curled up like dogs back of the stove, they made their departure, but not until we had given them a jawbone of some flour and sugar. I feared that this would not be the last of them, but, whatever their mission or wherever they came from, we never saw sign of them or anyone else again on our trip. As we saw a number of bands of sheep from our camp, I decided we would remain there the next day to overhaul our provisions and incidentally to secure some sheep meat as our larder was again empty.

The cache we had made in Ellis' cabin was in bad shape. Everything was soaked and many of the things had started to mildew. Unfortunately the roof of the cabin was a sieve. No doubt in the winter, at forty degrees below zero, it might have been tight, but now was useless as a shelter. While Gibson, Slim and Albert worked on opening up and drying our supplies, Andy and I climbed the peaks. Though we climbed high and traveled far, putting in a long hard day, we saw nothing but ewes and lambs. There was one large bunch that had several small rams which we attempted to stalk. We used every care and precaution, but something must have gone wrong for they were up and started off before we were within half a mile of them. At last we gave up the sheep, and seeing a couple of caribou down below started for them; but long before we were anywhere near they had disappeared and never were located again. Just before reaching the river we came into some scattered timber and willows which was all tracked up with moose. We proceeded carefully in the hopes of seeing something, as we really needed meat in camp, but we were without any luck and finally reached camp late in the afternoon to be greeted by Jenny who turned away in disgust after she had smelled us over carefully and failed to get the scent of fresh meat.

On August 24th we made our final push to the head of the Tonzona and Mount Dall. It was but a short trip, even though the ground was quite soft. We passed a good-sized stream coming in from the right on the opposite side of the river and about noon reached the head of the main stream where two forks branch out, one to the left, or east and the other to the right, or slightly southwest. We made camp in some low cottonwoods about fifty yards below Capps' old camp. Some distance to the right at the head of the stream was a fairly good-sized peak which we were sure was Mount Dall.

Everywhere we looked there were white spots — sheep, sheep and even more sheep. One bunch on the hills directly across the Tonzona we were sure were rams, and then again all that we could see up towards Mount Dall looked suspiciously like sheep of the male gender.

We worked that afternoon fixing up camp in a substantial manner as I thought that we would probably remain at this spot until Daly and Burrows caught up with us. On our entire trip to date we had seen less ptarmigan than in one day on the trip three years previous. In talking this over with Mr. Capps he was sure that some disease was killing them off and said that some he killed could not be eaten on account of their condition.

My first day hunting at Mount Dall was for meat, pure and simple, so starting early with Andy and Gibson we proceeded upstream towards the base of Mount Dall. We passed many bunches of rams but decided our best bet was to go on up to the glacier. We were still some distance from it when we located a large ram lying on a pointed rock and several others just below him. These lower rams were traveling down and finally disappeared in a deep draw. There was some discussion as to how we were to reach the rams, and finally I told Andy to lead on. We started up a stream bed with high, rocky sides which appeared to head towards the draw we wanted to investigate. The wind was blowing a gale down the side of the mountain but we were sheltered for most of the distance until we came out on a shale slide which had to be crossed in order to reach that draw.

We crawled over the slide as best we could, and reaching the edge looked down into a basin that was literally covered with rams. They were lying down unconcerned and protected

Motion picture enlargements

A friendly ewe　　　　*The two Indians*

Cathedral Mountain on Tonzona

from the wind, and sad to relate there wasn't a real large head in the bunch. We examined them carefully for several minutes and Andy suggested that I kill the lower ram as he thought it was the largest. The ram on the rocky point across the draw was still lying down though showing much interest in our doings. I suggested shooting at the one across the way, which met with much disapproval.

"We need meat," Andy declared. "Get that first, then waste all the ammunition you want on that fellow over there."

I shoved the rifle ahead and crawled to the edge to find the lower ram had risen and was looking directly towards us. I took a hurried aim and the gun cracked just as the ram jumped, but only to collapse and roll down about fifteen feet stone dead.

Our friend across the way had risen, and giving him one hurried look through the glasses I pulled up the rifle and let go. The bullet struck at his feet and the spattering rock made him jump and run. From then on until he went out of sight back of some rocks near skyline I kept sending a liberal supply of lead after him, but all too low. Once he flinched and I was sure he was hit, but Andy and Gibson, who were both watching through their glasses, said it was a rock splinter and not the bullet that hit. After it was all over these men asked why I wanted to waste ammunition on a sheep at such a distance. It was not until then that I actually realized how far off that ram had been. At least I had the satisfaction of replying, "Well, I came darned close to him every shot anyway."

We went down to the dead ram and while it was being

butchered I noticed a ram come out from some rocks and go up into a cave-like opening high above us. There was a deep patch on its right side that looked like blood and I was quite certain it was the ram I had been bombarding. After we were through with our work we climbed clear to the top to put this wounded ram out of its misery. We finally came quite close to the ram which had gone into the cave-like formation and was lying down sheltered from the wind. After considerable noise we succeeded in arousing our friend, who came slowly out, stopped, looked us over carefully and then walked by and on up over the top. It was not the ram I had shot at, and further he was in a perfectly healthy condition, though there was a deep stain on his side from lying on reddish shale. Worse to relate his head was quite small. We packed the dead ram to the bottom of the draw leaving him in a safe place so he could be brought into camp next day on a horse. With sufficient meat for our immediate requirements we started back to camp.

On our return we traveled slowly as we were looking over the various bunches of sheep scattered about the hillsides in hope that we might locate a fine big head for the next day's hunt. We saw several that looked to be the right sort and at last we located a bunch of three consisting of one small, one medium and a grand old-timer.

"That's our boy for tomorrow," remarked Andy, then turning his glasses to the opposite ridge he looked hard for a few seconds, and remarked, "Do you see that large moose up there?" pointing in the distance. I saw a large black animal but couldn't make out just what it was.

"It's a huge grizzly coming this way," Andy announced.

We were out in the open and the wind was blowing hard directly towards the bear.

There was no chance to do anything but take a crack at him from where we stood. The bear was high up on the mountain side, going along slowly with his huge head swinging from side to side. We wondered what the distance was. Someone guessed about two hundred yards, so I took aim and immediately realized that he was further off than that as the front sight completely covered him. I held about a foot above the bear's back and let go only to have the bullet strike some distance below the bear. I then raised my sights to four hundred yards, and the bullet struck below the bear though considerably nearer. At the splash of the bullet on the rock the bear came rushing down to investigate.

Gibson took me by the arm and said, "Come on and leave that bear alone; they have a jinx on you."

I'll admit I was inclined to feel that way myself and started to go on, but as the bear had returned to his former trail I changed my mind and decided to get him. I raised the sights to seven hundred and fifty yards and let go again, the bullet striking directly behind the bear. Hurriedly loading I aimed slightly in front of Mr. Bear and on the report of the rifle there was a dull thud and the bear came rolling down the side of the mountain like an express train.

There was more or less panic in our ranks. Only Andy appeared calm; Gibson began hurriedly to load the 22 Winchester he was carrying, while I filled up the Mauser, then pulled out a handful of shells to have in easy reach. I looked about for a sizeable rock behind which to make my stand, but nothing short of a fair-sized cobblestone was in sight.

The bear, as I said, was coming down fast, rolling over and over until he landed on a bench whereupon he proceeded to drag himself into a clump of alders. We waited for a long time for we figured that if he wasn't badly hurt he would come out, and if he was we would leave him until the next day. The shooting had disturbed our big ram and we watched him make for the highest, most inaccessible place on his side of the Range.

After about half an hour we went on our way to camp which we reached in time for a late supper of sheep meat that was none too tender. We discussed plans that evening and finally concluded that the bear, if still in the alders, would be dead, and that Gibson and Slim when they went for the meat should give the alders the once-over. Andy and I were to go after the big ram with the intention of finding him if he were still in the country. When we started off next morning there was snow in the air, and the weather looked pretty mean generally, but we were not to be discouraged. Andy and I climbed to the top of the mountain where we had last seen the big ram and wandered over every nook and corner, but no sign of him; in fact the sheep had very nearly all disappeared. Eventually we located a few bunches hidden away in the most secluded of spots, which convinced us that a storm was on its way.

Toward late afternoon we saw two fair-sized moose, just at the willow line on the right branch. They were still in the velvet and in any case too small. We reached camp late that evening and were quite discouraged at not having found our fine ram. Gibson and Slim had returned with the sheep meat, but claimed to have forgotten about the bear. Maybe so; I don't know. Jim Gibson then admitted that if they waited until the next day it would give him longer to die and further he didn't like a wounded grizzly at any time and least of all in a bunch of thick alders. The next day was impossible. It just poured, and the wind nearly took us out of the country. Needless to remark we holed up in camp. Towards afternoon it let up a bit so Gibson and Slim went out to get the grizzly, but without success. They returned late in the evening and claimed not to have found any sign of it.

August 28th being fine and clear, Andy and I started for Mount Dall. On our way to the glacier we located three rams which corresponded to the three we had seen, but on carefully examining the large one we could not decide that he was what I was after. As they were in a safe position and could not have been successfully stalked, we passed them up. Upon reaching the glacier we traveled well up the ice in the hopes of locating some rams we had seen several days before, but without success. We saw rams lying on a grassy slide directly under Mount Dall. I looked them over and thought they were small, but Andy was not satisfied and he suggested that I wait until he should cross the stream to get a better look at them. He also wanted to take a look into a basin and canyon which were alongside the grassy slope.

It was but a short time before Andy returned and informed me that there was one very large ram in the bunch and that they were easy to reach. Off we went and I found that Andy was not so truthful, as the climbing was anything but easy for me; but as Andy is like a goat it didn't seem to bother him at all. When we were part way up we discovered that the sheep had gone. Desiring to get a little more exercise we continued to the spot where the sheep had been lying. We searched everywhere but no sign of them; they had literally been swallowed up. Andy explored a miserable steep and uninviting canyon, with no better success.

We stayed up on our exposed roost until four-thirty, with the wind trying to dislodge us every minute. We noticed that the three rams we had passed up had come down to feed and were going lower steadily. Andy proceeded to give me a dissertation on sheep hunting to the effect that it was more or less useless to climb these high mountains, instead of which we should wait until they came down to feed when it would be easy for us to get within reach of them. While we waited, a fair-sized ram came down within a short distance of us, but across the canyon. He looked us over carefully and then lay down, occasionally looking up towards Mount Dall.

"That ram," said Andy, "is watching us and if we keep quiet and wait, those other rams will come back."

I had no desire to contradict Andy, but for some unknown reason the ram we had passed in the morning was steadily growing larger in my estimation and I was more than confident that we were prejudiced owing to the position he was in; but now that he was coming down I was sure he was the real king of Mount Dall; and just then a cold blast almost rolled me from my perch.

"Let's go for that other fellow," I said. Andy agreed.

When we reached the river bed we gave one last look back. There away up in the snow and ice of Mount Dall we saw the rams we had been looking for, and before we started our stalk for the downstream ram we saw them come down and pass within thirty yards of where we had been waiting.

Well, we sat down and waited and waited. Seven o'clock came and about half-past Andy started and at the same time remarked, "We have had a hard day. That is a big ram and I wanted him to get down in a good position so we wouldn't have to climb too high."

I should say that we went up two to three hundred feet, everything going well until we stumbled upon the small ram of the trio in the hole in which we wanted to hide. Of course he stampeded and we concluded that the jig was up, so we lay quiet for some time. Then we crawled out of our hole to find the three rams tranquilly feeding, but above us. Andy whispered, "We can't move. Can you shoot through those rocks?" I looked over the ground with my glasses and, though there were several vertical rocks, the head and shoulders of the big ram were clear.

That one glimpse settled me on the size of the head, so getting in the best position possible, I held on the shoulder, and as the gun went off I saw the ram jump and go between the two rocks, the lower part of his rump showing. Shooting again I dislodged him and he came tumbling down the mountain and passed us, bringing up on some rocks below. The ram was all that I could have hoped for, as he was a very old one with curl over 41 inches and base 14¾ inches. The first shot had really killed him as it entered a little low on the shoulder and passed through the backbone, tearing a hole large enough to push your hand through. We skinned out the head and dressed out the carcass, though it was only good for dog food, as both hindquarters had been ruined with the second shot. It was again late when we reached camp, but that made no difference as a hard day's work had been well ended. Next day Andy, Slim and Gibson were off for the ram while I laid in camp catching up on my photographic work and repairing odds and ends.

Then Andy, Gibson and I went down to the right branch and followed it up to the head, while Slim went further downstream to locate the country below us. We saw quantities of sheep on both sides and all looked very much like rams. By noon the wind was blowing a gale and as we had to buck it we made very slow progress, especially as the fine sand the wind carried cut sharply. Capps had described the head of this stream and as there was a very interesting glacier towards the head of another stream on the left-hand side which he called Surprise Glacier owing to its being unobserved until you came directly upon it, I was particularly anxious to see it.

At the extreme head of the main stream there was a break in the mountains and a fine low pass which should lead down to the head of the Yentna on the south side of the Range. So far as is known this pass had been undiscovered until this year when Capps explored it and went through to the south side. For many years the Indians from the south side of the Range would go up to the head of the Yentna and return with sheep. This puzzled the Alaskans, as no sheep had ever been seen on the south side, so it is fair to presume that this pass must have

Surprise Glacier

Mount Russell from the Chedotlothna

been known to the older Indians and used by them. As we had seen many meat racks that had not been used for years we felt sure our supposition was correct.

After securing some pictures of Surprise Glacier, we started downstream in a light snow which quickly turned into a teeming rain with the wind stronger than ever; fortunately our backs were turned to it and the horses traveled fast. We picked up Slim at the mouth, a very wet and bedraggled individual, as he had forded the river waist-deep and deeper, while the rain completed the wetting down.

The rain kept up all night with the wind every moment threatening to send our tents to the upper reaches of Mount Dall. Fortunately we weathered it. As the rain continued most of the next morning we laid up in camp and began worrying about Daly and Burrows. We had been at the head of the Tonzona for ten days and we were wondering how much longer it would be before we could leave and push on down to Rainy Pass. Toward afternoon the rain let up, so Gibson, Slim and I started out for a walk while Andy worked on the scalps of my rams. We had wandered but a short distance when we heard some ptarmigan and we at once hustled back to camp for the 22. You may imagine our surprise on reaching camp to find two pack horses with Burrows driving them. Daly had arrived in seven days, two days shorter time than we calculated. There was much rejoicing, and about that time the clouds broke away so "everyone was happy and the goose hung high."

After the greetings, Daly in a questioning manner turned to me and wanted to know if the object of the trip was to discover difficult country, or just to try one's patience; at any rate he allowed he could stand it if we could. It seems that my friends had been assuring him that if he ever located me it would be a miracle. I fooled them for once.

We decided to put in one more day at that camp, and then turn downstream and into the Tonzona Basin. The next day was a glorious one—a clear blue sky and a bright shining sun. Andy declared that he would take Daly to Mount Dall and get him up to the large ram that had fooled me, while Slim and I went off to the right branch to look over some willows for moose. Gibson decided meantime to follow on downstream to try and locate a way into the basin. Slim and I climbed high above the willow patch, sat down, and waited. About three o'clock the willows here and there began to show signs of life which turned out to be moose. We saw eleven that afternoon, of which nine were bulls but none of the size I was after. It was after six when we pulled out for camp and although I had seen nothing that I wanted I nevertheless considered it had been a most successful day. Gibson overtook us on our way to camp and said that he had seen many rams, several of which were large, but there was no place to enter the basin until we went well downstream below Cathedral Creek.

As we came near camp we spied Daly and Andy coming with something white on Andy's back which seen through the glasses, turned out to be a sheep head.

"Well," said Andy, "we have your friend."

"Yes," remarked Daly, "and what's more Andy hunts sheep in the right way."

It developed during the evening's talk that when Daly and

Andy reached the glacier, there stood the band of rams that had eluded me. "What shall we do, go up and probably stampede them or wait until they come down?" asked Andy. There was but one answer; they waited quietly behind a rock, smoking cigarettes and spinning yarns. Around three o'clock the rams came down and after they were well established on their feeding ground Andy took Daly up a draw for possibly a hundred feet and the big old ram of Mount Dall bit the dust.

"That's the only way to hunt sheep; let them come down to you," was Daly's closing comment.

On the way back to camp that day I had a wonderful view of Mount Dall, the first really clear one, but as it was late and as I was sure the fine weather had set in I let my photographic work go until next day.

Bright and early on September 5th we broke camp for our final attempt to reach Rainy Pass. Slim and I were off with the dogs and cameras for that picture of Mount Dall, but, sad to relate, though the sky was clear of clouds the mountain was completely covered by a bank of fog that had risen from the valley. I waited until the last minute in hope of it clearing, and finally had to shoot Dall enveloped in fog. We went on downstream until we thought we could get into the basin, but after stumbling into some dry, soft ground we gave it up and camped on a small clear stream that emptied into the Tonzona. As Daly and Andy were off in the mountains after sheep and expected to find us in the basin, we started a great smoke, which they fortunately saw, and made camp after five o'clock. They had seen several bunches of sheep but all were small, though there were some in the basin that looked to be the right sort.

Next day our horses had gone and it was one o'clock before the two Jims returned with them. Not discouraged, we packed up and started downstream until we came to some old camp grounds unused for many years; one of these we felt sure had been Dr. Brook's when he made his reconnaissance of Mount McKinley in 1902; the others had belonged either to sourdoughs or Indians. We followed the stream into the basin and kept on until late, when the going became very soft and rain began to fall. Picking out a fairly dry spot we made what was destined to be our most westerly camp.

Andy was anxious that Daly come with him to investigate a bunch of rams he had located the day before, and they were off before camp had been pitched. Well after dark they returned with a magnificent ram head with a curl over forty inches and a spread of twenty-seven inches. This ended our sheep hunting. For days we remained at this camp waiting for the weather to clear. During that time there were but two decent days, on one of which Gibson and I climbed the high ridges above camp and made a general exploration of the country. We could plainly trace the various branches of the Tonzona, three in number, and further on the Dillinger, and in the distance were peaks that Andy told us marked Simpson Pass. During the rainy days I worked on the maps and figured out our best plan. Rainy Pass could not be over forty to fifty miles away, which meant three days travel at best. On all the mountains I could see many sheep, and among them, perhaps, the world's record was still roaming at large.

On our other clear day Andy, Burrows and I made a fair reconnaissance of the Tonzona Basin and located the pass which Dr. Brooks had traveled. We also found an old camping ground of white men with a cache and quite a quantity of grub in good condition, which we were unable to understand, as all signs pointed to the camp's not having been used for years. Our conclusion was that it was likely a trapper's camp and the cache had been used by someone else who might have camped nearby. This branch of the Tonzona which drained the main basin, was a fair-sized stream which, passing on through a steep canyon, emptied into the Tonzona several miles below Cathedral Creek on the west side. We saw many moose on this day's trip, most of them bulls, but all too small; we were ambitious for a head of 70 inches or better.

It was now nearing September 15th, the date we had set as the latest that it was safe to remain down the range, and after considerable vacillation it was decided that we had better start back. On September 12th the weather cleared. We broke camp and, cutting through some woods at the base of the mountains, made the river bar, covering in a couple of hours ground which had taken us a day and a half to make coming in. We found the Tonzona in bad shape, the water high, and quicksand at the only available spot for crossing. There was nothing to do but tackle it and fortunately we made it without any serious mishap, though for a short time it looked as if one of our pack horses was gone. Teddie, who was always the leader, wandered out of line and struck some quicksand, going down and under; but in some inconceivable manner he got on his feet again and made the shore. The dogs had a very bad time of it and Spot positively refused to tackle the stream. We went off and left him emitting the most pathetic howls I have ever heard a husky turn loose. Slim remarked that if he didn't have the nerve to tackle it he could stay there. His courage must have returned for it was not long before he caught up with us.

We came to Ellis' cabin early that afternoon and at once proceeded to replenish our supplies from the cache and also to celebrate with a bath. We were all set for an early start next morning with the intention of camping near Giles' cabin on Rock Creek to hunt moose for a couple of days. Again a downpour that continued all day upset everything. Again we changed plans, and when we had a fine day following we packed up and pushed on as far as possible, passing Giles' cabin and eventually camping in a swamp where we found plenty of horse feed. That afternoon the range stood out clear as a bell, and from our position Foraker appeared to tower over McKinley. Of course we couldn't take time to unpack the cameras and when we reached camp the clouds had begun to gather, so another golden opportunity had gone.

As we were coming down the ridge into the Chedotlothna, about noon the next day, we spied a large grizzly. We made every endeavor to get Daly within range, but Mr. Bear was too canny and made his getaway down a steep draw. After we made camp and had lunch, Daly and Andy crossed the river, going downstream in hopes of coming across the bear again. Slim, Gibson and I went upstream to try to definitely locate Mount Russell. We saw quantities of sheep, mostly ewes and lambs, and on our way up to the high places came across the head of a large ram which appeared to have been killed in the early spring. The clouds were breaking, and finally getting a fairly good view of Mount Russell, I used up my films only to have it clear perfectly a little later on.

Returning to camp, Daly and Andy reported having seen many moose signs and one good head. Far below us, possibly ten miles, they also saw huge bands of caribou, all traveling to the eastward, no doubt on their winter's migration. We decided to remain another day at this camp so as to hunt downstream in hopes of seeing a large moose or possibly getting in with the caribou. Again the fates were against us for the rain was coming down next morning, if possible, harder than at any time on the trip. We remained close in camp all day, but towards evening the barometer began to rise and our spirits with it, for we were now determined to push on to the mouth of the Muddy and there put in our remaining days before hiking it out for our steamer. The next few days were fine and we made our old camp in the cottonwoods the first night; on the second, after trouble crossing the main Foraker, we reached our east Foraker camp.

On the third day as we were nearing Birch Creek we saw a large grizzly feeding with his long hair waving in the stiff breeze. We were within the Park and all guns and ammunition were stowed away. As we had to pass close to where the bear was we decided to yell so as to scare him. Our efforts had the opposite result for in the next breath Mr. Grizzly was coming directly for us as hard as he could. There was a wild scramble to get our guns, and fortunately Andy remembered I had a box of cartridges in my saddle bags. Things looked rather unpleasant for a few seconds, but the bear changed his mind and was off in some willows not to be seen again. As it was, the horses had become quite nervous and if that bear had charged through us, I am sure it would have taken till Christmas time to have gathered up our outfit, if nothing worse had happened. After a long day we reached Bill Shannon's cache on Slippery, only to find no water within a mile and practically no horse feed; so we traveled down to a lake where we camped with our horses tied to trees, there being no sign of feed within miles.

"Tomorrow night," Jim Gibson remarked, "they will have fine feed on the river bar at the mouth of Muddy."

Again we were doomed to disappointment for when we reached the mouth of Muddy, after traveling for hours through huge bands of caribou, we found that all the feed had been either eaten or trampled under the hoofs of the migrating caribou. Again the horses had to be tied and early in the morning Gibson and Burrows, went off with the horses to Shannon's cache on McKinley River bar, leaving two poor animals with us. They were to return on the third day which we were sure was sufficient time for us to secure fine specimens of caribou.

There was no difficulty in locating caribou, but to get a worth while head was another proposition. We looked over many bands and at last I picked out one that seemed to be a fair specimen and killed him. Daly and Andy then departed for across the river, while Slim and I went in for the horses and packed the caribou into camp. Again we went out in hope of finding some feed for the two horses and ended by tethering them in a small bunch of grass and pea vine that probably lasted half an hour. Andy and Daly appeared from the woods across the river, Andy with a head on his back that looked larger than he. Slim and I concluded it must be two, but upon their crossing the river we were shown one of the finest caribou heads you would want to cast eyes upon with fifty well-defined points. It seemed that in shooting at the large head Daly thought he had not dropped him, and with his second shot brought down another which turned out to be a nice head but much smaller. As we had agreed between ourselves to kill but two caribou, this finished his bag.

The following day Andy and I traveled miles in a heavy snowstorm trying to locate a large head. We saw many, many bands and crossed the river three times, finally getting mixed in with a band of several hundred, and though there were numerous good heads we could not decide on any of them. We hurried back to camp to get the others out to see the large band but the barking of the dogs must have scared them for they turned and went back across the river. I felt that I couldn't leave that camp without making every effort to secure a large specimen, so Andy and I were off early on the morning of September 23rd, the day the two Jims were to return to us. We traveled not more than half a mile up the bar before we saw a large band coming directly towards us. We looked them over very carefully and picked out several fine bulls; one in particular met our fancy as his horns crossed in the rear and appeared tight together. I decided to take him, and, sitting down, I waited for an opening of the bunch so that I could reach my bull. At last two cows that were feeding alongside of him separated and my opportunity came. Upon the crack of the rifle the band stampeded, my bull with the bunch.

"I guess you missed him," Andy said, and then, "Run out and get the best shot you can; it is the only chance."

As Andy spoke I saw the bull slow down, stop, jump in the air, and fall. When we came up to him he was dead, shot through the heart. The head turned out to be all that I had hoped for; it was rangy with forty-five points, and the rear horns not only crossed but were firmly against one another; when I pulled them apart they snapped back in place again. It did not take long to remove the head and make for camp where we found the horses and the camp well on its way to demolition.

That afternoon we reached Shannon's cache on the McKinley, my wife and Daly traveling with Slim, as the fresh snow made good going for the dogs. We had caribou with us all day long; in many bands reindeer were seen; one in particular was a fine bull with a grand head, and as white as snow. We were within the limits of McKinley Park again, so our guns were packed away. It seems too bad that these reindeer should be allowed to range with the caribou.

From Shannon's we went to Wonder Lake, where Polly's Roadhouse is located, stopping over night with the Andersons. There we saw caribou again in countless thousands, as Slim remarked, and pictures galore were shot, both still and motion. Unfortunately after all films were exposed the range cleared and we had a magnificent view of McKinley and its shadow in Wonder Lake. That evening we returned to Shannon's camp where the caribou were still rambling by; one bunch took over three hours to pass.

We left Slim and his dogs at Wonder Lake which made us realize that the trip was nearly at an end. From Shannon's it took us four days to make the road camp at Savage, and during those four days we passed through many sheep. At Sanctuary and Savage the caribou were in endless procession. We drove in from Savage by automobile, while the men brought the outfit, arriving early in the afternoon. That night we stayed at Merino's McKinley Park Hotel and the greater part of the time was taken up in discussing the disposition of Jenny. Being of a tender nature I said I would take her home with me.

We had traveled between four and five hundred miles through country practically unknown to white men, and I feel safe in saying that Mrs. Beach was the first white woman who has ever been to Mount Dall, though possibly Fanny Quigley may have reached it on one of her many wanderings. We saw sheep, moose and caribou in countless numbers and a country that for years will be just about impossible to reach for hunting. It was a never-to-be-forgotten trip, and even though we failed to make Rainy Pass, we did live for nearly sixty days in the Shadows of Mount McKinley.

Jenny of Mount McKinley

JENNY OF MOUNT McKINLEY

NESTLING at the base of Mount McKinley on the north side of the Alaskan Range is a large and impressive mass of ice known as Peters Glacier, from which emerges, roaring, a dirty body of water which goes by the expressive name of "Muddy." At the head of this stream and alongside of the glacier there was camped a long and lanky son of Wyoming. This man had been prospecting the McKinley Range for several years, his only intimate companions being a bunch of half-wild huskies. One beautiful morning a few years ago the huskie family was increased by some seven or eight puppies, and their master, looking over the new arrivals, picked up a little black lady who attracted his attention and remarked, "Well, you are the Queen of the bunch." From this the puppy was known as "Queenie." She rapidly began to show promise of becoming a wise and well behaved sled dog. Somewhere back in the ancestry of this wild wolf dog, high breeding and class must have existed.

As Queenie's accomplishments developed it was not long before a nearby neighbor on the Clearwater, some twenty miles off, wanted her. Our Wyoming friend had many dogs, and feed was scarce and hard to get; finally he parted with Queenie.

Things progressed favorably for a time and Queenie became a personality in her new home. She had developed the keen scent and hunting prowess of her wolf ancestor and could bring a rabbit or gopher down with little effort. In the team, things were not progressing so well, for Queenie was unable to control her wolf howls when traveling over the crisp trail. Beatings only cowed her; she learned to howl without opening her mouth. Finally there came to Queenie a family of wonderful wild wolf dogs with straight ears and slant eyes. After the puppies were able to care for themselves, Queenie's master decided he had no further use for her and gave her to a friend who lived in a mining town about thirty miles to the north.

New troubles arose. Soon after her advent at the new home Queenie saw a horrible beast about to attack some of her master's belongings. With the courage of her distant ancestor she made one dive for it only to meet an impenetrable wall of sharp needles which readily came off and remained imbedded in her face, mouth and far down her throat. Poor Queenie had had her first experience with a porcupine and had come off second best. Her new master, failing to remove the quills, had made up his mind to put her out of her misery, but a miner came along and begged him not to shoot her; he would remove the quills. It took him over two hours to perform the operation, and even then it was impossible to extricate them all. After this Queenie was taken into town on the railroad and given away.

For a time Queenie enjoyed quiet and comfort but it was to be short-lived. Her new owner had a child who tried to make friends with her, but as Queenie was not accustomed to that sort of treatment she did not respond, and finally ended by either growling, snapping or biting the youngster. Whatever happened only Queenie and the child will ever know, but the act brought severe chastisement. That was the last seen of Queenie by her erstwhile owners.

About five weeks after her disappearance our pack outfit was traveling down the Alaskan Range over high benches on its way to Mount Dall, many miles to the westward. On approaching the head of Muddy River, the men saw what they thought was a wolf lying on the ice on Peters Glacier. As they came near the animal moved off and they saw it was a dog. Thinking she was lost they began calling, using such names as came to their minds, without effect. Finally one of the men hit on Jenny. With that the dog came running towards them wagging her tail and showing all evidences of friendship. She looked lean and half starved, and as the men were big-hearted they decided to give her a square meal. Jenny at once considered herself part of the outfit and traveled majestically at the head of the train. She quickly made herself a valuable asset by standing guard at night, and woe to the rabbit or gopher that attempted destruction! One night the men were awakened by a loud rumpus from Jenny and upon investigation they found her driving a porcupine out of camp. No chance of her getting fooled a second time.

They returned from Mount Dall to the railroad where I joined them and heard of Jenny's wonderful achievements and the necessity of taking her along with us on our trip. I looked her over and, though she showed no marked signs of friendship, I took a fancy to her. Up to this time we did not know the history of our watchdog, and it wasn't until ten days later, when the Wyoming prospector joined us with his dog team, that we discovered that Jenny of Mount McKinley was, or had been, his Queenie.

Jenny guarded the pack train and worked like a Trojan at her job. Every little while she would circle and come to the rear of the train to look things over and then trot to the head again. She had a strong objection to game, ever fearful, no doubt, that they might charge, with the result she chased various caribou and other animals to the high hills, returning with her head in the air and her tail curled tight over her back, very proud of her performance. This did not suit our views, so poor Jenny was harnessed as left wheel dog to the sled.

As we had to pass through Mount McKinley National Park where no living thing can be disturbed, we had secured dog feed (dried salmon) for a sufficient number of days to cover our passage. The unexpected is always happening in Alaska, and this time a very severe storm laid us up for five days. Dog feed was exhausted and likewise our supply of corn meal and rice, which went to help appease the hunger of the poor huskies. At last the Park boundaries were behind and a short trip from camp enabled the dog musher to secure a caribou. Upon returning to camp for a horse to pack in the meat he was met by Jenny who carefully smelled his hands and without ado took off on his back track. When they reached the caribou Jenny was enjoying a hearty meal.

From this you might think that Jenny was the usual huskie type of glutton, but such was not the case. She was a small

eater and very particular in what she would take. A great deal
of her time was occupied about camp in making caches for
future use. There was no doubt she intended to winter in that
country, and knowing the Alaskan Range, took no chance.
Poor Jenny! Little did she know what was in store for her.
As a privileged character she was allowed to wander about
camp, the other dogs being tied. Twenty-four hours a day
she was on duty and never once did she allow anything to
happen, nor did she steal any meat though many opportunities offered. Whenever anyone returned from a hunt Jenny
would be on hand about a mile from camp and at once would
come up and smell. If she caught the scent of a fresh kill no
time was wasted, off she would go on the back track. If it
happened that nothing had been secured, which was more
often the case, a disgusted look would be cast at the returning
hunters and back to camp she would go. When meat was to
be packed into camp Jenny was always on the job and came
in with two hind quarters strapped on her sides.

In the team she was a tower of strength. She never shirked,
always willing to do more than her share. When the dogs
were about to be harnessed in the morning Jenny would disappear and only a diligent search would reveal her hiding
place. It wasn't that she wanted to sidestep hard work, but
I am sure she felt that her responsibilities were in other directions such as guarding the caravan while in motion. One
morning she did elude all searching parties, and for a time
we thought she again had a taste of the wanderlust. We had
been on the way only a short time when with all possible
importance she appeared and at once took upon herself the

responsibility of leading the dogs, between times watching the pack train. This continued for a part of the day until in a burst of importance she came within reaching distance of the dog musher who wasted but little time in shifting Jenny back to her old place at wheel. The music that was wafted over the McKinley River for the rest of the day far outstripped the singing of a large band of hungry wolves on the track of a long-deferred meal.

Coming to a camp on the bar of McKinley River we met a friend whom Jenny greeted most affectionately. It turned out to be the miner who had removed the porcupine quills some months previously. She had never seen him before or since, until this day.

We bade adieu to our Wyoming friend and his dogs at Wonder Lake for we knew there would be no further need of them for the balance of the trip. As our journey was nearing the end Jenny seemed to sense an approaching calamity. Her behavior was above reproach and on the first command she would respond instantly. Within three days of the railroad, as we were traveling up a long steep grade and Jenny was on duty, we saw in the distance an object which we made out to be a man with a bunch of dogs. Suddenly Jenny got the scent and acted most peculiarly; she slunk to the off side of the train with her tail tight between her legs. At last we passed the man, who turned out to be one of Jenny's former owners. He called her a few times without result. It was not until we had passed well on our way that Jenny came to life and ran off to a high knoll looking down on her late master with her head up and that tail in a tight curl on her back.

Jenny in a friendly mood

At last we reached McKinley Park Station and everyone was busy as the party was to separate the next day. Poor Jenny couldn't make out what was happening. Doubtless she felt that if she could only keep track of the duffle, eventually she would be with us. It was almost impossible to separate her from it. That night there was a serious conference concerning what was to become of Jenny of Mount McKinley. Having a soft spot for dogs and having become very much attached to this wild wanderer, I finally consented to take her home with me. When I broke the news to the long-suffering lady of the party, my wife, she responded with some remarks about a letter I had received from home advising me that my canine population now consisted of twelve huskies and a police dog.

But little more remains to be told, for Jenny stood her journey like the thoroughbred she is. First Curry, then Seward; at Juneau she called on the Governor; at last Seattle, Chicago and finally New York was reached and Jenny acted as if she had been accustomed to large cities and traveling all her life. A twenty-mile motor ride, which was her first, to Long Island, finally brought her to her new home. With proper dignity she made friends with the other dogs, and today enjoys her new surroundings. But I can imagine that there are times when her thoughts must wander off to those wonderful ice-covered mountains teeming with sheep, caribou and moose in the land of our last frontier, Alaska, with the wish to be home once more uppermost in her dog mind. Since this was written poor Jenny has passed on, a much lamented companion.

CHAPTER V.

RAINY PASS, SADDLE OF THE RANGE

STORY OF THE EXPEDITION OF 1926

DURING the winter evenings following our trip to Mount Dall my thoughts wandered to the talks I had had with Stephen R. Capps of the United States Geological Survey while we were stormbound in the cotton woods on the way to Mount Dall. Capps was very much interested in the section of the Alaskan Range to the west of Rainy Pass. Little was known of this country, and it was his intention to make a trip there in 1926 if his appropriation would permit.

Andy Simons had also told me of a most interesting trip he had taken into about the same section with a Captain Hubback, who was collecting specimens for a British museum. From Andy's tales the game was really too thick to be comfortable, and as to the size of the heads, well, if they weren't all records, at least they were in the record class.

Again there persisted in coming back to me the memory of a beautiful clear day that I had put in with Jim Gibson on the high ridges about the Tonzona Basin. There was not a cloud in the sky, and as we looked towards the west and south it seemed as if the peaks about Simpson Pass were but a short day's mush, and beyond was Rainy Pass with its protection of ridges and peaks. It was a never-to-be-forgotten day.

I finally decided to have a talk with Mr. Capps, so on to Washington I went. A short talk brought out the fact that Capps was in an uncertain state, as Congress was cutting down on all expenditures and the United States Geological Survey was to suffer somewhat more than seemed wise. Capps thought there might be some scheme worked out so that we could combine. His last words were that he would "make medicine" and let me have the result as soon as possible.

Also, to our best knowledge and belief, no prospector had ever gone through the country, so there was a possibility of mineral discoveries.

As the winter drew to a close Capps and I had come to an agreement, and a general plan for getting into the country was decided upon. The pack train was to be sent in light from Beluga on Cooks Inlet, in charge of the head packer, and along with it were to go the assistant packer, the cook, Mr. Trimble the topographer, and his assistant. They were to follow as far as possible the old Indian trail that Dr. Brooks had used years ago when he made his reconnaissance of Mount McKinley, until they came out on the Skwentna River. The duffle and supplies were to be taken up the Skwentna River by boat. Capps would be in charge of the river expedition.

I had secured Andy Simons and his boat, and Jack Lean who, in the old days, when the trail to Iditarod crossed and followed up the Skwentna, ran a roadhouse at Happy River. Andy Simons had a splendid knowledge of the Skwentna and, what was still more valuable, a proper respect for its peculiarities. Jack Lean knew the river from its mouth to

Happy River as he had traveled it for many years; possibly he knew it too well, as a man who is constantly handling dynamite can't see how it will go off unless properly detonated.

Andy Simons had been on a spring bear hunt to the Alaska Peninsula, so was unable to connect with Capps on the first trip up the river. It was planned that I should come in later, and take up the last of the supplies that Capps was to leave at Susitna Station. In order to help us up the Skwentna (as we had been told it was a swift, treacherous piece of water) we had one of the large Johnson outboard motors. Capps planned to reach the head of the Skwentna, map it, and make a survey of the geological formations and be back to some point where I could connect with the party before crossing to the north side of the Alaskan Range.

The personnel of the expedition was as follows:

Stephen R. Capps, of the United States Geological Survey, was in command; a more experienced hard working man would be impossible to find. He travels over the mountains like a goat; there was never a piece of rock or a formation he did not reach. The marvelous part of it to me is how the Government seems to be able to retain men of such calibre.

Next came K. W. Trimble, the topographer, a man of untiring energy. He was out on his work every day to the top of the highest point wherever we camped, and there he established his station.

Then there was William T. Mulkey, the assistant to the topographer. Later on the trip he was nicknamed "Spuds," and thus he was known.

The head packer was Seward Old from Kodiak Island, better known as Sid, very quiet but most efficient. Not once on the whole trip was a horse bothered with a sore back. This means a great deal, especially in such a country as we traveled, for there were no trails and at best the going was far from simple.

Alf Norman from Browning, Montana, was assistant to Sid. Alf was handy at anything, and everything he did was quietly and efficiently taken care of.

Bud Farrell, he of the bushy shock of brick red hair, and better known as "Red," hailed from Great Falls, Montana, and was chef, or possibly better described as "meat slinger."

Andy Simons and Jack Lean I have already introduced.

During my talks with Capps we figured that it would be possible to get up to Happy River in four or five days. You can imagine my surprise when I received a wire from Capps as I was leaving to bring eighty shear pins for the motor, and to allow eleven days to reach Portage Creek.

I left New York on July 26th, via Chicago and the Northern Pacific to Seattle, and sailed on July 31st on the Alaskan Steamer, *Yukon*, Captain Glasscock in command. Andy and Jack met me at Seward, and no time was lost in getting on to Anchorage. Noel Smith, the Manager of the Alaskan Railroad, had the gas car waiting at Seward. As I was unfortunately forced to visit a dentist in Anchorage we were delayed and did not leave until August 8th. The gas boat *Alert*, Captain Bill Austen and his tailless dog, skipper and mate respectively, that carried the mail to Susitna Station, were waiting for us, and at eight o'clock we bade adieu to the shore line of

Susitna Station
Left to right: Indian Jimmie, a trapper, Mr. Healy,
Billy Dennison and Jack Lean

Skwentna Crossing

Anchorage and headed across Cooks Inlet. The dog and the skipper were inseparable. Having got him as a pup, Bill proceeded to break him into the ways of a seafarer. Everything went well for a time until one fine day in some unknown manner the dog caught his tail in the propeller shaft, which promptly wound it up and snapped it off close to the poor animal's body. At first Bill felt he should put his friend out of misery, but kept putting it off from day to day until the dog finally recovered. It was interesting to see the pains with which that dog avoided the shaft, whether revolving or still.

In crossing the Inlet it is quite necessary to take advantage of the tide, which was going out. At the mouth of the Susitna River we anchored for the tide to come in, as it is impossible to enter the river against both tide and current. We anchored at nine forty-five and in due course were high and dry on the mud flats. It was a bright clear day and very warm. In the distance McKinley, Foraker and Russell stood like marble statues. Mount Dall could not be seen. Further to the west Mount Spur and its surrounding peaks first showed faintly through a haze that seemed almost like a fog, which later disappeared so that the Chugach Range rose clear and majestic above us. By three o'clock the tide was sufficiently on the return for us to be on our way again, but for a short time only. As we entered the mouth of the Susitna we ran high on a bar and lay there twenty minutes before the incoming tide released us. As we entered the Susitna River we saw a large bunch of hair seal on the west bank. The movie camera came out and many shots were taken. On being disturbed the seals flapped into the water, coming up all about us.

The rest of the afternoon was passed in traveling through low uninteresting country. Jack helped pass the time in telling of the trials and tribulations which Capps and he had had on their trip to Happy River. Upon bringing out the Johnson motor at Susitna Station the people there, both whites and Indians, had made fun of them and said it wouldn't last ten miles on the river. When they reached Skwentna Crossing they elicited the help of Jack Rimmer, who still holds forth at his old roadhouse. He and his partners, McElroy and Heffner, were surprised to find a motor still running. Well, the motor came through without a hitch, and was about to go back to Happy and beyond.

The Susitna River is a wide, swift-running stream of light brownish color, the water being heavily laden with glacial silt. When Jack left Capps and came down to Anchorage to meet Andy and me, he crossed Cooks Inlet in the boat under power of the Johnson motor. We were now towing the boat, so we made very slow progress, but nevertheless kept moving in the right direction, and at eleven-fifteen at night, but still in daylight, with a light drizzle falling, we reached Susitna Station. It was very warm, and plenty of mosquitoes filled the air.

Before the construction of the Alaska Railroad, Susitna Station was an important town on the trail to the gold mining town of Cache Creek. There are several imposing buildings, a good-sized school and church. Both are now closed as the government has closed the school, and I imagine there is not sufficient population to keep a church going. The population today consists of about five white men and thirty-five or

forty Indians. The leading citizen is R. R. Healy who, besides holding all the important political positions, is Manager
of H. W. Nagley's store. Healy is a well-educated interesting personage, and why he remains there is a mystery. There
is a large hotel (or what was formerly one) going to pieces,
as the owner, a woman, had shortly before departed this life.
Mr. Healy very kindly asked me to stop over night in his
house, which was immaculately clean, and of course I accepted. On our return I was to see more of the town, but
just now I had no sooner turned in than it was time to be up
and starting, or so it seemed.

Bill Austen agreed to take us up as far as his boat could
navigate. We were under way by seven-thirty, and going on
up the Susitna until the mouth of the Yentna was reached,
and then up the Yentna, passing many old and deserted
places. We reached McDougall, where the trail started for
Cache Creek, at five-thirty in the afternoon. Here we found
a town, completely deserted except for one old man who
lived there with a bunch of dogs. A deserted river steamer
was going to pieces above town, and many of the houses still
had furniture and supplies in them, just as they had been left
by their owners. About an hour later we passed what looked
like an old ranch with several buildings, all deserted and
going to ruin. This was known as Grays. At eight-thirty p.m.
we tied up alongside a sand bar, and Bill Austen informed us
we were just sixteen miles below Skwentna Crossing. We put
up my tent on the bar, while the boys slept on the *Alert*.

I have neglected to say that we arranged at Susitna to have
an Indian named Jimmie come along with us to help on the

river. Jack's tales of his trip with Capps made us somewhat apprehensive, especially as our load was a very heavy one. We had supplies to be cached for the pack train on their way out, in addition to further supplies for the expedition in the field, and my dunnage and moving picture cameras and accessories. Our first attempt to secure a helper was in Anchorage. We talked with a good husky Indian and made him liberal offers to join us. Of course he agreed to do so but that's the last we saw of him. I guess he is traveling yet in the opposite direction. Jack also told us of the numerous shear pins that were destroyed, and if it hadn't been for some 22-calibre brass cleaning rods which were cut into the proper length for pins, we would have been out of luck. I discovered next day when we were about to start that the motor was set straight down on the stern of the boat, so I adjusted it to as great an angle as we could carry and get results, which cut down the number of pins that were sheared; but at that we used plenty.

We were under way by seven next morning and soon entered the Skwentna River. We noticed the difference at once. The water was a dark muddy color and much swifter than anything experienced to date. It now began to rain but we kept going along in a slow even way, and by noon Bill Austen said he could go no further as it was the end of navigation for his boat. We transferred to the river boat, and after adjusting the motor we waved good-bye to Bill and his dog as he disappeared downstream. When I was informed that we were only four miles from the mouth of the Skwentna and we had taken four hours to make it I began to appreciate there was work ahead for us. On the second turn the Johnson began to purr and kept it up steadily, except when we had to refill the gas tank, until five minutes after four when we pulled alongside Skwentna Crossing, to be greeted by Jack Rimmer, Joe McElroy and Heffner. The motor had heralded our coming for sometime back.

It was still raining so we took ourselves (and in my case, my sleeping bag) to the old roadhouse. An old Eskimo igloo had nothing on that roadhouse, for the upper floor was filled with dried salmon which had just been secured for the winter's dog meat. The evening passed most enjoyably, especially as McElroy had satisfied our appetites with a fine dinner. Tales of the old trail days and of experiences prospecting and trapping made the time pass very quickly. I was overcome by the actions of the three old-timers. They were inveterate smokers and cigarettes were constantly being lighted and thrown on the floor when about half smoked. What particularly interested me was the fact that they never put out a match or cigarette—just tossed them carelessly in any and every direction.* I expected to see a blaze at any minute, but none occurred, and upon my venturing to remark on it Mac volunteered, "We've been doing that for years." As it was necessary to make an early start in the morning I finally took courage, and grabbing an apology for a broom, cleaned a space on the floor free from butts and matches, spread out my bag and turned in.

We were up at six o'clock next morning, and McElroy

---

* Skwentna Crossing roadhouse has since been burned to the ground and the owners are still wondering why.

served one of the best breakfasts it has ever been my luck to sit down to. His sourdough flapjacks beggar description. There was no difficulty in understanding why Skwentna Crossing had been such a popular roadhouse in the old trail days.

The weather was warm, and a heavy mist was thick upon us, so much so, in fact, that it was eight o'clock before we made our start and left behind us our last trace of civilization, until we should connect with the main party. According to a letter from Capps that I found awaiting me at Anchorage, we were to meet the outfit at the mouth of Portage Creek on August 17th, or eleven days from Anchorage. I read this letter to Andy and Jack, and then added, "Just a good day's trip above Happy River."

"Like hell it is," was Jack's comment; "I've been a great many years on this river but never up to Portage Creek, and believe me we will know we have traveled some when we get there."

It didn't seem possible that it would take seven more days to make between fifty-five and sixty miles. Little did I know what was in store for us, or I wouldn't have been so skeptical. We had hardly left the crossing behind when we struck a rock and a shear pin let go. This meant getting into the river and dragging the boat to shore; otherwise in a few seconds the current would carry us back a distance that we had made only after hard work, and possibly cost us an hour or more in time. We put in a new pin, but had only gone a short distance when we struck again. We really were making exceptionally good time, and about ten o'clock we passed the mouth of the Talushulitna River. The change in the setting of the motor helped considerably, and the old boat was plugging along at a great rate. It was a little after three o'clock when Andy and I, walking considerably ahead of the motor, happened to look across the river and on the opposite bank saw a good-sized grizzly bear looking at us. We stared at one another for a few seconds and then Mr. Bear quietly melted into the brush. We passed Capps' old camp and at seven at night camped about a mile and half above. As we were fixing up the tent two beaver played about in the stream, paying no attention to us.

Jack said we had made splendid time, covering about twelve to thirteen miles. I was sure then that it would not take us six days more to navigate the remaining forty or forty-five miles. I neglected to say that the weather had cleared by noon and we had a splendid view of Foraker, Russell and Dall, all the afternoon. The next day was clear and hot, uncomfortably so, and Jack quietly remarked as we got under way that from here on there would be little chance of using the engine; the order of the day would be lining and pulling the boat upstream. We were able to use the motor for some time, though we made but slow progress. Nevertheless, it was better than lining.

By noon we reached the place where we were to cache provisions for the pack train on their return. As the cache had already been made we were not very long in loading it up with a goodly supply of provisions, more in fact than Capps had instructed, as we were desirous of lightening the boat as much as possible. The entire afternoon was one continuous

fight against that down-rushing water with the engine per-
forming beautifully. We camped below Hayes River, all
thoroughly tired. We had a fine salmon for dinner that night
and there was a feeling of satisfaction as we had covered a
good nine miles that day.

We were off again next morning with somewhat dampened
spirits as our gas now began to run low. A case of ten gallons
that had been cached by Capps for our use, had been washed
away and we had several miles to go before reaching the next
cache. The river seemed pretty fair to me and I am sure if
we had had sufficient gasoline we could have run all the way
to our next cache. We stopped for lunch just below the mouth
of the Hayes River, and then proceeded to line until five
o'clock, when we camped, having made a total of six miles
for the day. We had plenty of mosquitoes and "no-see-ems"
that night and I thanked my stars that the tent had a mosquito net.

Next day we were off again with hardly a cloud in the sky,
and now there was no using the motor; it was just plain tugging on the line, ploughing at times in water nearly to our
waists, then again along sand bars. To break the monotony
we were continually stumbling into quicksand. Both Andy
and Jack kept warning me against falling as the water was so
saturated with silt that they claimed it was impossible to swim,
and there was slight chance of ever coming up if I was
carried into the channel. We stopped for lunch with a feeling
of having accomplished a good morning's work, possibly three
or four miles. At two o'clock we reached our next gas cache
and found the five-gallon can intact. In this case it had been

Left to right: Heffner, Jack Rimmer and Joe McElroy

One of our camps on the Skwentna

cached high on the shore. We started up the motor, and, though we had it wide open and there was plenty of water, we made little or no headway. Finally Andy and Jimmie went ashore and proceeded to tow, and at last I did likewise. With the three of us on the line and the motor wide open we could just about hold our own with the boat out in the current. After tugging away for half an hour with a possible advance of a couple of hundred yards, Jack shut off the motor and pushed the boat into shallow water. For the balance of the day it was towing all the time, though the motor came in handy crossing the river from sand bar to sand bar to enable us to get footing to handle the line.

It was very hot all day, and we were all beginning to get sore shoulders and arms from the infernal towline. The Indian, Jimmie, who had hardly spoken, began to grumble and remember things he had to do at home. We camped that night below the mouth of a large canyon. There were many tracks on the bar, moose, lynx and bear predominating. Just before we made camp a large bear looked us over and slowly drew off into the bush, to circle and come out again near camp; it was a nice big black fellow, full of curiosity.

It seemed to us that the canyon would be reached the next day in short order, but we were doomed to disappointment. The current was too much for the power of our motor, so it was just tug and pull, and after three hours rather strenuous exercise we reached the mouth of the canyon to find our next cache of gasoline had vanished to parts unknown. We made about a mile up the canyon and then stopped for lunch. The weather was very warm and the sky overcast, with a fine rain falling. It really was a relief to trudge through the river as it was cooling, and in any case we were wet from perspiration. In the afternoon after getting by a mean, crooked, steep part of the river, we were able to run the motor for quite some time. We were making slower time than if we had been out on the line, but at least we were making headway and getting a rest for the next day's work, which Jack said was going to be a pippin. We made camp above the canyon at half-past five after accomplishing a well-earned seven miles.

"Next day Happy River and the day after Portage Creek," I remarked, which elicited from Jack, "Maybe." I noticed we were all getting rather quiet and as soon as we had eaten we turned in. Sometimes it was seven o'clock, but never later than eight. As we sat eating our evening repast, with the rain coming down gently but soakingly, Jack blurted out, "I wonder where Capps gets that easy day stuff from Happy to Portage? I wish he was going to tackle it instead of me." We now had two days in which to reach Portage Creek if we were to be there on the day named by Capps. We had been making six to seven miles a day, and, as Jack said, it was seven miles to Happy River and possibly ten miles more to Portage. I was certain we could make it in the two remaining days.

August 16th broke cloudy with the rain falling, and as my alarm watch started to go off at six o'clock I piled out of my blankets and soon had the rest of the bunch hustling. Jimmie was completely down on his luck and was grumbling about being a "damn fool for coming." To brighten him up I said, "This is a fine morning, Jimmie. Sun will soon be out, and tomorrow Portage Creek." Jimmie looked at me in a hopeless manner and answered, "Me tired; water too quick."

The thought of Happy River and clear water put new life in us. We had been drinking the river water for the last few days and as it was the color of mud and thick with silt the thought of clear water meant a good deal to all.

By noon we reached another canyon and after pulling a short distance up it we stopped for lunch. The rain was now coming down in earnest, and as I looked at the bunch I couldn't help but feel that we were a lot of drowned rats. Jimmie had shrunken perceptibly, Andy was beginning to have a drawn look, and Jack, who had been a constant source of amusement on the early part of the trip, had become quiet and a little inclined to be annoyed at small difficulties that were every now and again bobbing up to try our patience. That afternoon was one that is pleasanter to forget as we just could not seem to make any headway. Alders along the bank had to be cut to get a footing; the channel that Jack used when Capps went up was now broken into many sloughs. Whenever we came to a bad turn in the river big sweepers would also be there just to make it a little more interesting.

After three hours of this sort of work I had about enough, but in making another turn Jack called out, "There's Happy. Now you know how it came to get that name."

New life came to us all, and in a burst of energy we made a landing just above the mouth of Happy River. I went to the deserted roadhouse and started a fire in the kitchen stove. It was a real job but eventually I succeeded, and then had a chance to look about. The building had half fallen down and was filthy, as the porcupines had been using it as a home. In the main room of the bunk house there was a huge smear of blood over a bench and on the floor, which Jack later informed me came from a porkey that Jack Rimmer had murdered when they stopped there on their way up with Capps.

Of course the roof leaked like a sieve, so I gathered up a lot of tins and old plates and placed them under the worst leaks, and plugged up the others as best I could. While in the midst of cleaning up the place Jimmie appeared. He greeted me with, "Me going to die; me very sick." I looked him over and discovered that he had a slight temperature and a bad cough. I dove into my bag and brought out some aspirin, and quickly had him swallow ten grains. "Now lie down and a little later I will give you some more medicine," I remarked, with the mental reservation that I would shoot a good stiff dose of castor oil into him. Jimmie was in a deep sleep in a few seconds in the cook's bunk off the kitchen, and he never stirred until we wakened him next morning.

Any idea of proceeding further that day had vanished. Before we reached Happy River I had come to the decision that we could but do our best and if we were late in meeting Capps we could not help it, as human endurance has a limit. The night was one of bad dreams and nightmares, with an awakening in the morning to low-hanging clouds and heavy rain. Though we were up at five o'clock it was past eight before our eternal struggle began. Jack informed us that from here to Portage Creek, which was possibly ten miles, we had new fields before us, as no boat had ever navigated those waters. A short distance up river we could see a dirty, swift stream tumbling down from a high glacier and emptying into the Skwentna, and beyond, the entrance to a high canyon. I figured that we should reach the stream in about an hour, and the canyon mouth surely within two to three hours. Our engine now was but an ornament, for with full speed and three of us on the line we were unable to budge the boat upstream while in the current. We were later informed by Mr. Trimble that at this point there was a drop of fifty feet to the mile in the Skwentna.

We tugged and pulled so that by noon we had reached the mountain stream. Much difficulty was experienced in crossing it; in fact we had to line up quite a distance, then drop down, with Andy and Jack rowing against the current so as to guide the boat to the opposite side. We reached the mouth of the canyon shortly after one and lunched there, while the rain came down in sheets. To enter the canyon it was necessary to cut down many overhanging alders so as to be able to walk in the shallow water and line the boat along. Finally a bar appeared which we reached with the aid of the motor, and we were then able to line again.

By two o'clock the sun was shining brightly and our spirits rose as the clouds had broken, and all indications pointed to clearing, but by four-thirty it was raining harder than ever. Coming to a somewhat protected bar that was much higher and looked safe from any sudden rising of the river we decided to camp. It was rather a desolate outfit, but a good roaring camp fire and a sudden letting up of the rain helped towards restoring our equilibrium.

Jack told us that Portage Creek came into the Skwentna just above the canyon and that it couldn't possibly be more

than four to five miles farther. This news was most com-
forting, especially as the next day, August 18th, was the
appointed time for meeting the pack outfit. The night passed
without excitement, except that Jack had a bad nightmare
about three in the morning, and it took both Andy and myself to convince him that he was not on the river. As there
was a heavy fog over the canyon next morning, we were
unable to get under way until eight o'clock. We made splendid progress, there being convenient bars to walk on, and
several times we were able to run the motor. About noon we
could make out the end of the canyon and the open country
beyond. A stop was now made for lunch, and while we were
in the midst of our meal we saw something white come out
on a meadow about a mile above the canyon.

"There's the outfit," exclaimed Jack, and sure enough that
white object turned out to be a horse, which was quickly followed by others. We wondered how long they had been waiting for us. The river now was in a deep channel, and we decided to start the motor, with the result that we went sailing
along, shortly coming out of the canyon and into the clear
waters of Portage Creek. I jumped out of the boat and
started for shore to find it quite a different proposition walking in clean water; the rocks were so slippery I could hardly
keep my feet.

Upon reaching the bank I found a blaze on a tree with a
note left by Capps, and by following the blaze came to the
cache. While Andy and Jack were unloading the boat I struck
out to find camp. The note advised me that the pack train and
packers would meet me at Portage Creek on the 18th, and

that the expedition had had a most successful trip to the head
of the Skwentna. I picked up some tracks which I followed
upstream in the general direction of the horses. The tracks
disappeared but by circling I picked them up again heading
back towards Portage Creek. Coming up over a little rise I
looked down, and there sat Seward Old, the head packer, and
Alf Norman, his assistant, just about to consume huge bowls-
ful of huckleberries. We all quickly gathered about and
helped devour those berries. Sid (Seward Old) told us they
had arrived the evening before and that the Survey party
was at the head of Portage Creek waiting for us to join up.

That afternoon was used in repacking the cache and putting the boat and motor in a place safe from high water.
Jimmie, our Indian helper, was to leave us at this point and
return down river. He decided that the best plan would be to
build a canoe, so we let him have an extra "Mantie" and he
was now hard at work.

Next day it was still cloudy and raining, but we were off
at ten o'clock, after bidding Jimmie good-bye and good luck,
and up Portage Creek over what might be called somewhat of
a trail as this was the third time over it. A good part of the
distance was through thick willows, with here and there soft
ground; but, generally speaking, the going was fine and we
made splendid time. We saw a lynx sitting quietly under a
tree watching us, and further upstream we saw a few scattered
caribou. We reached the main camp at a quarter after three
and were enthusiastically greeted. Capps said it would take
one more clear day for Trimble to finish his map, and that
then we would pull for the north side of the Range, passing

over at the head of Portage. Our next day was put in exploring the pass, and incidentally, on my part, in trying to break
in a new pair of shoes which resulted in my being pretty badly
crippled for several days thereafter. As usual it rained during
the morning but cleared beautifully in the afternoon, and
this enabled Trimble to clean up on his map work so that we
were all set for our hop across the Range in the morning.

August 21st was as clear and fine as anyone could ask for.
Shortly after five the hustle started, though it was nearly ten
o'clock before we were under way. Following upstream an
old moose trail that we had located the day before, we wound
our way through some very thick alders which in places had
to be chopped out, and navigated some soft ground. At last
we began to climb an easy slope and came out above the
alders. A long gradual climb brought us to the top and our
pass, which we hoped would permit us to reach the north side
of the Range. We came through an old caribou trail, but now
the real difficulty confronted us. Below lay a large basin with
a lake covering the greater part of it. On the left there was
no chance of getting down, while on the right there was a
long boulder slide. Sid decided to try the slide, and I must
say I admired the way he brought the horses over those
rocks. Fortunately the horses were old-timers and accustomed to Alaskan traveling, which helped greatly.

Coming to the end of this basin we found there was more
difficulty ahead. Down below was a stream but how to get to
it was another matter. Sid led on again, taking the right side,
and in some way the horses kept their feet and reached the
banks of the stream. One horse was hit by a rolling rock and

Four curious rams

Head of Portage Creek

for a second it looked as if he would lose his balance and tumble headlong to follow the rock; but he miraculously kept his feet and continued down. Sid's saddle horse made a slip, and the next thing we knew he was going down like a goat, jumping from rock to rock. It seemed impossible for him to make the bottom, but he never lost his head, and with a regular landslide of rocks following, he reached the smooth ground below, none the worse for his experience.

It was after five o'clock when we made camp that night, a little over seven hours on the trail. Our barometers showed an altitude on the pass of 4,220 feet, but later Trimble determined the altitude by triangulation at 3,834 feet.

As we came to the north side of the Range, game began to appear. We found many ptarmigan, and saw at a little distance across the valley seven bull caribou but all with small heads. Capps told me that they had seen over fifty bear before my arrival, mostly of the black variety. On our way up the Skwentna we saw numerous bear tracks on the bars, some being of great size. Our camp was scattered through the alders which lined the banks of the stream, and incidentally the stream was alive with Dolly Varden trout. We planned that night that I was to break away from the party next morning with Andy Simons, Jack Lean, Alf Norman and five horses. We were to head eastward towards Rainy Pass, while Capps was going to the west to look over the Stony and Styx Rivers.

As the barometer was falling our chances for a start in the morning were slim, and when we wakened to a heavy rain it was not unexpected. We put in the greater part of the day catching some of the Dolly Varden, and were more or less successful, with a total of a hundred and eighty fish. I have to admit that our only real angler was Trimble, as he used nothing but flies. Mine were taken on salmon eggs for bait, I am ashamed to confess, but I was trying for food, and not doing scientific fishing. My recollection is that Capps was high man, and as he was fishing some distance above us I won't make any accusations, but we were all suspicious.

Red, our cook, for some reason forgot lunch that day, and as we were all interested in fishing it was past two before we realized it. I suggested to Red that we should have trout for dinner and supper combined, and he agreed—if we cleaned them. It did not take us long to accomplish this. I know that Capps, Trimble and I did our share of the work and saw that the trout were all turned over to Red as per specification. That combined meal kept Red busy cooking fish, and it only finished when the last of them were consumed. An average of twenty fish to the man may seem high, but the fish were not too large, and the meal consisted of fish alone.

August 23rd was cloudy but clear and much colder, and as the barometer was rising, we decided to make our start for Rainy Pass. We were packed and under way by nine o'clock. After saying au revoir we started downstream until we came to Ptarmigan Valley and then headed due east. Andy remembered the country perfectly, and of course Jack Lean knew it like a book as he had been the proprietor of Pass Creek and Happy River Roadhouses, and also at one time had been dog musher over the trail to Iditarod. On the whole the traveling was good, although at times we came across soft ground that delayed us. In one place Frank, one of the pack horses, went down, but Alf brought him out without harm.

Game could now be seen on all sides. Scattering bands of caribou would come towards us, look us over, then trot off to a safer distance, and give us another look. All the bulls being in velvet, we paid no attention to them. According to my records we counted over fifty caribou that day, and in addition, eight bull moose, two of which had fair-sized heads, somewhere in the fifties we thought. We saw numerous bunches of ptarmigan and secured five for that evening's meal. By three o'clock we decided to camp on a bar towards the head of Happy River. After everything was shipshape Andy and Jack proceeded to point out to me where they expected to head for the next day. "Over that ridge is the greatest ram range in Alaska," said Andy. "It's the headwaters of the south fork of the Kuskokwim."

Our trip next day was a short one, possibly five or six miles, to a willow patch alongside of a stream teeming with trout, where we made our camp. Andy and I started for the ram range as soon as we had had a bite to eat. The travel was slow over a heavy rock slide and on a good incline towards a pass. We were camped on waters flowing into Happy River on the south side of the range, while we headed towards the Kuskokwim watershed on the north side. We saw caribou scattered about, but no sheep until we went over the pass, and then the white spots began to appear on the mountainside. We counted some thirty sheep, mostly rams, and in addition must have scared an old grizzly from his haunts; the signs were so fresh that we expected to come face to face with him at any moment. We turned up another valley where more sheep could be seen, but again our too familiar friend, the rain, came down in torrents forcing us to retrace our steps to camp, where we arrived thoroughly soaked. We had seen tracks and trails of several grizzly bear and were camped alongside the deeply worn trail of an old-timer.

The next day the rain was still coming down as if it had never rained before; everything was fairly well dampened. About all we did that day was to land twenty-seven nice trout and watch our horses depart over the skyline with a big grizzly hastening their going. A few caribou wandered about, and a bunch of five almost walked into camp in an endeavor to satisfy their curiosity. The trout failed to appease our palates. I am afraid our orgy of a few days previous had killed our taste. Alf returned in the later afternoon with the horses which he placed below us in Ptarmigan Valley in a bunch of luscious feed.

Though the rain was still coming down the next day, Andy, Jack and I started for the sheep mountains and on our way disturbed our grizzly friend, who took to the high mountain side and made a great get-away. Andy informed me that the new Alaska game law did not permit shooting grizzly bear until September 15th, so no attempt was made to kill a bear though many opportunities offered. Our day after the rams was most disappointing as the wind was switching in every direction. We made three stalks in all. Our first two were unsuccessful owing to the wind swirling on us, and the third, though successful, found rams smaller than I was after. We saw in all between sixty and seventy sheep, but none of the heads came up to my mark. There were two bunches, one of four across the stream and high above us that we were sure included some old-timers, and one of five, which we located on our way back to camp, that certainly had enormous looking heads as seen through the fog.

We reached camp after eight o'clock in the dark as the sky was black and the rain still falling. There being no change in the weather the next day, we decided to reach the bunch of five rams that lay nearest to camp. We found that our rams had shifted their position and were perched high up on an unapproachable peak. After waiting quietly for a time in the hope that they would change their position, we decided to try to reach a point from which I could secure a rather long shot. In climbing that side hill we encountered some of the worst going I have ever experienced; the rock would break away, and large pieces were constantly rolling down, bumping and jumping like rubber balls. Andy, in attempting to locate better going, succeeded in getting to a spot where he couldn't go either up or down; it took some manipulating by Jack to get him down to our none-too-sure footing.

I finally reached the spot we were heading for and crawled out to try for my shot. It was an overhanging shelf and as I crawled in position I hoped it would not break away. We realized by this time that the rams were a fine lot and that there was one that had an enormous head. My shot hit just below the big ram, possibly two inches, as nearly as we could judge. The rams were out of sight in a jiffy, and, though disappointed at the outcome, I was so glad to get off that ledge that I really forgot about losing the big ram. As the rams did not appear on the other side of the draw, Andy felt that I might have nicked the big fellow. We climbed down from our perch and hurried over to the other ridge up which we started, and were about half way when I saw the head of a ram appear towards the top of the draw; shortly after the four others appeared and they then all lay down. This time the position was different for I had a splendid grass slope from which to shoot. I crawled out and, lying prone, killed the big ram with my first shot.

"There's another just about as big; give it to him also," said Andy.

Another shot bowled the second ram over.

We then sat down and ate our lunch as it was after two o'clock and we had left camp early in the morning. To tell the truth, curiosity had the better of me, and a sandwich was hardly swallowed before I wanted to get to the rams. I kept putting my glasses on the first, or big one, and then on the second one which began to look larger than the first. I was wondering if I could have made a mistake on that first ram. I was after only a very large head—a record if possible—and I began to feel that I had made a bad mistake. Jack was the first to reach the ram and he stood looking at it so quietly that my fears were even more confirmed.

"Is he any good?" I tried to call without showing my feelings.

Jack's answer put all my fears at rest. "It's the biggest ram I have ever seen."

By this time Andy and I had reached the ram. My tape was out, following the curl which was forty-three and a half inches, while the base measured fifteen and a half inches, and the spread twenty-six inches. This came pretty near being a record Dall head, both Andy and Jack assured me. Even Andy said it was the largest head he had ever seen.

We had completely forgotten ram number two, but as I looked at him lying at a short distance I was somewhat uncertain whether I had measured the largest one or not. On the tape he turned out to be slightly smaller, though he had more than a complete curl.

Even the continuous rain failed to dampen our enthusiasm that evening. We decided the next day would be used in taking movies of the sheep and as the sky was now clear we hoped for the best. We were anxious to join up with the main party on the Styx and were behind our schedule owing to the rain, but of course the rain would also hold up Capps and his work.

It turned cold during the night, and next morning it certainly looked like snow, but we were off early with the movie camera while Alf took one of the horses to pack in the rams. We trudged to the head of the left-hand branch of the East Fork, and after taking a picture of a couple of ptarmigan I set up on a bunch of sheep, to have the camera stop after a few feet had run off. Try as I could, it would not run again; there was something wrong with the internal mechanism. We had to watch bunches of rams almost walk over us with no chance of recording their antics. Shortly after four saw us back at camp and at once a start was made to take apart the camera. As Andy put it, "The blamed thing is out of business now and you can't do more than put it still further out." We succeeded in removing the head of the camera, and as the spring motor went off with a great whirr I expected it to fly in all directions. We discovered the governor was broken, and after a little tinkering Andy removed the broken part and replaced the head. I wound up the motor and the thing ran, though at very high speed, so I threw over the control to half speed and had no further trouble; but of course, I lost my chances at rams as we did not visit their range again. By six o'clock that night it began to rain, and for the next two days we never budged from camp as the rain was coming down heavier than at any time. Our only amusement was to watch the caribou whose curiosity would bring them within a few feet of our camp.

On August 31st, even though it was still raining, we broke camp and started on our way back to join the main party. We reached Happy River and made camp shortly after two o'clock with the intention of stopping there a day to secure a couple of caribou specimens. I had promised to get a specimen for the American Museum of Natural History, as these caribou are the ones that at one time lived on the Kenai Peninsula and departed over night to parts unknown. For two days we hunted in the pouring rain and though we saw numerous caribou none were sufficiently large. On the third day the weather cleared beautifully. It was the first fine day in the ten we had been off on our side trip. That was the banner day of the trip for seeing game. Shortly after leaving camp to look over a bunch of caribou we had located, a wolverine came to look at us, but as we were very close to the caribou I did not shoot. Following the caribou over a

An Osborn Caribou, by Carl Rungius

ridge and down the other side we saw an old sow grizzly with two large cubs in the creek bottom far below. I suggested that if we went down to their level there would be little difficulty in getting the sow to charge, and of course in self-defense the law says one may protect himself. Andy couldn't see it that way, so reluctantly I retraced my steps.

The day was a busy one, for, between stalking heads that all seemed to shrink in size as we came up to them, I took a number of feet of moving pictures of the caribou. Towards late afternoon Andy located three bulls that really seemed worth securing. We made our stalk and came out above them, but they were constantly on the move, and when I took aim I noticed my front sight nearly covered the animal; we therefore decided to get closer if possible. Fortunately a deep draw ran down the hillside and this we used as a cover to get into a better position. We traveled as rapidly as we could but the caribou were making about the same speed, so I decided to start firing. It was offhand shooting and I really don't feel so proud of it, for it took seven shots to finish the first one; but with the second I was more fortunate as one shot brought him down and another finished him. They were both good average specimens. I could hardly expect to secure extraordinarily large heads as they do not come out before the middle to the last of September. My license entitled me to one more, but this I did not intend to kill unless I saw a most unusual head. Upon examining the two caribou I found the lungs of both were in very bad shape with huge white spots on them, and in addition the lung of one was fast to his rib. The caribou were outwardly in fine shape with huge rolls of fat over their backs. In addition to the caribou we saw four bull moose just out of velvet, one with a very large head that almost tempted me. Off on the ridges to the north, alongside the South Fork, we counted thirty sheep, very likely ewes and lambs.

The following day Jack and I remained in camp while Alf and Andy went for the caribou, returning with them by noon. Afternoon passed in skinning out the heads, taking pictures and packing up, for we decided to pull down to Captain Hubback's last camp and wait there until we saw Capps return from the head of the Styx. One of the caribou which I was bringing out for the American Museum of Natural History was completely skinned with leg bones to the joints. It was after dark when the work was completed and we gathered about the camp fire. That evening Andy told of some of the experiences he had when he and Captain Hubback were in this region some few years ago, when they were forced to kill their horses and go out by dog sled. The day previous Andy had shown me the exact spot where they had camped and where he had shot one of the horses. We searched for the bones without success, but two miles further on discovered them scattered about. Our conclusion was that a grizzly had dragged the horse to a more suitable spot for devouring. Andy also touched lightly on their trip down the river when their boat swamped and they had escaped drowning in some miraculous way. We finally turned in and it was but a short time before the stillness of the September night was broken by heavy breathing. None would admit snoring.

Next morning we were up at six, breakfasted at seven, and

by a quarter-past nine were packed and on our way. We traveled on a high ridge alongside the west edge of the valley, and, though we stopped two or three times to fix packs, before noon we reached the last camp of Captain Hubback where he cached his surplus outfit. The cache was partly standing, though some of the bundles (there were three in all) had fallen to the ground and were more or less destroyed by wolverines and porcupines. It had been constructed in the shape of a tripod, using long alders. The material abandoned was wrapped in canvas and the packages suspended from the tripod. There was very little that was of use; a few bars of soap was all that we salvaged, and they were partially eaten.

While in the act of examining the old cache and putting up our tents Alf, who had gone off a short distance below to look for horse feed, returned with the news that a fine black bear was feeding just beyond. I took my gun and a box of cartridges, for my eye had just lighted on a huge grizzly as he ambled over a slight rise in the ground almost into our camp. "Come Andy," I called, "this certainly is pretty near an attack; he is coming right into camp."

Andy looked up from pegging down a tent and replied, "Leave him alone; he is only curious."

Well, that grizzly just looked as if he wanted to join us and get some of the latest gossip. He would wander off a short distance, then stop, sit down, look back at us, then amble down to our camp again. We were one too many for his curiosity and I am sure he felt that he should know more about us. I can assure you that my gun never left my hands until he finally wandered over the top of the high ridge back of camp. I had a splendid chance to get a close-up of him through the glasses. He was jet black with a fine gold tip, and the coat exceptionally heavy for so early in the season. His face was kindly and had a very curious expression.

We had about forgotten our visitor when a second grizzly appeared. This one was smaller, of a dirty cream color, and looked moth-eaten. It was clearly frightened and had no use for us whatsoever; its one idea was to get out of the country as quickly as possible. I had a fairly good look at this bear also through the glasses, and it had an expression of fear on its face. I think that it had got our scent and was thoroughly frightened. Either one of these bear I am sure could have been secured if an attempt had been made. The thought of the movie never entered my mind until long after they had departed.

In the afternoon Andy and I took the movie outfit and climbed up a ridge back of camp where I took some very good sheep pictures, though of ewes and lambs only. There was one picture of a ewe going down the side of a canyon wall that seemed impossible to navigate. This picture fortunately turned out splendidly. In the late afternoon some sheep came down on a bench just above camp and Andy thought he could get a good still picture of them. We watched him crawl up gradually, and apparently unobserved, until within three hundred yards, when suddenly the sheep became nervous and began to wander off. There was one old ewe that paid no attention, so Andy kept on until within thirty to forty feet when he raised up and snapped the picture. When developed, nothing but landscape was visible. Besides the two grizzly visitors in camp, we had seen that day two moose, twenty-two sheep and over twenty caribou, and this without any attempt to locate them.

Next day Andy, Jack and I took a long mush over the ranges and came out on the banks of the South Fork of the Kuskokwim. We killed a few ptarmigan, seven in all. During the morning heavy banks of clouds drifted up Ptarmigan Valley and it was not until nearly eleven o'clock that the fog lifted. We were above the fog bank but the sky was well clouded and it looked like rain at any time. We had the movie outfit along with us in hopes the weather would clear. On the slopes of the Kuskokwim we saw many white spots, counting thirty in all. They were at quite a distance but we concluded they must be ewes and lambs. We jumped four large bull caribou, all with good heads. I tried to get a picture of them, without success. We saw ten other caribou scattered about although the visibility was poor. We really were out on an exploring trip, and as we had plenty of meat I did not intend to secure additional trophies.

When we left the main outfit we had hoped to join up with them again within a week but the weather had delayed us so we had been unable to do it. In any case we were to be back at the old camp at Dolly Creek not later than September 9th. Our present camp was almost directly across from Dolly Creek and we decided to remain here until we saw the survey party come back up the Styx. As we were returning to camp that afternoon and discussing the advisability of breaking camp and following up the Styx, Andy happened to look across the valley and remarked that he saw a large band of caribou coming down it. Jack and I tried to locate them, without success. While we were at it Andy remarked, "No, I'm wrong, it's Capps and the outfit returning." Sure enough, he was right, for his glasses, which were 10 x.p., showed up Capps on a white horse plainly in the lead. We returned to camp as quickly as possible and started a huge smudge in hopes that Capps would see it and know that we were not far off.

We were a few days ahead of the time set as the latest date for us to connect with the main party. Andy having had a very disastrous experience in this locality a few years previous, when he had taken Captain Hubback out, was now becoming anxious to be on the move for the south side of the range. I had been reminded many times that two or three feet of snow over night was not unusual. We well realized that such a storm would mean abandoning our horses and probably our entire outfit. Capps had set September 12th as the latest date for us to remain on the north side of the range. It was now September 5th and we decided to cross over the valley and join up with him the next day. If it was his intention to wait until the 12th to finish up his work I was satisfied that the time could be profitably expended in searching for an exceptional caribou.

The next morning, although a heavy fog hung over the valley, we made an early start. We fixed up the old cache that Andy had previously made when with Hubback and left about five pounds of flour, some baking powder, a small amount of tea and a quantity of candles and matches. We struck out directly across the valley, and I must say the fog was quite friendly as it kept gradually rising so that no difficulty was experienced in reaching our objective. Upon arriving at the old Dolly Creek camp we found everyone greatly surprised. Our great smudge had not been noticed and Capps appeared pleased at our unexpected return. Almost the first thing he said was, "Can you be ready to pull out in the morning?" Like ourselves they had been worrying about an early storm. As we had had so much rain a cold wave might precipitate the dreaded snow.

On our way across the valley we had seen several bands of caribou scattered about. In fact, in my notes I find that I have jotted down twenty-five as counted. We killed two ptarmigan at the foot of the ridge that led towards camp. After examining the specimens I had secured, we at once proceeded to get things in shape for an early start next day. That evening I heard all that had been accomplished by Capps and Trimble during my absence. Much regret was expressed at the lack of minerals, as we had hoped that this trip might open up great mining possibilities. A huge area had been successfully mapped and the rock formations carefully studied, all of which has been published in Geological Survey Bulletin No. 797B, entitled, "The Skwentna Region." Although the clouds hung low all day, with an occasional indication of rain, we nevertheless were hopeful of the morrow as the barometer was rising. The pass which we had come over and by which we had to return I have jotted down as "Portage Creek Pass." I was also advised that Trimble had discovered a new route to the basin which lies at the foot of the pass. This way enabled us by a gradual grade to negotiate the climb from camp and so avoid the rock slide that almost annihilated our pack train in coming down to Dolly Creek camp.

We were all up by half-past five on the morning of September 7th, and were ready to start four hours later. Everything went along smoothly until we reached the rock slide from the big basin to the top of the pass. This particular stretch seemed more uninviting, if possible, than when we came down. I left the outfit at this point and made my way to the top of the pass where Trimble, Mulkey, Jack, Andy and Red were already waiting. Capps stayed with the pack train which was in charge of Sid and Alf. Heavy fog banks were coming up from the south and completely blotting out the summit. They came in waves, alternately clearing and then closing down thick again.

I had about reached the summit when I saw a figure coming towards me. Owing to the distortion from the fog I was at first unable to make out what it was. Mulkey gradually began to take form and asked me if I knew what the trouble was with the pack outfit. In one of the clearing moments he had seen Capps, Sid and Alf all working over a horse that was down. "I am afraid one of the horses has broken his leg and they are going to shoot him," he remarked as he disappeared in a bank of fog that just then enveloped us. There was a long wait with everything completely shut out. Finally a light breeze sprang up and the fog once again lifted, leaving us in brilliant sunshine. Capps and the outfit now began to appear. He at once called out, "Smoky slipped and his hind leg became jambed between two large rocks. As he was down nearly to his thigh we feared it would be impossible to

The pack train on the summit of
Portage Creek Pass

At Happy River Roadhouse
Left to right: Andy, Jack, Sid and Red

save him, but Sid finally got him out." By this time the entire pack train was on the summit and a more careful examination was made of Smoky's injury. He was quite badly cut and very stiff though he was able to follow the pack train without carrying a pack and was as good as ever in a few days.

The delay with Smoky really helped as the fog had cleared and I was able to shoot some very fine movie film of the outfit on skyline. Our troubles were now about at an end for that day, as we followed down Portage Creek on the trail we had made and had fine traveling except for a stretch of soft ground through the heavy alder patch. The rain had not helped this particular patch; we found it much heavier going than when we went through before. We were all set at our old camp ground by half-past three and I had hardly sufficient time to change films in the movie before Red's dulcet fog horn sounded, "Come and get it."

The next day we followed down Portage Creek and reached our cache by two o'clock. We found the cache, the boat and the Johnson motor intact. All afternoon we worked steadily at separating the outfit as Capps, Andy, Jack and I were to go downstream by boat while Trimble and Mulkey were going with the outfit overland. We saw the outfit off the next morning, September 9th, at eight-thirty. They were to go back over the trail they had made coming up and were to meet us sometime that evening at Happy River Roadhouse. We had the boat all packed and ready to start before they left, and it was but a short time before we were gliding downstream. Jack and Andy were at the oars and would row hard upstream to keep the boat straight. We went downstream stern first, and in twenty minutes we passed our last night's camp on the way up. Entering the swift part of the canyon we saw white water over on the left, and Jack steered for it as he and Andy were sure this was the deep part. Before we realized it we were heading for a huge boulder with no chance to steer off. I was running off some film on the movies and was not aware of our predicament until we hit. The boat grounded and started to twist, and for a second it looked as if something might happen; then, with a lurch which almost swamped us, we were off again on our way.

Beyond this bit of excitement nothing much happened, except every little while there would be rather frantic rowing on the part of Andy and Jack to avoid a rock or a sweeper. The scenery was now passing too rapidly. We couldn't be satisfied; it had taken a full two days from Happy River to Portage Creek, and now on the way down we were lining up to the Happy River Roadhouse in one hour and thirty-five minutes. The channel of the river had shifted since we went up and now it was necessary to line up a slough for about a mile in order to reach the roadhouse.

At once we began to clean up the roadhouse, getting it in a more or less habitable condition. As it had been raining all day and the many leaks and holes in the roof were still there, I again gathered all the cans, plates and receptacles of many shapes and placed them so as to catch the volume of water that was making the floor into a lake.

We did not expect the outfit to arrive until at least six o'clock, so you can imagine our surprise to be called from our house-cleaning by the appearance of the horses at a little after three. The usual bustle took place until the packs were piled up and the horses turned out. I had already started in on repairs to clothing, mending socks and getting my personal outfit in shape. We, the river party, had plenty of time on our hands as we had to wait for the pack train to get down river to a bar from which we were to ferry them across to Canyon Creek where the cache had been made. Capps figured it would take two and a half days for the horses to reach the ferry.

That evening I conceived the idea of making Sid, Alf, Red, Andy and Jack play a game of "freeze out," the prize to be a checked mackinaw shirt that I had which had never been used. We fortunately had sufficient matches to give each one of them five dollars worth of ten cent chips. That was a serious game of poker with all the luck going to Sid who claimed he had never played poker before. What he didn't fill that evening wouldn't have been worth drawing to, and he finally ended by having all the chips. When I handed over the shirt Sid remarked, "Thanks, I just had to win as the only shirt I have is in shreds." Capps and I had tents up near the river while the rest seemed content to remain in the roadhouse.

The next day, after an all-night rain, was foggy with heavy clouds rolling up from the inlet. The horses had left fine feed close by and wandered off to poorer feed many miles away. Sid and Alf were already after them when I turned out at six o'clock. The fog began to lift and life once again became normal as the horses arrived. We all shot numerous pictures, and by nine Sid and Alf once again had the horses packed. As the outfit crossed the mouth of Happy River I shot several hundred feet of movie film at them.

Having all sorts of time on our hands, Capps and I did our mending and laundry, while Andy and Jack, with some thought to the future, repaired the roof of the roadhouse so far as material at hand would permit. It had finally cleared and the sun was shining, so I once again had that optimistic feeling and began to plan a quick trip to the Kenai after our return to Anchorage. Andy told me of wonderful opportunities for moving pictures and said that I was sure to get a moose fight.

Towards evening it began to cloud up and ended by raining hard all night. Andy and Jack continued their building operations the next day. We discussed the possibility of the pack train reaching the bar that night and concluded it would not be possible as the rain was bound to have made the old dog trail almost impassable. If it had not started to rain hard again in the afternoon I believe we would have dropped down to some convenient spot near where we were to meet the pack train. The rain was beginning to get me a bit, as I had had twenty-one days of it to date. This totally eclipsed our Mount Dall record of the year previous.

September 12th, the day we were to meet the outfit, dawned most disagreeably; after an all-night rain a heavy fog had settled down, only to be driven off by more rain. We were up at four o'clock and everything in the boat was ready for our start by half-past six. The first six miles were made in an hour and five minutes; then the fog began to bother so that the second six consumed nearly two hours and a half. We reached the bar where the horses were waiting at quarter to one, they having been there since ten o'clock.

The weather had now cleared and a strong head wind sprung up. We lost no time in starting to ferry the outfit; the boat was unloaded and the packs and saddles were piled in and taken across to a spot near the cache. After the duffle had been taken over the horses were led in and swam across. All this took us until half-past three when we were on our way downstream again. But things did not look so encouraging. The wind had become stronger and it was with great difficulty that Jack and Andy could do anything with the boat. At four o'clock we had to tie up alongside a sand bar where we camped for the night.

Off again next morning at half-past six; there was still some wind but it gradually calmed down. The day was simply perfect, not a cloud in the sky; McKinley and Foraker stood out in silhouette with their snow tops changing every few minutes as the sun rose higher and higher. We passed a fine yellow grizzly bear putting in a great feed of dead salmon as we were tearing through a stretch of swift water. There was no chance to get a shot as we were upon him and by, before we realized it. We stopped at Skwentna Crossing at twenty minutes to ten to find no one at home. We looked about and saw a case of eggs, helped ourselves to a dozen, and also to some potatoes. We left at ten o'clock. The current in the river was now much slowed, so our speed was cut perceptibly. We reached our last gas cache at half-past one, and rejoiced at finding our gasoline intact. We used most of the eggs for lunch. The box containing them claimed they were "strictly fresh," but that must have been written many months before they had been started on their way to Alaska.

We were about to leave when the whirr of a Johnson motor came to our ears. Shortly a boat appeared in the bend of the river and there sat Rimmer, McElroy and Heffner. They came over to the bar and we had a short conversation with them. They were short of shear pins for their motor. Further, they informed us that they had lined up that river for over twenty years, and now they purposed letting the Johnson take them back. They were getting a wonderful kick out of the change in conditions.

We made marvelous speed once we had fairly started. Our destination that day was to be Susitna Station and I can assure you we were not dallying any on our way. We left the bar at ten minutes after one and entered the Yentna at three. By this time Jack had the motor humming like an aeroplane so that our trip through the Yentna and into the Susitna seemed to take no time at all. As we came into the Susitna it was beginning to grow dark and I felt that Jack would have been just as well pleased to have made another camp, but we motored on and finally reached Susitna Station at seven o'clock our time (which was one hour earlier) on September 13th. Mr. Healy invited Capps and myself to occupy his upper floor, and you may rest assured we did not hesitate in getting our bags up there and opened for the night.

In the morning Capps and I joined Mr. Healy in a cup of coffee and then went up the main street to a house owned by Jack and a partner, Charlie Smith, where a regal repast awaited us. We were very much disappointed at hearing that the mail boat, with our friend Captain Bill Austen, had just left and was not expected to return for ten days to two weeks.

After some discussion we decided to try and make Anchorage in our small boat with the outboard motor. This meant much time adjusting duffle bags and packing part of Capps' equipment, to say nothing of many pounds of rock specimens that he had collected. We decided to remain that day at Susitna Station and start early next morning in order to catch the incoming tide at the mouth of the Susitna.

Our Indian friend and former companion, Jimmie, appeared, and told us of his experience coming down river from Portage Creek. He said that he completed his canoe shortly after we left and, packing in his provisions, a tarp and his rifle, he started downstream. Everything went splendidly until he came into some very rough water near the mouth of the Hayes River. He suddenly lost control and, striking a sweeper, was swamped. He held on to the sweeper and managed to get ashore, but all his food, rifle, and the tarp which he used to sleep in, were gone, and never recovered. In some way he crossed the river, just how we could not clearly make out, and striking the old dog trail reached Skwentna Crossing the evening of the third day. He was pretty well exhausted, but McElroy fed him up and after a few days rest he started off again with a fresh supply of grub, and reached Susitna Station without further mishap. What hurt Jimmie most was the loss of his old gun. After concluding his tale of hardship he hesitated for a second and then said, "River dam bad; me no go up again for million dollar." *

I ground out some movie film of the Indians, all of whom

---

* Poor Jimmie, I am afraid, will never again go up the Skwentna, for when I saw him last fall (1930) at the Station, he was in very poor health.

were more than anxious to be pictured. There were three old-time sourdoughs who were much interested in the Johnson motor and had to look it all over and ask many questions about it. They were positive that it was going to fall to pieces at any time; in fact had been predicting it ever since we had started up river. They had decided to order one, but about this time Charlie Smith appeared on the opposite bank of the river and called out for a boat. Jack started up the motor and crossed, loaded Smith and six dogs, everything going fine until his return trip. When about a hundred yards from the bank the motor went dead, and they had to row to shore. The three old sourdoughs shook their heads and allowed "they knew she would fall to pieces." It turned out that a piece of waste in some way had got into the gas line. In a few minutes it was cleaned out and she was running as sweetly as ever.

That evening we gathered in Jack's house, which from all indications must have been a gambling hall in the heyday of Susitna Station. There were parts of cloth-covered tables lying about, and many other evidences of former glory. We swapped tales and talked of old times, and I happened to mention Aleck Smith, better known as "Sandy" or "Scotty." This brought forth a howl from one August Tobin, better known as the "Gee Pole Swede." It seems that many years before Sandy and Tobin were sinking a shaft in frozen ground on a prospect. Tobin was in a hole about seventy feet below ground, while Sandy was tending the windlass on the surface. In lowering the bucket Sandy, according to Tobin, was not paying too close attention to his job and unwound the rope

Osborn caribou

Motion picture enlargements

Small bull caribou   *Ewe (Ovis canadensis)*

which dropped down the shaft. Some predicament! Seventy feet below the surface in solid frozen ground! When I saw Sandy he claimed that he ran back to their cabin some two miles, and returned with their blankets, split them, and after tying the pieces together, lowered them to Tobin who fastened on the rope, and the rest was easy. Tobin murmured, "Sandy said he ran to the cabin and back? Like Hell he did; I'll bet he had dinner and then read a book before he returned." "Just the difference between the fellow that's down in the hole and the one on top," Sandy remarked when I repeated the conversation to him some months after in New York.

Another told of the winter when Major Gotwals of the Alaskan Road Commission came over the trail with a doctor for the Iditarod. Leonard Seppala was the dog musher, and with him were his celebrated Siberians. Upon arriving at the Pioneer Roadhouse, Rohn River, which was being operated by French Joe (Joe Blanchell) they were greeted with great enthusiasm and invited to enter. Joe had a fine meal, consisting mostly of delicious juicy steaks, ready in short order. After a hearty feed they sat about enjoying their pipes. Joe broke in with the remark, "Pretty good meat, don't you think," and to this they all agreed. "I always knew one couldn't tell the difference between caribou and a good piece of lynx when properly cooked," continued Joe. The effect was beyond words. Those three husky, contented men were sure their time had arrived and that they had been poisoned. Of course Joe was just having his little joke. Months after I saw Seppala in New York and told him of the tale; he said, "Yes, Joe put one over on us; I was pretty near sick."

Capps and I started for bed at ten o'clock but no doubt those boys kept at it until all hours. Since leaving the pack train the weather had been clear and cold, and we were now sure the next day would be likewise. Our prayers went forth for calm weather to cross Cook Inlet.

Seven-thirty on September 15th saw us waving good-bye to our friends, all of whom seemed skeptical as to our being able to get across the Inlet. The last words that came over the air to us were from Mr. Healy, "Don't take too many chances."

The motor was singing an even purr as we struck out into the current, and looking back, towering over all we saw the great McKinley, with Foraker almost as grand, while Russell and Dall seemed dwarfed alongside of them. Our boat was very heavily loaded, and we four were not light-weights. We literally whirled along with the swift current of the Susitna, and it was but a short time before we reached the mouth, to find that the tide had not yet started to come in. We waited some time before the water began to rise, but finally we started, at first dragging, but eventually riding in deep water. We were making good time, but not as fast as we had planned owing to the boat's being loaded to within four inches of the gunwales. We watched every breath of air, every cloud, every least suggestion of a blow. Ahead of us was Turnagain Arm, looking harmless in the sunshine. We had one or two qualms as a small squall came up and the waves started to splash over the sides, but fortunately they did not amount to anything. The tide turned before we reached Anchorage and for about two hours we had to buck it, but fortunately we were in the lee of the land and reached Anchorage about two o'clock.

Andy, Jack and I did some hustling the balance of that day as I had decided to go to the Kenai and hoped to connect with Capps again on the Steamer *Alaska*. We arranged to ship the boat next morning on a flat car to Lake View on Kenai Lake, we to go along with it. That night at the Parsons Hotel a room with bath sounded good to me, and believe me I enjoyed the bath and also the good bed.

Before going on with my trip to the Kenai let me set down from my notebook some of the records of game seen and taken on the trip:

KILLED

1 Ram—43½" Curl, 15½" Base, 26" Spread
1 Ram—39¾" Curl, 14¾" Base, 23" Spread
(The meat of the Sheep was entirely consumed.)
2 Bull Caribou, one of them for the American
    Museum of Natural History
(The meat of the caribou was not edible as both
    had badly affected lungs.)

28 Ptarmigan } For food
207 Trout

SEEN BY ACTUAL COUNT

14 Moose		6 Grizzly Bear
371 Caribou		2 Black Bear
231 Sheep		1 Wolverine
	1 Lynx	

The moose I did not hunt, but just stumbled across. There are many in that section, but I was too high for them, and as I was planning the trip to the Kenai I was not interested.

Just a word before I depart for the Kenai. My trip to Rainy Pass was made possible through the courtesy of the United States Geological Survey. Its success was entirely due to the splendid preparations made by Stephen R. Capps. His experience and knowledge of the country were responsible for solving many difficulties that otherwise might have turned success into failure. Everything was carried out in a quiet, efficient manner, and never once did I hear a cross or discordant note. The entire company was a hard-working, active lot of men who looked upon all obstacles as mere troubles to be overcome with a smile. I consider it was quite a privilege to have been permitted to be one of the party.

We said good-bye to Capps on September 16th, as the freight pulled out at eleven-forty. It brought the first realization that the trip to Rainy Pass was over, and I wondered whether I would ever look down Ptarmigan Valley and mush over the old Alaskan Range in the shadow of Mount McKinley again. I had plenty of time for thoughts as the freight was not celebrated for its speed. At three o'clock we reached Tunnel where we had a fine dinner with the train crew. Depression had come over me which I couldn't shake off, but I tried not to show it to Andy and Jack. We reached Lakeview at six o'clock and unloaded the boat and our duffle. I went to the section house for mail which I had telephoned from Anchorage to have forwarded to me from Seward. I found none of the letters I had expected, which did not help to lessen my depression. We put the boat in the lake, loaded her up, started up the motor and went over to Andy's house, where we spent the night. I had been craving for eggs, and I particularly asked Andy to get some *fresh* eggs at Anchorage, and I believe he tried his best.

At five the next morning we were up and lightening our outfit to a minimum, as it was now back packing. We left Andy's house at a quarter-past seven and stopped a few minutes at the Lake View Station, but fifteen minutes later saw us heading across Lake Kenai. There was a heavy fog which, as usual, lifted sufficiently for us to hold our course. The old boat was making excellent time, the motor going like a charm. We reached Cooper Landing in two hours and forty-five minutes, which Andy said was fast time. Jack had to look over things in his cabin at Cooper Landing, so we stopped there for half an hour, then headed into Kenai River with the motor wide open, and we were traveling, for in thirty minutes we came to the entrance of the canyon. We had passed several clearings, some with cabins in more or less abandoned condition. At one spot there were several buildings, the remains of a questionable gold mine.

As we came to the canyon the motor was shut off and tilted clear of the water. Jack and Andy once again took to the oars, and we began to shoot through. I was in the stern of the boat trying to get moving pictures of the rushing water. The weather was clear and quite warm with plenty of black flies and no dope to help combat them. We stopped for a few minutes in the lower canyon at noon to talk with some men we had passed further up the river. Many sheldrakes and a few mallards had risen as we shot by, and on the river bank our first porcupine wabbled slowly along near the water's edge.

When we came through the lower canyon to the more level water entering Shilak Lake, great quantities of dead salmon lay on the banks. Many gulls were having a battle royal for the fish carcasses, while the odor was stifling and the black flies increasing in numbers. We had some difficulty finding the proper channel through which to get out into the lake. When the deep water of the lake was reached we all drew a sigh of relief. The motor began driving the boat rapidly away from the odor and the flies. When half way across Shilak we stopped at Lucas and Nelson's cabin, which we found deserted. We immediately started a fire in the stove and began cooking our lunch. While waiting for lunch I began to look about, as I knew that Lucas and Nelson had some hunters out in the hills. I came across a field glass case with George Burghard's name imprinted on the top, so I had one of the men identified. I looked still further to try to identify the other, but had no success. There being a fine Victrola with many records, we had music also. Jack and Andy knew, so they claimed, that there should be some fine home-made wine, and we searched everywhere without finding it, much to our disgust when later on we were told it was in a box outside of the cabin.

At quarter of three we were off again and, as we entered the lower river, stopped at an old salmon drying rack to cache ten gallons of gas for our return trip. Quantities of duck rose and flew downstream, while a few circled and came down again behind us. We reached the mouth of Killey River at half-past four as the shadows began to fall.

Our going now was not quite so simple, for there were constantly changing channels, with sweepers, rocks and sand bars looming ahead. We worked up possibly a mile and a half when we decided to camp, as a mean bit of river appeared, and it was now very nearly dark. The weather was still fine, though quite foggy in the morning, and the black flies were getting worse by the minute.

Next morning saw us plugging on up Killey River until nine o'clock when we reached a high bank where Andy thought we should camp. As soon as camp was fixed up we started off to hunt moose. We traveled in a southerly direction for something like seven or eight miles without seeing any, though there were plenty of fresh signs. Finally, on a far distant ridge we picked up four cows, but there was no bull with them. Andy said that we would have to pack in five or six miles, in order to reach better moose country. On our way back to camp we discovered it would be possible to run the boat some three miles further up stream. The black flies had now become unbearable; they were literally chewing Andy to pieces, while they drove Jack and me nearly crazy.

The next morning a fine rain was coming down as we broke camp. This time we pushed up too far so that we had to cross a wretched swamp in order to reach a small lake where Andy desired to camp. We tied up at eleven o'clock and after making up packs and having a bite to eat we started on a foot race over about as mean a swamp as one would want to tackle. After that we came to the down timber for which

Kenai is celebrated. We located the lake and made camp in the early afternoon. It was really a most interesting spot as the high mountains stood out in the distance and the lake was an attractive body of water.

By this time I was becoming quite nervous about missing the Steamer *Alaska*. That evening we turned in early as we intended to put in a long, hard day on the morrow. It meant that I could hunt just two days more if I were going to catch that steamer.

I have no idea how long I had been asleep when I was awakened by splashing in the lake. It was a fine moonlight night and I could see the dark forms of three moose walking in the water. I gave a low call and it was immediately answered by the bull. I was having quite a conversation with the moose when Jack stuck his head out of their tent and wanted to know what all the noise was about. The moose stayed about for some time but it was not very long before Jack and I turned back to bed. Andy slept through the entire incident.

The next two days were put in climbing over the worst mess of down timber I have ever been unfortunate enough to encounter. This could have been endured but for the pest of black flies that literally devoured us. They raised welts on Andy, and, though they did not poison either Jack or me, nevertheless they made life scarcely worth living. To top all this we were unable to find any large moose, and in fact there were few in that part of the country. By actual count we saw five bulls, eleven cows and three yearlings, but none of the bulls had any sizeable heads. We watched a nice, fat,

Mount McKinley after the snow

Typical group of rams in the McKinley country

black bear on the second day for fully half an hour. He was eating berries and having a fine time generally. It was a simple shot and the pelt was fine, but the season on black bear does not open until October 1st. I wouldn't have shot him in any case, as I enjoyed watching his antics. He suddenly saw us but he kept on feeding, pretending he hadn't, until he worked over a slight ridge; then he beat it for all he was worth.

Upon return to camp on the second evening we had a most serious discussion. If I was to catch my steamer we would have to pull out the next morning. Andy and Jack both felt that we had played in hard luck as the moose had all moved across Funny River. They were both emphatically opposed to my leaving the Kenai until I had secured a fine specimen. It did not seem fair to the country, I had to admit, but then I should get out on the *Alaska* as there were many matters needing my attention.

As we were discussing the pros and cons of whether I would return or remain we lay on our backs watching some of the most wonderful displays of northern lights I have ever seen. It seemed as if the heavens were covered with great wavy veils that were constantly swishing and changing colors. Suddenly they would snap out, and shortly again would be followed with more and greater varieties of waving colors. It was a wonderful night, brilliantly clear, with a keen snap to the air. Is it surprising that with such influences I was finally prevailed upon to remain?

In the morning we made up light packs, taking one tent, our bags and sufficient food to last three days. We crossed

Funny River and packed about five miles towards Tustamena Lake. It was a blistering hot day and the black flies were still doing their bit. We made camp near a glistening stream of water bordered on either side by sizeable standing timber. When we started to make camp I placed my rifle alongside a scrub tree, and Andy did likewise with his. We pitched the tent and as it was about noon, and hot, we decided to take a snooze, then a bite to eat before going out to look for that big bull. We had cut up a mosquito bed net into three pieces. This we wrapped about our heads and tried to get asleep. Andy and Jack quickly dozed off, but not I. It suddenly occurred to me that it was quite foolish to lie out there in the sun for fly bait, so I scrambled into the tent and soon passed out of the picture also. I was the first to awaken, a little after one o'clock. Andy and Jack were still in the land of nod and it took some persuasion before I had them back to earth.

We were eating a light lunch of cold meat, bread and cheese when I heard a movement of the brush just beyond us; looking up, there not thirty yards away stood a huge Brownie. Andy and Jack spotted Mr. Bear about the same time, and there was one fine bit of excitement for a few seconds. I don't know which of us was the more scared, the bear or we three. Andy grabbed his rifle and tried to throw a shell into the chamber; the gun jambed. I rushed for my gun, but it was gone, while Jack dove into the tent. The bear rose on his hind legs, let out a couple of "woofs" and was out of sight. Jack appeared from the tent with my rifle which he had carefully put away after the tent had been pitched. After a little trouble Andy succeeded in getting out the shell which proved to be badly split. What a pretty mess that bear might have made of us if he had wanted to! But he was a good bear and only curious. We discovered later that we were camped alongside of a bear trail; it must have belonged to old Mr. Brownie.

That afternoon we saw moose aplenty, some of them with pretty good heads. By actual count we looked over fifty-two moose, of which eleven were bulls. The rut was just getting to its height, and we watched several bulls working themselves to the proper state of excitement. The air reeked of moose, and if you are familiar with their odor at that time of the year you know it was none too pleasant. There was one solitary bull with a huge head off some distance in a meadow. I wanted to try and reach him, but Andy thought we should only look them over and really start hunting the next day. On our way back to camp as the shadows began to fall, the moose seemed to be everywhere. Three bulls, one with a pretty good head, almost accompanied us to our domicile. When we reached camp it was black night, and no water. Someone had to go to the stream. As I recollect, it was Jack who went; Andy and I felt that we were the competent ones to make fire and clean the dishes; any excuse was better than none. We turned in shortly after supper, and believe me our guns were loaded with shells that had been carefully examined, and placed close to our sleeping bags.

The next day, my big day on the Kenai, was September 23rd. At quarter of seven we were off for a high ridge which we intended to use as our lookout. We did not put in any great length of time in locating; it wasn't necessary for there were moose everywhere. The annual convention was under way and it seemed as if they were coming from every direction, and heading towards us. We did some traveling that day, for every patch of timber had a bunch of moose in it. From one patch of timber to another we went, and one bunch of moose after another we looked over,—great bulls with harems of from three to six cows.

They did not appear to pay any attention to us; in fact several times some of them must have scented us, but it seemed to make no difference. One bull looked very fine to me; he had an evenly balanced head with wide palms and sixteen points on each side. I put my gun up to shoot, but Andy said "No," and insisted it was too small. I was seeing so many moose that I was losing all sense of proportion. On and on we went looking over moose and still more moose. We had about concluded to call it a day and put off the deadly massacre until tomorrow when Andy spotted two bulls squaring off for a fight about two miles away. We all looked those bulls over through our glasses and decided they were owners of great heads, and we decided to work closer. The nearer we went, the larger the heads seemed to grow, until we were satisfied that either one was well past the sixty-inch mark and heading towards the seventy. The next problem was to get near enough to examine the heads closely, and this was not such a simple matter. There were cows scattered about; no doubt the unpleasantness was caused by these lady spectators.

We came along splendidly until we all but bumped into an old cow and calf. To get by these it would be necessary to pass to windward and so frighten them, and it was more than likely they would stampede in the direction of the scrappy bulls, and then all chance of getting close would disappear. Andy decided it would be better to let the cow see us and trust that she would depart in the opposite direction. A slight interruption was caused by Jack seeing something curled up at the foot of a couple of trees that greatly resembled a bear. I was not to be taken from my moose stalk, and said so. The bulls had stopped their fight and one wandered off by himself while the other proceeded to confiscate the cows that had remained. We now had a fine chance to look the head over in detail, and it certainly came up to our previous impression. Andy and Jack figured the head at about sixty-five to sixty-eight inches, while it seemed larger to me; at any rate it was a fine specimen of a Kenai moose.

We bided our time and gradually worked closer until the bull and cows lay down. We then worked up to within about a hundred and fifty yards, and I regret to say the head began to shrink. It was plain that though the head was large, the spread would not be so great, as the points all turned up. I decided nevertheless that he would do, so leaving Andy and Jack I worked over to where I could get a clear sight of the shoulder. At about seventy-five yards I carefully placed a shot, and the old bull gave a bellow, at the same time trying to make a lunge, but it was all over. The head measured sixty-two inches and had fifteen points on each side; a splendid massive specimen. It was now too late to skin out the head and make camp, so we left the carcass after opening him up and placing the head so the scalp would not spoil. The weather was still warm, and the black flies, if anything, on the increase.

On our way back we ran across a very angry bull, and at the first grunt Andy gave, he came for us. His eyes were blood red and quite small; there was mud plastered on his neck and strips of willows hanging on his horns. A short distance off a large cow was quietly feeding, and directly behind the bull stood a calf. As the bull started towards us the calf gave him two or three butts on the rump, but he paid no attention. Andy by this time tried to entice the bull a little closer, and was quite successful as he came towards us on a trot with his head down and rolling from side to side, with a deep grunt at each step. When he was within twenty feet I threw a cartridge into my rifle, as I did not like his looks. I noticed Jack glancing about trying to locate the best place for a getaway. I yelled and waved my arms, but the bull only stamped the ground and let out husky grunts.

"If he comes any closer, Andy, I am going to shoot," were my words. Just then the cow came trundling over and undoubtedly said something to the bull, for the next instant he turned and they both crashed off, going like a couple of high-powered shells. That evening as we were seated at the camp fire there was a heavy tread on the trail alongside camp, followed by a crashing in the brush; our friend the Brownie without a doubt.

The next day passed in getting the moose head into camp and skinning it out, and then packing the skull as far as Funny River. On Saturday, September 25th, the day I was to have sailed from Seward, we broke camp, and just as we were adjusting our packs I heard a noise in the brush on the edge of the woods. I looked up quickly and there, not twenty yards off, stood our friend the Brownie. He had probably been watching us quietly for sometime, wondering what we were doing now. I grabbed my gun and threw in a shell, but at the movement the bear made a quick turn and melted into the woods before I could get the gun to my shoulder.

We were on our way by seven o'clock, with Jack in the lead, hitting up a fine pace to follow. We crossed Funny River and headed straight for the lake, passing two cow moose on the way. We reached our former camp on the lake at ten o'clock, and after resting there for a few minutes were off again, following a new trail that Jack had made which was shorter and better. At half-past eleven we were back at our cache on Killey River, with the boat nearby. It was now storming in the mountains but down where we were the weather still held fine.

There is but little more to recount of this trip. It was now but a matter of a few days to run up the lower Kenai, Shilak Lake and then the upper Kenai, finally crossing Kenai Lake. All of this was accomplished without much effort, as the motor worked beautifully and bucked the swift waters well. Of course through the canyon we were forced to line for short distances, but from our camp on Killey River to Andy's house on Kenai Lake it took exactly seventeen hours and twenty-five minutes running time. The elapsed time was longer as we stopped over night at the Lucas and Nelson cabin, and then made another stop at Cooper Landing. There we saw the trophies secured by George Burghard and Art

Norcross (the other hunter whose identity I had been unable to discover previously) and they were a fine pair of moose heads.

My first desire on reaching Andy's house was to get some fresh eggs. About two miles down the track was a chicken ranch, and I went down there with Andy's stepson, Buster Revelle. I bought three dozen eggs and packed them back to Andy's and cooked them all. There were now five of us as Buster and his brother had come in. We ate every one of those three dozen eggs at one sitting. Andy and Jack complained about their having no taste, but believe me they were good, and went to the spot. I now received a batch of mail, most of it having arrived before I left for the Kenai, and so the next few days passed until Sunday, October 3rd arrived, when I departed with George Burghard and Art Norcross on board the Steamship *Northwestern*.

As I look back on my trip those countless days of rain and fog have totally been eclipsed by the sparkling bright days of sunshine. That grand old range of mountains, rugged and snow-clad, with McKinley towering above often comes back during spells of reverie. As for the Kenai with its lowlands nestling amongst high snow peaks, with its countless moose wandering about, with hot sunshine and black flies galore, "a part of the banana belt," as Jack Lean put it, comes often to mind. So many pleasant memories of friends that I have made, and recollections of the sheep ranges and the wide valleys, keep coming up from time to time that I fear I am weakening and that once again I hear the call to the shadow of Mount McKinley.

Jack in a serious mood   *Andy*   *Jack*

Motion picture enlargements

Lee   *Charlie*

CHAPTER VI

EXPLORATION OF 1930

NINETEEN THIRTY has rolled in, some four years since I last wandered the grand and glorious hills on the north side of the Alaskan Range that are so well watched over by the great McKinley. The lure of those hills and the great game herds call and the wanderlust slowly but surely gets the better of a poor, weak vagabond.

Stephen R. Capps of the United States Geological Survey put on the finishing touches by telling me I should explore a pass at the head of the Tonzona that undoubtedly leads to the headwaters of the Yentna River. And again, between our last camp in the Tonzona Basin in 1925 and Rainy Pass there still remains a great blank space.

To locate a high line trail from Tonzona Basin to Rainy Pass was a fascination. We knew that Dr. Alfred H. Brooks had made the trip through the lower passes, but to be the first to discover a new short cut through that blank space became an obsession.

Curiosity and the call of Alaska were uppermost, and so after definitely deciding not to try the trip and turning over my horses to friend Capps for his trip, I fell. Night letters to various men who had been out with me began to speed over the air, Andy Simons at once said he would go, and also Jack Lean, and then I arranged for a pack outfit from Bob Bragaw.

Andy secured Lee Hancock and his brother Charlie as packer and assistant. This happened late in the spring so that all arrangements necessarily had to be made by wire.·

I planned to send the horses in via Beluga and the old trail used by Dr. Alfred H. Brooks in 1902, and by Capps in 1926 when I was along. Jack Lean with McElroy and Buster Revelle were to go up the Skwentna with a boatload of provisions and turn them over to the pack train after they had crossed the Skwentna at our old ferry. The pack train was then to relay the provisions over the old dog trail to Happy River Roadhouse where we were to meet them later on.

My return to Alaska was one grand reunion. Everywhere I went old friends were on hand to greet me. It was "old home week" for me. At Chitina Oscar Breedman greeted me as the long-lost prodigal, and on the trail it was the same. The Alaskans certainly have a way of making one at home.

At McCarty a fishing party had been arranged by John and Melo Hajdukovich, and a wonderful day was enjoyed by all. "The finest fishing in the world," as John Hajdukovich described it, and I can only say I have never had anything like it. District Attorney Collins, better known as E. B., ran me in to Fairbanks. We arrived in time for breakfast, and dropping into the Model Café, I just had to tell Berney Carr, the proprietor, all about my fishing trip. Later in the day Berney formally notified me that he had called a special meeting of the Chatanika and Summit Lake Rod and Gun Club, and that by unanimous vote he had been authorized to issue me their "Fish Liar's License."

Time fled more rapidly than I wished, and it was not until July 31st that I arrived at Anchorage. Andy Simons, Jack Lean and Bob Bragaw all were on hand at the Station to meet me. Everything was in shape for a wonderful and successful adventure. My wife and her sister had accompanied me on the trip to this point, but in the morning they left for the outside on their way home. Andy, Jack and I had to lay over in Anchorage that day as Bill Austen, the captain of the gas boat *Alert*, which was to take us to Susitna Station, did not like the looks of Cooks Inlet.

We finally left Anchorage about nine o'clock on August 2nd under a clear blue sky, and reached Susitna Station at seven o'clock that evening. Again I was greeted by enthusiastic friends, headed by Mr. Healy, the Mayor. Andy and I passed the night in the old deserted roadhouse and Jack went up to his own house.

The next morning we fastened our 18 H.P. Johnson motor on the rear end of the boat that we had towed from Anchorage. The rain had started but only in a gentle way. We had more or less trouble with our motor all day. It commenced kicking up as we left the Station, and kept at it. I am not going to tire you with the details of our trip up that miserable Skwentna, but will only touch on the high spots.

In pouring rain we pulled into McDougall about noon the second day, and for three days we remained at that desolate spot with the waters of the Yentna rising higher and higher. We first stopped in a deserted cabin, and were forced to move the second day as we were flooded out. There were three trappers there, and they were pessimistic. They moved their supplies and bedding up into their caches. Our next move proved to be temporary as the water again drove us out. On the third day we took to our boat, and with our load lightened by one of the trappers we ran ten miles upstream to Gray's, a deserted camp. Though this was on higher ground, the river again threatened to drive us up into the mountains. Precious days were passing and we were helpless against the flood. At last the waters began to recede and we started on. Eric Oman with his boat and motor, took part of our load and helped us nearly to the mouth of Hayes River. Here again we were delayed by rain followed by an earthquake.

Even though we had an 18 H.P. kicker we could use it only on short stretches. The good old line with man-power was our only hope. And how I hate that infernal line! Four years ago on our way up the Skwentna I had watched Jack Lean on the gee-pole; it seemed a cinch. The gee-pole is used to keep the boat off shore while it is being hauled upstream by the men on the line. Oh, why did I ever envy Jack? The job was wished on me, and then my troubles began. Before we reached Happy River I gradually became more or less proficient. At any rate each day I required less aid to help me get that boat out of the trouble I would permit it to swing into. The gee-pole job I will sell short to any young ambitious man who wants to take a trip up the Skwentna River.

The day we reached Happy our spirits were high, our troubles were over and the sun shone brightly; it always does when you arrive at Happy. Lee Hancock appeared after considerable hallo'ing on our part. He had about given us up, and was sure that the Skwentna had again taken her toll.

Charlie was at the cache above Pontella's, just off the old trail, on a lake that the planes use as a landing place. Pontella's Cabin was so named from the trapper who originally built it. In the days when the trail was in use the musher would stop at Pontella's and telephone to the Pass for weather conditions, and when he started Pontella would advise the Pass. In this way many a musher was kept from disaster. The telephone wires were trailed along the ground, and this would have worked splendidly if the caribou hadn't taken it into their heads to wind the cable about their horns. We followed the cable for long distances, but here and there it had been broken by the caribou. We found a shed antler with a huge coil of wire wound about it.

The bear had played havoc with our cache, and so Charlie had to sit on the job.

The horses having strayed, we were late in getting off the next day, and in the afternoon of the second day, after having wallowed through some of the worst going one would ask for,—mud, belly deep on the horses,—we reached the cache. After taking stock of our provisions we found the bear had relieved us of all our dried fruit, several sacks of sugar and all of our oatmeal.

In the morning we started early and decided we would move all our supplies to the Old Pass Creek Roadhouse at the Pass. The traveling was much better though still soft. We reached the Pass in early afternoon, and Lee and Charlie at once returned with the horses to the cache. The rain was with us again, and so it was not until late afternoon next day that the boys returned with the balance of the supplies.

On August 21st, another fine day, we went through Rainy Pass, and while traveling down the Dalzell River on the north side we saw a grizzly bear quietly feeding. There was no way to avoid it, we had to pass directly by that grizzly as there was a canyon on the other side. When within a couple of hundred yards of the bear we stopped, and the movie camera was unloaded. I had a peculiar feeling about that bear, and made Andy get his rifle and handed mine to Jack. Crawling over a low ridge I set up the camera and started grinding. The bear saw us, raised on his hind legs, looked us over for a second, and then started. It was a perfect stalk as he crawled through brush, keeping out of sight, and rising every once in a while to make sure he had us located, and then coming on again as rapidly as possible. When he was within a hundred and fifty feet he broke from the brush and headed directly for us. By this time, though the camera was grinding on, I was yelling to shoot. At about fifty feet Andy shot and turned the bear, and almost immediately after Jack shot and broke the bear's neck, killing him instantly. The horses were bucking and stampeding, food stuffs were being scattered over the landscape. Gradually things quieted down and we were under way again.

It was about that time I spotted a nice fat bull caribou. The season opened August 20th, and we had been without meat for nearly a month. Jack and I started off to get the caribou and suffice it to say we had fresh tenderloin for dinner that evening.

We made camp at the ruins of the Rainy Pass Roadhouse and for three days we remained there. During that time we explored the surrounding country and discovered two passes towards the head of the Dalzell River. One pass leads back into Ptarmigan Valley and the other over to the Kuskokwim. Sheep were scattered about on all the high ridges. Many fine rams were there, but none that came up to what I was looking for. We went back to Rainy Pass and looked over a bunch of rams that we had seen when we came through. There were two fine heads in the bunch; one of them was well over forty inches on the curl, but I wanted a forty-five or forty-six, so was content to shoot several pictures which I regret to say did not turn out satisfactorily. There were a few scattered caribou wandering about the hills also, but no large bands had as yet put in an appearance. We had also seen several black bear, and the one grizzly that met his end as he charged.

We left Rainy Pass Roadhouse and followed down the bar of the Dalzell until we located the old dog trail on a bench on the left hand side. The old trail had been cut out of the high hillside and was still in good condition. Our pack horses never seemed to appreciate the necessity of traveling, and would wander into a bunch of luscious grass and linger on to feed. They certainly had no regard for their figures for they continued to put on fat right up to the last we saw of them as they crossed the Skwentna on their way back to Beluga.

My saddle horse, Dolly, would eat anything and always cleaned up the bacon and eggs (and such eggs!) while they lasted, finishing off each morning with the remnants of the sour dough cakes. One day while traveling I picked some blueberries and was blowing off the small leaves preparatory to eating them. Dolly put her head over my shoulder and lapped them up before I knew what was happening.

Towards afternoon we came to the mouth of the Dalzell, and there before us the Rohn River opened up with high pinnacled peaks towards its head. There, too, were sheep on the high peaks, well up near its source. We stopped and carefully looked over the country through our glasses. There seemed to be a low pass leading over into the unknown country. My first decision was to work up the Rohn and explore the pass, but after a conference with Andy and Jack, I finally decided to keep on to the Kuskokwim, and then return to the head of the Rohn. This was where I made my fatal error, for my opportunity of getting into that new country passed then and there.

We kept on until we reached the Rohn River Roadhouse which had been burned to the ground. We found delicious raspberries growing amongst the ruins, and splendid rhubarb in the old garden. A little above the old roadhouse we discovered a trapper's cabin that had been occupied the previous winter and still contained a goodly quantity of supplies including a portion of a case of "Strictly Fresh Eggs." Though we looked through papers, magazines and books no name could we find. We signed our names, with date, so the owners would know of our visit.

Next morning it was raining again, and the head of the Rohn looked threatening. Besides, we would have to return to get around the canyon near the mouth of the Rohn, and also, the horses had wandered off. The river was too deep to ford, and the current was swift as it came through the can-

The sign on the summit

Refuge hut near summit. Rainy Pass

yon and entered the Kuskokwim. It was August 25th and to follow Dr. Brooks' trail around the foothills to the Tonzona Basin would have taken ten days, and possibly as many more to get back. It was too much of a gamble, and with regret at having to change our plans we headed up the Kuskokwim. On the first day we had our own troubles in trying to get around a series of lakes formed by beaver dams. After wandering for sometime with the lakes behind us we discovered a well swamped trail which we followed nearly all the rest of the day. At spots it was blocked off by wind falls and landslides, but on the whole was in very good shape, though from all indications it had been cut many years before. It had unquestionably been cut for pack horses, and looked very much like the work of a United States Geological Survey party.

We wondered who had been in these parts for I knew there was no record of any party having been up the south fork of the Kuskokwim. We stopped at an old camp ground undoubtedly made by a Survey party. There was a pile of wood, now nearly decayed, cut for a stove. Again we speculated as to who had been in these parts as we were certain we were the pioneers. At this camp while packing up next morning our head packer, Lee, almost passed out with an acute attack of what I diagnosed as ptomaine. We had with us some canned oysters and Jack had made a soup of them the night before. Lee ate most of it, while the rest of us went very light or passed it by. I made a few suggestions but Lee didn't think much of me as a doctor.

Andy, Jack and I went off on a reconnaissance, leaving Charlie feeding Lee quantities of hot water and mustard.

We wandered further than we intended as new sights were constantly coming to view. There was a low pass on the opposite side of the Kuskokwim that called wistfully. It must lead into a wonderful country, and it seemed so near and easy to negotiate. Unfortunately the old Kuskokwim was high and literally boiled downstream on its way to the Bering Sea, and there was no way we could cross. We saw a cow moose feeding on the bar near us but we did not disturb her. There were sheep on the hills both sides of the river. We discovered a sheep lick with trails two feet deep leading to it. There were no sheep using it, but the signs were fresh as if many had been there but a short time before.

We located a stream that we were sure headed up in the general direction of Sheep Creek on the opposite side of the range, where I had hunted rams four years ago. As all chance of making my original objective had gone I decided to push on to the head of this creek in an endeavor to locate a pass to Ptarmigan Valley, and to spend the balance of my time there.

Returning to camp we found Lee still quite miserable. I put my foot down and made him take two tablespoonfuls of epsom salts in a cup of hot water, following that shortly after with another cup of hot water. In about an hour after it began to look as if our sick man would recover. In the morning he was much better. Though weak, he was able to travel and in a few days he was as well as ever. I found six cans of oysters and two of clams in the outfit which I promptly ditched with some miserable looking cheese, and no further trouble was experienced by anyone.

We camped near the head of our stream and found a pass into the head of Sheep Creek. We spent several days at this camp in a splendid stand of spruce all of which was dying or dead. This we found to be the case with all the spruce in this section; some sort of scale is killing it. We looked over many rams but none came up to my expectations.

One day when we were on a high peak the clouds cleared and the blue sky was everywhere. There stood McKinley, Foraker, Russell and Dall, and there stood the peaks about the Tonzona Basin, so near that it hardly seemed a day off. On our way to camp that evening we spotted fifteen rams on a high mountain across the stream from us. We looked them over carefully, and though they were far off we could make out horns, two or three of which were big. "Now," said Andy, "those rams are in a place we can't reach from here, but we will put one over on them tomorrow." He then explained there was a canyon back of camp and that he was sure we could go through there and come up easily to these rams on the back of the mountain.

Early next morning we started, and after steady climbing until noon we found ourselves in a rough slide with a large basin opening up below us but no sign of the sheep. A little further on was a deep canyon, and beyond was our bunch of rams, further away than they had been when we located them the night before, and just about as impossible to reach. We were puzzled and unable to make out the topography, though the basin seemed familiar. After many minutes of survey it suddenly dawned upon us; it was over on those rough ridges above the basin that I killed the large ram in 1926. Those hills and mountains certainly had done some fearful twisting and turning when they were being formed. The rain started in again and the fog came down over the tops of the hills, so we wended our way back to camp.

The next day, September 1st, we decided to try getting up the pass and into the head of Sheep Creek. The clouds hung low and rain was falling, but undaunted we packed up with little difficulty, only a few slipped packs, and made up a steep grassy hill, following alongside a canyon down to the head of Sheep Creek. We passed an old camp ground that Andy told me he had used the year before, when he had taken James A. Stillman there to hunt sheep. We made camp in the pouring rain on the bar of the stream about fifty yards below. For firewood we had green willow that would not burn, so preparing meals became hectic. We put in another day at this camp, and towards late afternoon of that day Andy told me I had better come and kill a fair-sized ram that was above camp. It was still raining, though not quite so hard. The ram looked small, and high up. "What's the use," I thought.

Andy said about this time, "Come, we have to have meat, and sheep is good." I realized that we had been living on caribou, and I suddenly wanted to taste a good juicy mutton steak. Off we went, and as there was a small canyon near camp it looked as if the stalk would be easy. We finally came out on a ridge that brought us within two hundred yards of the ram, with a deep ravine to another ridge, and just above the latter, the ram was quietly feeding. I wanted to make the other ridge as I dislike to shoot over an intervening piece of scenery. It was raining hard again, and the clouds were slowly coming down. Just then a small ram appeared and fed directly towards us. There was no chance to move, and each second the rain was getting wetter and colder. "I am going to shoot anyhow; I probably will miss, but there's no other chance, Andy," I mumbled. As the shot rang out the ram jumped, so I let another go that hit amidship. Thereupon I let loose some off-hand shooting that would have disgusted a novice. The less said about it the better.

On September 3rd we packed up and started back to Pass Creek. The rain was still with us. Down Sheep Creek we traveled, and in nearly two hours we passed my camp of 1925. How we mushed from that camp each day and went up to the head of Sheep Creek and back, seemed incredible. We had some very soft traveling, but reached Pass Creek Roadhouse in the early afternoon.

For six days we remained at the Pass, going out each day in hopes of getting a record moose or caribou and possibly some pictures. Conditions for photography had been almost impossible, with only an odd day now and then when the camera could be used. The caribou by this time were appearing daily in larger bunches, and many fine heads amongst them. Here again, I was looking for the unusual and was hard to satisfy.

Aeroplanes were constantly (at least one each day) going and coming from the Iditarod. One day returning from Six Mile Creek we saw a ship come out of the Pass and head directly for our camp, zoom down and circle it, then off again headed down Happy Valley towards the Skwentna. Suddenly it veered and turned towards the lake.

"That's Mat Niemenen on his way to Anchorage; he just wanted to look us over," remarked Andy; and then, "Guess he decided to land on the lake and stay at the cache over night rather than tackle that fog."

We later discovered that Andy's surmise was correct. Two days later Mat came over camp again with Ernest Walker Sawyer and Charles Flory on their way to Bristol Bay. He zoomed down within a hundred feet, waved something and then rose over some brush where he dropped a package of papers, straightened out again and was gone in a bank of fog through the Pass before we realized what had happened. They had left Anchorage about two hours earlier, and we had the morning papers. It had taken us over three weeks to reach the Pass on our way in. Some difference!

After reading the news of the day I decided to pull out and catch the Steamship *Yukon* as I found that the Steamship *Aleutian* which I had planned to return on had been taken off. We moved camp to the mouth of Moose Creek and put in the balance of the time there. It was necessary to cross Happy River to get to our camp on Moose Creek. The river was high, and just as Dolly, with me on her back, reached the deepest part of the river she slipped and went down on her knees. There was an unpleasant second, and then she recovered and was on her feet again, but I was thoroughly soaked.

Up Moose Creek I secured a very fine specimen of caribou with forty-five points. The meat was all packed out and consumed, one hindquarter finally landing in New York in splendid condition, where it was greatly enjoyed.

Going up to Simpson Pass and also another pass that leads to Rohn River, we saw black bear galore, from ten to fifteen a day, but made no attempt to secure any. We also saw one fair-sized grizzly a long way off towards Simpson Pass, and several bunches of sheep, ewes and lambs. Of moose, there were many, and they are grand animals, larger by far than those on the Kenai. They are more of a mouse color than any moose I have ever seen. Sixty-inch heads were an ordinary occurrence. We almost walked upon one fine bull with a grand head, which Andy and Jack said would go a full 65 inches; but it was too small.

At last we saw what I was looking for. Such a head I never expect to see again. The first time we saw him was just after I had killed my caribou, and the shot had made him nervous. At any rate he gave us the slip and made his getaway in the high alders. Jack was certain the head would go over seventy-five inches, while Andy, always conservative, said it was well over seventy inches. It was so large and massive that it was hard for me to estimate, though the bulls we had seen were but playthings to this fellow.

Toward dusk the next day we saw him again, and unfortunately it was raining. We made the stalk, which seemed easy, but when we were near the bull he shifted into dense alders. They must have been well over seven feet high and so thick we had to work our way through them. Suddenly a grunt; we were within a few feet of the bull. We saw the horns crashing against the alders but they were too thick for us to make out the animal. We attempted to draw back with the intention of climbing higher so we could look down on the alders. The bull heard us; there was a grunt and a huge head rose above the alders about fifteen to twenty feet away. There was nothing I could see to shoot at. For just a second that huge head appeared, then another grunt and he disappeared. My chance had gone and never again did I see him, though another day was put in trying to pick up his tracks.

At last our time had come to pull out. The snow was gradually climbing lower on the high mountains but none had come to stay on our level. We went back to our cache on the lake and discovered that bears had again visited us, and also found two cases of gasoline that Mat Niemenen must have left. Then for two days we wallowed through muck and water with the horses up to their bellies. Finally, on one of our clear days, and such a day as only Alaska can produce, we came down the steep hill to the remains of Happy River Roadhouse. The next day we packed up, and the pack train started off for the crossing.

Andy, Jack and I left in the afternoon via boat, and on the first turn in the river there, within twenty yards, stood two fine grizzly bear on their hind legs. Alas! My rifle was packed away, and they had gone before I was able to reach for it. We camped that night on a bar near a bear crossing. During the night the wind shifted to the north so that in the morning a cold gale was blowing downstream. The air was thick with the fine sand from the bars; in fact, so much so that it was like a heavy mist. It stung and cut both hands and face, but fortunately it was on our backs so we were able to travel.

The canyon below Happy River on the Skwentna

Bar tracked up by old grizzlies

As I have explained in the account of my previous trip, it is necessary to row against the stream in order to control and steer a boat going down those treacherous swift waters. I doubt if we could have rowed in the usual manner and withstood that sand-laden blast. We reached the Crossing early, and I at once went ashore to seek cover from the wind and sand. Andy and Jack wandered off to see if by any chance the horses had as yet arrived. None of us ever thought of taking a rifle, which was next to madness as the bar was all tracked up by old grizzlies. I found a sheltered spot and built a fire to warm up. Andy and Jack had by this time disappeared. I had quietly settled down by the fire for reverie when I happened to look across the bar in the direction of the boat, during a slight let-up in the sand storm, and saw a large grizzly that seemed to be standing in the boat. I let out a yell which, of course, didn't carry ten feet in that storm, and ran towards him. I can't say just what was in my mind, but my only thought was to scare off the bear from the meat we had in the boat. I then noticed Andy and Jack running towards the boat, and they too were yelling and waving their arms, as I afterward was informed. The bear was a well-behaved one and turned and ran when he saw us.

I now saw that the bear was not in the boat but on the opposite bank of the river. From where I had been, he had appeared as if standing in the boat. What his intentions might have been we will never know but it was more than likely that he smelled the meat and was about to investigate, when we appeared. When we assembled and found everything intact Andy remarked, "We would have been a swell bunch if that old grizzly had gotten into the boat with our outfit, meat and guns. He certainly would have had the laugh on us." Thereafter when I left the boat I always took my rifle along.

The day passed on and in late afternoon we pulled into the shelter of some alders, and made camp. It was just after seven o'clock in the evening and beginning to get dark when the pack train made its appearance. Fortunately the river was low, and the horses were able to ford it, and so through the sand clouds I saw the last of the pack train disappearing in the woods across the Skwentna. Before five o'clock next morning we were up at breakfast; it was still dark and I am sure from after effects that Jack gave us raw sour dough cakes. Later in the day I felt like the boy who ate dried apples and followed them with a couple of glasses of water.

We had been under way hardly an hour before we saw a grizzly traveling along the bar towards us, stopping now and then to feast on dead salmon that had washed up on shore. We tied up the boat and headed for him, but about that time he changed his mind and began wandering in the opposite direction. At each opportunity when the bear's head was down we would run towards him. At one time we came within two hundred yards of our quarry. As he was in a hollow, we tried to get nearer. When he appeared again out of the depression he was farther off than ever. Finally we decided to return to the boat and drop down river to intercept him farther on. I guess he had been playing with us for we never came within a quarter of a mile of him again. That was our last excitement though we did see another bear near the mouth of the Susitna River about dark.

We stopped a few minutes at Skwentna Crossing to leave McElroy's grub box that he had forgotten when leaving Happy River earlier in the summer. We lunched near the mouth of the Skwentna River, and then put on our motor. After lunch we opened it up and all but flew down the Yentna, passing Gray's and McDougall's before we realized it. We reached Susitna Station at seven o'clock, and there was Bill Austen in the *Alert* just pulling in with a bunch of trappers and their outfit. He was going to haul them next morning up the Yentna as far as he could navigate. After a conversation with the trappers they agreed to wait until Bill took us to Anchorage and returned for them. Some more Alaskan hospitality.

We left early next morning, and after rather a rough trip reached Anchorage by one o'clock, in time for lunch. My first move was to the Alaska Steamship Company's office where I discovered that the Steamship *Yukon* was to sail the next day. There was some tall hustling to get things in shape, but I succeeded, and headed homeward on the *Yukon*.

Before concluding, just a few reactions on my trip.

Andy and Jack need no comment and are splendid companions and excellent men in the hills. Lee and Charlie Hancock are enthusiastic, hardworking young men, and have the making of wonderful packers.

I want to mention that upon my return, on a visit to Washington I told Philip S. Smith and Stephen R. Capps of the old trail I had found on the Kuskokwim. They looked up records and from what was unearthed it must have been the workings of Lieut. Joseph S. Herron in 1899. This ill-fated expedition discovered Simpson Pass and then wandered about the Kuskokwim, finally abandoning their outfit and attempting to raft down the river. The rafts were wrecked, and the party started back by foot. His Indian guides had deserted him and disappeared one night. Another native found one of his caches and trailed the six white men until he came up with them and guided them to Telida, a native settlement on Tatlothna River, a tributary of the East Fork of the Kuskokwim. The records of this expedition are meager; no doubt they were lost. Sufficient to say I am sure this old trail had been swamped out by Lieut. Herron's party in their wanderings along the Kuskokwim.

I often wondered when in the hills what would have been accomplished in exploring a high line trail from Rainy Pass to the Tonzona Basin. I have my doubts of it ever being of any value in travel, for in fact the condition of the country is about the same today as when I first started rambling those hills many years back. True it is that the government is building a road into Copper Mountain, Mount McKinley National Park, now called Mount Eielson after the pioneer Alaskan air pilot who was lost in the Arctic in 1930 endeavoring to rescue a ship that had been frozen in.

The tourists will overrun those hills and passes possibly as far as the Muddy. It is going to be many years, if ever, before hunting parties will be able to get into the hills between Mount Dall and Rainy Pass. The aeroplane may open up the inaccessible spots, but who would want to miss that delightfully miserable trip up the Skwentna on the end of a towline?

CHAPTER VII.

EARLY EXPLORATIONS AND LATER DEVELOPMENTS IN THE McKINLEY COUNTRY

THE Mount McKinley region was the last American wilderness to yield its secret to the explorer. It was 1902 before the first white man, Dr. Alfred H. Brooks of the U. S. Geological Survey, set foot upon the great mountain's flanks. It brings the spirit of early exploration so near to us that we can better realize the hardships and heroisms which inspired those who broke the immensely greater wilderness, now the United States, for the homes which cover it today. Stories like the one that follows help make us, I think, sturdier men and better citizens.

In his published report of 1911, Brooks says that there were more natives on the slopes of the Alaskan Range and in the adjacent lowlands before the white man came than afterward. A great game country like that north of the McKinley group probably supported a comparatively large population. But none of the rivers or other greater features had names which were recognized outside of certain localities. Every tribe, probably, had its own names. The big mountain was in part an exception. All the tribes east of the great central group called McKinley Traleika, while those on the northwest side called it Tennally.

The relationship between the latter name, which Brooks reports, and Denali, which Archdeacon Stuck and others have given as the Indian name for the great mountain, is apparent. Archdeacon Stuck lived as a missionary among the Indians for many years and no doubt is a better authority on the pronunciation of the name than Dr. Brooks at the time he wrote his report. The spelling is arbitrary in both cases.

Behring, in 1741, is credited with being the first white man to get anywhere near this region, which wasn't very near. He probably sighted the mainland, or some of the islands near Cook Inlet, but he made no explorations, nor are there any records which can identify his location with points ashore.

Captain James Cook, whom George III. sent out to look for the west end of that fabled northwest passage, the eastern end of which so many navigators tried for so many years to locate, thought that he had found it in May, 1778. He had sighted the American coast probably where Oregon now is, and had followed up through the sound known as Prince William into the water now called Cook Inlet. Looking for a river, he missed the Susitna and entered what he thought was a river but wasn't. On discovering his mistake he named it Turnagain River and sailed away. It is called Turnagain Arm on today's maps.

It is interesting that Cook was several days in waters from which, far to the north, the snowy summits of the McKinley group are plainly visible in clear weather. From his failure to mention mountains in a carefully detailed log, we may conclude that the Alaskan Range hid behind a blanket of clouds during all his stay in those waters.

Meantime, when the survivors of Behring's journey got back to Siberia with tales of a great fur country, the Siberian fur traders operating on the Kenai Peninsula extended their activities to more northerly shores; but the Russian government checked exploration by granting a monopoly to one company which confined itself strictly to the fur business. Here Dixon and Portlock, two of Captain Cook's officers who returned on a commercial expedition, found them in 1786 and no doubt traded with them. The two did a little useful exploring and recording on the side, but they did not see the mountains either.

In 1794 another one of Captain Cook's officers, George Vancouver, completed the survey of Cook's Inlet and undoubtedly got a glimpse or two of the great range from the water, for he referred to lands west and northwest of him as "bounded by distant stupendous mountains covered with snow and apparently detached from one another. But possibly," he added, "they might be connected by land of insufficient height to intercept our horizon." It is evident that Vancouver conjectured correctly. From his ship in the sound he was unable to see the Alaskan Range but did see the peaks of McKinley, Foraker, and others rising above the general range level.

What the greatest of these peaks looked like to Vancouver, its first recorded observer, may be got from the description many years later of another Cook, who was to be identified with the scandal of a false claim of climbing it.

"The shore line at the head of Cook Inlet," wrote Dr. Frederick A. Cook of his approach to it by sea in 1903, "was screened by a blue haze, but several times during the night of twilight we got a peep at a snowy crest which pierced the blue dome far northward. This peak, like a star on a cloudy night, would blink and disappear with marvelous quickness. It did not seem to us as being very far away, nor did it give the impression of great altitude, but there was a mystery about the thing which kept one's attention pointed. This in reality was Mount McKinley, a hundred and fifty miles away."

"Like a dim cloud on the northern horizon," wrote Belmore Browne, who later exposed Dr. Cook's faked pretension, of the same view from Cook Inlet.

Even Vancouver's successful surveys did not inspire the commercially-minded Russians to carry them further. There are reports that Malokoff, who hunted for gold in the Kenai Peninsula in 1848-50, visited the Susitna basin, but he did not say so in his records. The Russians overran the great Kuskokwim basin, but they were not interested in snowy mountains. In a Russian summary of Alaskan geography published in 1852, the range was located under the name of the Tchigmit Mountains, and there are references to Bulshaia Gora, or Big Mountain, which probably meant McKinley. In Russian maps published in 1860 and later, the Susitna and Matanuska were well located.

In 1867 Alaska passed into the possession of the United States, and American prospectors began to overrun the country. This led, in the eighties, to the beginning of government explorations, geographical and geological, which give us to-day's still limited knowledge of the McKinley country.

One of four rams at Rainy Pass

*A moose in the Rainy Pass
country*

Motion picture enlargements

The caribou of Rainy Pass

In 1878, Harper and Mayo, prospecting for gold up the Tanana River, reported a snow-covered mountain in the north, which of course was McKinley. They described it to E. W. Nelson of the Biological Survey as "one of the remarkable things they had seen on this trip."

Another prospector, Frank Densmore, crossed from the lower Tanana to the Kuskokwim in 1889, and described it so glowingly that the Yukon pioneers called it "Densmore's Mountain" for years. Surveys on both sides of the region noted the existence of the range without adding to knowledge of it. Stories of its great height circulated all over Alaska.

The finding of gold on Cook Inlet in 1894 began a new era, but until W. A. Dickey, a prospector of a different type, organized an exploring expedition in 1896, definite knowledge was lacking. Though Dickey did not get very near the mountain, he not only named it, but, without instruments, calculated its great height within three hundred feet!

When Belmore Browne asked him, some years later, why he chose the name McKinley, Dickey replied that he was so disgusted with the free silver talk of prospectors whom he had met on the trail that he named the biggest mountain he ever saw after the strongest gold standard man he ever heard of. When Dr. Brooks asked him why he guessed 20,000 feet for its altitude Dickey said the calculation was based upon his probable distance from the mountain with careful consideration of atmospheric conditions. The actual altitude is, let us recall, 20,300 feet. But the public paid no attention to the discovery of a mountain 20,000 feet high, considering this just another wild western tale.

In 1920 I crossed the Gulf of Alaska with Dickey on board the old Steamship *Alaska*. He gave me some very interesting descriptions of McKinley. Curiously he told me he named it after President McKinley as he was the outstanding man in the country at that time, just as that grand mass of ice and snow was the outstanding mountain in North America.

During some years before and after Dickey's adventure, many parties of prospectors and geologists visited parts of the general McKinley country. Official surveys all around it gradually reduced the size of the unknown. In the winter of 1901 a man named Dalzell arrived at Cook's Inlet overland from a steamer on the Kuskokwim River, saying that he had crossed the high ranges probably not far from Rainy Pass.

The United States Geological Survey began exploring, surveying and studying Alaska in 1892, and by 1902 most of the exploring had been done. Previous to 1902, according to Dr. Alfred H. Brooks, the McKinley region was "a great block of unexplored territory."

A determinative exploration, plans for which had been begun in 1899, left Seattle by boat on May 13, 1902, steamed up Cook Inlet May 28, and landed at Tyonek, on the west shore, that same night.

It consisted of Dr. Brooks, in charge, D. L. Reaburn, topographer, L. M. Prindle, geologist, a recorder, two packers and a cook. The party carried three small tents, sleeping bags, a shoe repairing outfit, mosquito headpieces, a folding canoe and oars, large and small axes, and provisions for a hundred and five days. There were two 30-30 carbines and a 22 rifle to provide fresh meat. The food weighed 2,300 pounds and the rest of the outfit 700 pounds. Each horse carried 150 pounds.

The natives at Tyonek, after the fashion of natives, prophesied misfortune as the seven men and twenty horses took the trail, a thousand pounds of their duffle going up the Skwentna by boat convoyed by Indians so as to save their horses as much as possible upon starting into the wilderness.

The plan was to travel around the lofty peaks in the direction of the hands of a clock, as close to them as possible. Starting through swamps abounding in ducks, geese and sand hill cranes, taking advantage of Indian trails when found, cutting trails through heavy forests, the expedition used up nearly a third of the season with a sixth of the journey done. It began to look as if the native predictions might come true. Failing to ford the Skwentna, they had to go downstream to meet the boat. They forded the Kichatna often, and sometimes both men and horses had to swim. Birds and an occasional moose helped their larder. At an altitude of three thousand feet, with the low crest of the range nearly attained, Brooks commented in his diary: "This region appears to abound in white Alaskan sheep." A plain sportsman like myself would have said it "abounded." The scientist Brooks only dared say, without careful survey, that it "appeared" to abound.

On the first leg of Brooks' journey, Robert Dunn, who faced and dreaded it years later, wrote in *Shamless Diary of an Explorer:*

"Tundra, strictly speaking, is the coastal marshland of Siberia, yet any vast low and ill-drained country in the north, frosted or no, is called tundra. It was considered almost madness to venture into the interior from Tyonek. Stories were told of men who had set out from there to be driven back crazed by mosquitoes. I had traveled over tundra in Alaska, and knew its hateful yellow moss bordered by white skeleton spruces, its treacherous ponds sprinkled with white flowers, its willow thickets concealing abysses of red muck. The buzz of bull-dog flies, the hot anger and desperation of burdened cayuses kicking helplessly in a mire, were familiar enough."

Three years previous to the Brooks expedition, Lieutenant Joseph R. Herron had preceded them on much the same route and had found a way over the range into the valley of the Kuskokwim which he called Simpson Pass. As soon as he had got beyond the sheep country his two native guides deserted him, and he had rather a desperate time finding his way to civilization down the Kuskokwim on a raft; but finally he met natives and they took him to the Tanana by way of Lake Minchumina.

Brooks had intended going up the Skwentna but was unable to make a crossing, so followed down until he reached Skwentna Crossing. He then decided to cross over to the Kichatna River and followed the bars of this river to its head, then up the Morris River and through Simpson Pass, down Moose Creek and out on to Happy River. From there he followed what afterwards became the dog trail over Rainy Pass.

The Brooks party crossed Rainy Pass on July 15th and went down the Kuskokwim about twenty miles, touching country traversed by Herron, and turned northeast into virgin country. For two hundred miles they followed almost an airline through the unknown along the base of snow-covered mountains with broad gravel plains on their north.

"Our only serious interruptions," writes Brooks, "were the glacial streams which emerged from the mountains, many of them with the volume of good-sized rivers, directly athwart our course. Fortunately on each a ford was found, for the turbulent waters threatened a perilous passage to so frail a craft as our folding canoe." They never used the canoe, and finally abandoned it. At the greater rivers, native boats were found. Many of their camps were above spruce levels, but there was always willow for cooking. The foothills furnished big horn mutton and the lower lands moose. They lived well.

Mount McKinley and Mount Foraker, called Denali (or Tennally) and Denali's wife, respectively, looked even larger as they rapidly advanced. They were the first white men to set foot on McKinley's flanks. On August 4th they camped fourteen miles, as the crow flies, from McKinley's summit. They took a day off here and Brooks climbed to within nine miles of the summit, much to his satisfaction.

They covered the next hundred miles rapidly. On August 15th, they camped on the Nenana, and the next day passed again out of the utterly unknown into explored country— surveyed by Eldridge in 1898. From there they followed trails not unknown, and on August 24th encountered a white man with a band of Indians, the first human beings they had seen in nearly three months.

"They directed us," writes Brooks, "to a trail long used by Indians and recently improved by a party of white men who were reported to be making a survey for a railway. We followed this trail for thirty miles across the lowland of the Tanana. Broad meadows of magnificent grass alternated with belts of birch, cottonwood and fine spruce, or with large marshes dotted with lakes." The timber was unusually large for the Yukon basin, trunks measuring eighteen to twenty-four inches not being uncommon.

On August 29th they emerged from the forest on the south bank of the Tanana at the small native settlement of Tortello. Their coming seemed miraculous to the natives, as all previous visitors had come via the river. The Indians fortunately had a canoe in which the party crossed the river, there unfordable.

From the Tanana, against the advice of the Indians who considered a northward journey in September utterly foolish, they started for the Yukon, and reached Rampart September 15th. From there they took the river steamer to Seattle. In a hundred and five days, the party had covered eight hundred miles making ninety-four camps. It had traveled every day except nine. Eleven of the original horses reached Rampart. They brought home six hundred geological specimens and three hundred photographs.

"The party numbered so few men," Brooks reported, "that one of the geologists could not be spared from the pack train while it was on the move, and his geologic observations had to be subordinated to this task. The other geologist and the topographer made such digressions as time would permit. On the north side of the range the average airline distance between camps was ten to twelve miles so it was seldom possible

Sketches of Ovis dalli, by Carl Rungius

to extend observations more than four or five miles from the route of travel. Even on these trips it happened several times that one of us missed camp, and was forced to spend an uncomfortable night under a spruce tree, with a scanty supply of food. During the summer the writer's own traverses aggregated some 800 miles."

One of them collected plants and made a daily weather record. "Only those who have participated in an exploration of this kind can appreciate what it means for any member of the party voluntarily to burden himself with additional duties."

Thus was America's ultimate and most difficult wilderness first subjugated by hardy government scientists in an exploration unexcelled for its speed, geographical and geological achievement. Its story will hold for all time a high place in the literature of scientific discovery.

My own interest in this remarkable country was first inspired by several long talks with Alfred Brooks on board the steamer returning from the North. These conversations were supplemented by the interesting narratives of Belmore Browne. Brooks' reports and Raeburn's maps are to me nothing less than miracles. They did about twenty hours work a day, moving camp in the bargain. Many years after, traveling by those maps of Raeburn's, I found them most accurate; in fact they stand today as the authentic maps for that country.

Four years after Brooks' exploration, one of his party, L. M. Prindle, made an examination of the new gold placer district of the Kantishna. At least four other geologic surveys and reconnaissances were made during the next four years, covering particular districts. In 1907-08 Charles Sheldon, sportsman and student of animal life and conditions, spent nearly a year in the upper Kantishna basin largely in the area since covered by the national park. Mr. Sheldon died in 1927 and his valuable book has only now been published during the preparation of this manuscript.

Construction on the government railroad now operating from Seward to Fairbanks by way of the Susitna, Nenana and Tanana Valleys was begun in 1915, which led to several geologic and topographic expeditions in the Kantishna region. The principal topographic party was in charge of C. E. Griffin, and the principal geologic party was led by Stephen R. Capps, who has made several later trips, and is again in the field at this writing. Dr. Capps will pass into history as the explorer, geologist and observer to whose splendid work the perfecting of modern knowledge of the McKinley region will be due.

Meantime several parties have attempted the colossal task of climbing Mount McKinley, three of which have been successful. Only one of these, led by the late Archdeacon Stuck, made the south peak, which is the supreme summit. Another was driven back by an overwhelming blizzard when within three or four hundred feet of the top. Still another climbed the north peak, which is five hundred feet less in altitude.

The first try was made from Fairbanks in May, 1903, by Judge Wickersham and four men. Ascending by the Peters Glacier, they were stopped by an enormous wall of ice supporting the north peak. On our trip in 1922 we found some old pack saddles, blankets, etc., in a tree at Peters Glacier. It was undoubtedly part of Judge Wickersham's outfit. It was a cache, so we left things as we found them.

The very same summer Dr. Frederick A. Cook made two attempts. Starting at Tyonek he crossed the range by Simpson's Pass, ascended by the headwaters of the Tatlathna, and was stopped at eight thousand feet by an impassable chasm. Descending, he came across a camp deserted by Wickersham a few weeks earlier and tried it again there. The same ice wall that stopped Wickersham stopped Cook. Returning, he crossed the Muldrow Glacier ignorant of the fact determined by later parties that only by it is the summit of McKinley attainable.

In 1906 Cook tried it still again from the impossible southern side in company with Dr. Hershel Parker of Columbia University, and Belmore Browne. They approached from the south, failed, and returned to Cook Inlet where the party broke up, Parker leaving for home and Browne remaining to hunt. Cook, leaving him there, ascended the Chulitna River to Tokasitna late in August accompanied only by his packer, Edward Barrell. He told Browne that he meant to reconnoiter for another attempt the following year.

A few weeks later reports came down the river that McKinley had been climbed by Cook who followed and confirmed them. Seeing an opportunity, he explained to Browne, he had made a dash for the summit with Barrell and had attained it on September 16th.

A great amount of discussion followed. The public naturally accepted the newspaper reports as true, but the sourdoughs of Alaska didn't. Cook's story as reported in the western press, and later told in detail in his book, which appeared in 1908, was increasingly disbelieved. It was pointed out that, beyond a certain point known to several explorers, his details became suspiciously vague; doubt also followed his description and picturing of the summit of the great mountain as bare granite. A photograph in his book showed a man waving a flag from a granite summit which Cook declared was Mount McKinley's.

In 1909 the Explorers' Club of New York invited him to show them his proof, but he made no appearance.

In 1910 following his book, Parker and Browne explored the south side of the mountain on the trail of Cook and discovered the evidence of his faking. In New York before starting they had figured out, from the evidence of text and photographs, the probable location of the photograph of the alleged summit on what they called "glacier number 2," about nine miles from the real summit.

And so it proved. The photograph which Browne took of one of their own men waving a flag was identical in every topographical detail to that which Cook had taken of Barrell waving a flag. The spot was not even on a slope of McKinley.

So that ghost was laid and the way cleared for the real achievements to follow.

The first of these took place the very same summer as the Cook exposure. It was an Alaskan try for the prestige of the first ascent, and was led by Thomas Lloyd of Fairbanks, accompanied by Charles McGonogill, William Taylor, Peter Anderson and Bob Horne, prospectors, and E. L. Davidson, a surveyor; but Horne and Davidson quarrelled with Lloyd and returned soon after the start was made. Long familiar with every common aspect of the great mountain, the adventurers had reached the correct conclusion that the Muldrow Glacier originated at the summit, and had determined roughly the lines of general approach to its head, above which they assumed that the way would be reasonably clear.

At Muldrow's head, they left Lloyd, who found himself unable to go further. The others went on without ropes, every man for himself. Thus, together, they reached the immense slope known as the Grand Basin which, at its height, divides the north and south peaks. Why, on the morning of April 10th, they chose the slightly lower north peak for their ascent is not precisely clear from the insufficient and unscientific records of the splendid adventure. It is probable that they thought the north peak the higher. Anyway, McGonogill is quoted as wanting to plant the long flag pole, which they had dragged all the way up, so that it could be seen through glasses at Fairbanks—a hundred and fifty miles away. He complained to Archdeacon Stuck long afterward that, on their start homeward, from the summit, they failed to see it even from the upper glacier.

"The men who accomplished the astounding feat of climbing the north peak in an almost superhuman march from the saddle of the northwest ridge," wrote Archdeacon Stuck in 1914, "could most certainly have climbed the south peak too." On another page of his book the Archdeacon called this ascent "unique in the annals of mountaineering."

At the end, McGonogill outstripped Taylor and Anderson

and was the first man to stand upon a summit of McKinley. The three planted the flagstaff firmly. The entire top of the mountain was heavily plated with ice and snow.

That same notable year, E. C. Rust of Portland, Oregon, attempted the climb from the impossible south side.

In 1912, Parker and Browne, not content with exposing Cook's fake, made a vigorous bid for the honor of being the first to stand on McKinley's extreme summit. They left Seward late in January and started their ascent on June 4th, where Lloyd had started, following his course up to 15,000 feet in altitude. The next 2,000 feet were difficult in the extreme. From that point, by way of the northeast ridge, they made their grand assault upon the south peak.

Only three or four hundred feet below the extreme top, a blizzard struck them, of such bitter cold and violence that human flesh and blood could not stand it. Feeling themselves literally freezing, even with the end just before them they were obliged to retreat, making their way down with what speed they might to save their lives.

A tragedy, this, for which, nevertheless, they had reason to be profoundly thankful, for there followed close upon their heels an earthquake of such violence that Archdeacon Stuck, who followed their course up step by step the year after, was unable to identify several important miles of it by reason of the terrific upturning of the rock. Had they found clear weather at the top instead of a murderous tempest which drove them violently back, it is practically certain that scientific and other examinations would have held them until too late.

So it was left to Archdeacon Stuck, the celebrated Alaskan missionary, to attain first the supreme summit of McKinley. He accomplished it on June 7th, 1913. His companions were Harry P. Karstens, years afterward first Superintendent of Mount McKinley National Park, Robert G. Tatum, a young ecclesiastic, and the half-breed, Walter Harper. Preparations were undertaken many months ahead, caches of food were made covering all eventualities, and much of their personal equipment was made to order. Nothing was left to chance.

The Archdeacon's book, "The Ascent of Denali," tells a story of excessive toil with remarkable vividness and charm. Relaying supplies so that every stretch of the arduous climb must be covered three or four times is so common a story of high mountain climbing that few dwell upon it. The earthquake-shattered ridge made especially heavy going. "We must cut steps in those ice blocks, over them, around them, on the sheer side of them, under them—whatever seemed to our judgment the best way of circumventing each individual block. Every ten yards presented a separate problem. Here was a sharp black rock standing up in a setting of ice as thin and narrow and steep as the claws that hold the stone in a finger ring. That ice must be chopped down level, and then steps cut all around the rock. . . . Steps had to be made deep and wide; it was not merely one passage we were making; these steps would be traversed again and again by men with heavy packs."

At the top of the Grand Basin, 19,000 feet above the Arctic Ocean, breathing was difficult under the best of conditions. To men staggering under crushing packs it was painful. "If we could advance but a couple of hundred feet a day, we were still confident that, barring unforeseeable misfortune, we could reach the top."

With the top actually in view, perfect weather, and hardships nearly passed, "the author began to have fears of personal failure." There were fits of smothering, "and the medicine chest held no remedy for blind staggers."

Success was achieved on June 7th. "At last the crest of the ridge was reached, and we stood well above the two peaks that mark the ends of the horseshoe. Also it was evident that we were well above the great north peak across the Grand Basin. Its crest had been like an index on the snow beside us as we climbed, and we stopped for a few moments when it seemed that we were level with it. We judged it to be about five hundred feet lower than the south peak. . . .

"But still there stretched ahead of us, and perhaps one hundred feet above us, another small ridge with a north and south pair of little haycock summits. This is the real top of Denali. From below, this ultimate ridge merges indistinguishably with the crest of the horseshoe ridge beyond it. With keen excitement we pushed on. Walter, who had been in the lead all day, was the first to scramble up; a native Alaskan, he is the first human being to set foot upon the top of Alaska's great mountain, and he had well earned the life-long distinction. Karstens and Tatum were hard upon his heels, but the last man on the rope, [meaning himself], in his enthusiasm and excitement somewhat overpassing his narrow wind margin, had almost to be hauled up the last few feet, and fell unconscious for a moment on the floor of the

The two upper sketches are Grizzlies and the lower one is a Black Bear, by Carl Rungius

little snow basin that occupies the top of the mountain. This, then, is the actual summit, a little crater-like snow basin, sixty or sixty-five feet long, and twenty to twenty-five feet wide, with a haycock at either end—the south one a little higher than the north."

After a prayer of thanks, Tatum thrust the flagstaff deep in the Summit snow and they said a Te Deum.

Archdeacon Stuck testifies to the visibility from the south peak, of the Lloyd party's flagstaff on the north peak. Even from there, it could be clearly seen only with the aid of glasses. But it was there. Harry Karstens told me that Harper and he were able to make out the flagstaff with their naked eyes. The author also described the sky from the summit, which there assumed "a blue so deep that none of us had ever gazed upon a mid-day sky like it before. It was a deep, rich lustrous transparent blue as dark as a Prussian blue, but intensely blue; a hue so strange, so increasingly impressive that, to one, at least, it seemed like special news of God."

My old friend Slim Avery (better named by my wife "Skyline Slim") told of having found the Archdeacon's old camp. Some of the provisions were still intact, and to prove it he and his partner boiled a cup of tea from the old supplies.

Meanwhile, rapid development of the Gulf shores and the valley of the Yukon, both of which were in communication by steamer with Seattle, the increase of prospecting and mining, and the growing demand for better direct communication between gulf and river, gave impetus to the old project for a government railroad between Seward and Fairbanks. Surveys made while the later events of this story were in progress were followed by two acts of Congress passed in 1912 and 1914 respectively. The first authorized the President to appoint a Commission to examine into problems of transportation. The second directed the President to appoint a Commission to locate the route. The Alaska Railroad Commission and the Alaskan Engineering Commission came into existence, and construction was begun under authority of President Wilson, in 1915, and concluded with the golden spike driven by President Harding July 15, 1923.

Up to the time of this writing $67,500,000 have been spent for the purposes of the railroad, including telegraph and telephone lines, wharves, hospitals, townsites and dwellings for employees, from which it may be inferred that the wilderness east of the great McKinley group has rapidly become a surprisingly well populated and busy country for one so new. There have been many hunting and exploring parties also. The advent of thousands of laborers on railroad construction, and the need for their "living on the country," which means feeding on the game of the marvelous wilderness, endangered the immense caribou herds and the uncounted thousands of mountain sheep which composed the bulk of the animal population north of the range, and hastened the creation of Mount McKinley National Park. Congress created the Park in 1917, eight years before the railroad opened for business.

It will surprise most persons to know that saving the game from destruction by hunters, rather than conserving the greatest mountain country in North America, was the actuating reason for Mount McKinley National Park, which otherwise probably never would have been created.

This country was overrun for many years by prospectors, trappers and government meat hunters who literally slaughtered the sheep and caribou to feed the railroad construction gangs. Nevertheless, as these same men completely wiped out the wolves and other vermin, the game held its own. I have visited meat hunters' cabins on the Savage and Sanctuary Rivers that were literally covered with old antlers of sheep and caribou, while the ground for several hundred yards about was well carpeted with discarded skins of the same animals. It was just one year since the killing had stopped when I first saw these places. You may well imagine my surprise at finding quantities of sheep and caribou, both at the headwaters of the Savage and the Sanctuary.

Since that time all hunting and killing has been stopped; the prospectors and trappers have gone, but in spite of this control I am advised that the sheep and caribou are on the decline. The answer is simple. The wolf, the coyote and wolverine have again come into their own. Woe to the game that must give toll to these destroyers!

The Alaska Railroad, which has so extraordinarily developed the country immediately tributary to it, has proved an exceedingly expensive luxury. Its passenger traffic has increased from $188,000 in 1925 to $231,000 in 1926, which is eloquent of the changes it is making in population. But its annual cash loss of $1,670,000 in 1925, the year it opened to business, only decreased to $954,000 in 1926. None except rich modern governments can do business on those terms, and there are those who predict that this part of Alaska is not capable of sufficient development ever to make it profitable.

This is not the place to exploit the government's pictur-esque adventure in railroading. The figures at least suggest that it is making great changes in the colossal wilderness of which McKinley is the center. And yet this wilderness remains today practically unbroken. The thousand visitors brought to the National Park by the railroad in 1929 were lost, so to speak, in the vastness of the country.

As I have traveled over various sections of Alaska and have seen the great possibilities that stand out on all sides, I have often wondered what the next hundred years have in store for this vast garden spot. Its soil will grow about anything that our western states do. Alaska is a continent in itself, and why, tell me, shouldn't it develop and become a prosperous country for all time? Its climate in summer is glorious, with twenty-four hours of wonderful daylight and growing weather. Its flowers far surpass in size and color the same species grown in our so-called milder climates. The scenery has nothing that can compare with those wonderful lights and changing colors on the high outstanding ice-and-snow-clad peaks, with the valleys a riot of wild flowers.

As to the winters, they are cold but not any more so than in our western mountain states. The days are short, but so are the winter days in Norway and Scotland. This great northern possession of ours will in the future pass from the public mind as an ice-clad, snowbound, "ungetatable" country which even our post-office until a few years ago classified as a foreign country. Its strategic position for the east alone would make it a valuable possession.

What will a hundred years mean to Alaska, for when all is

said and done a hundred years is but a short period in the development of a country. Why shouldn't Alaska be well populated? I can see no reason. Her stores of mineral wealth which today cannot be economically obtained will, in the future, as the country has a greater population and better transportation facilities, be opened up.

Vast McKinley Park is but very little different from our Yellowstone Park when Lewis and Clark first traveled through that wilderness. It makes me shudder even to think of it, but I fear the time will come when automobile roads will be twisting and turning through those grand hills, and there will be hotels at all the wonder spots. One will be able to drive in his car from New York across the continent, continuing north to Alaska. And what finer trip than through the Park and see the grandest of all North American mountains, Denali! One hundred years roll around rather quickly, and many things happen. And why should not this great country come into its own?

Evening view of Mount McKinley from the Clearwater

Mount McKinley from the Clearwater

CHAPTER VIII.

MOUNT McKINLEY NATIONAL PARK

As early as 1915, after the immensity of Mount McKinley had been advertised by unsuccessful attempts to climb it, by the Dr. Cook controversy and his exposure, by the nearly successful attempt of the Parker-Browne expedition and finally the successful ascent of Archdeacon Stuck, and by the beginning of the Alaska Railroad, talk began about making it the center of a national park.

Not much was known publicly of the country's qualification for such a purpose. Eminent topographers and geologists had reported on its geography and its mineral resources, emphasizing coal, without celebrating its beauty. Even Charles Sheldon, who had made two trips in its vicinity, being deeply absorbed in the study of its big game animals, made slight mention of its scenery. Nevertheless, with the railroad planned for so close an approach, it seemed possible that some day it might figure in the country's recreational equipment.

This being recognized, men who were interested in national parks urged that the project should be undertaken promptly in order that an adequate area could be secured; later on commercial interests might oppose. This kind of comment was in the air at that time. It was remarked that Yellowstone, Yosemite, Sequoia and Glacier Parks would not have been nearly so large had they been created at later dates than they were. Rocky Mountain Park had been originally planned on a much greater scale which could have been adhered to if pushed at that time. Certain interests were holding up, at this very time, the wonderful canyons of the kings in the Sierra, which could have been added to Sequoia for the asking ten years before. The struggles of contending interests were still keeping the Grand Canyon out of the National Parks system thirty-one years after William Henry Harrison introduced the first bill.

It was high time to start the movement for a McKinley National Park.

In the end it was not national park sentiment that put over McKinley National Park, but the desire to preserve big game from destruction. While national park people were talking, the Camp Fire Club of America with the help of other game preservation associations became active. The increase of Alaskan hunting parties to the great caribou and mountain sheep country north of the Park, the coming of parties from a distance, even from abroad, and the organization of professional hunters by the Alaskan Government for the purpose of feeding at so much per hundred-weight the thousands of men about to be employed on building the railroad, foreshadowed the rapid destruction of the greatest game herds left in North America.

It was certain that with the rush of these hunters ordinary game reservations couldn't protect. If shooting were to be allowed at all it would require an army of guards to hold it within prescribed limits, which was impracticable. On the other hand, if made a national park, no shooting would ever be possible, but at least these noble herds would annually breed game by thousands which would spill over the boundary line and keep up the neighborhood shooting indefinitely.

Specific credit should be given to Belmore Browne and Charles Sheldon for the work they did to secure the passage of the legislation creating the Park. The initiative for this legislation came from Charles Sheldon. He secured the first meeting in Stephen Mather's office, and Belmore Browne was also present. The Camp Fire Club of America, Boone & Crockett Club and the American Game Protective Association were united in a committee to secure the passage of the legislation, and John Burnham had charge of the legislation and put it through. Wickersham, who was then delegate from Alaska, had at first refused to introduce the bill, but John Burnham got Charlie Hamilton, a friend of his and a Congressman from New York, to agree to introduce the bill in the House, and in this way forced Wickersham's hand. He did not think the time had arrived for such legislation. He wanted first to know what the Alaskan sentiment would be. To give Judge Wickersham credit, however, when he once took hold of the bill he handled it with energy and effectiveness. The bill was passed in 1917 without opposition.

All the arguments before the committees of Congress and on the floors of both houses were game preservation arguments. Congress, always alive to the interests of miners, specified that legitimate prospectors should have the right to shoot up to their requirements of meat in the field. There is no doubt that this latter provision gave rise to a certain amount of illegal slaughter, which did not, however, make a dent in the game supply, and in 1929 the permission was revoked in part because by then it was apparent that there were not sufficient minerals to make mining worth while, at least in the eastern half of the reservation.

In any event, the National Park Service of the Interior Department, under whose administration Mount McKinley National Park was placed, could not have protected the enormous area with the appropriations Congress provided. Eight thousand dollars a year for salaries of officials, rangers and laborers, buildings, road and trail making and upkeep, purchase and care of horses and dog train, guns, ammunition, and everything else besides, sounds ridiculous. It was ridiculous, but years passed before Congress would consider increasing it. At this writing, including the annual cost of building the motor road, (which is following approximately the line of the trail which was in the process of being laid out at the time of my first trip, from the Park entrance westward to the bar of the McKinley Fork, about thirty miles from the base of the great mountain) the appropriation for 1931 is $46,700, and for 1932, $31,100.

A thousand people a year, more or less, go there now and usually come back hugely disappointed. There are rather meager accommodations for taking care of the ordinary tourist. There are not sufficient horses for riding, nor are there other conveyances. Sheep and caribou are seldom visible where it is possible for tourists to go, and then only one or two at a time. There are few guides or other facilities. Mount McKinley is many miles from the ordinary routes taken by the tourist, and is frequently hidden under clouds in summer, so that many people who go there get no glimpse of it.

Not one person in ten has been warned of the climate and goes improperly clothed for comfort. Those whom I have talked with in later years were prepared for extreme cold, with possible snow and ice. In reality the summer weather is beautiful and warm, and summer clothing is comfortable. The nights are cool, and may be even cold, but the air is invigorating and even a spell of cold weather is not noticed.

At this writing, and perhaps for some years to come, Mount McKinley National Park has not justified its making from the point of view of the average visitor to a National Park. Some day, when the government auto road is finished and comfortable camps are established, with guides and equipment for getting around readily, the National Park will fulfill its mission to the people. The sight of the mountain alone is worth the trip and some discomfort. If camps are properly located, for instance, one at the head of the Muddy River alongside the Peters Glacier, one could spend weeks wandering over that mass of ice that heads up into the mighty McKinley itself. It would be a mountain climber's paradise, and when tired of that particular bit of scenery, in a day, or certainly not over a day and a half, Mount Foraker could be reached. Foraker has never been climbed and it is nearly as high as McKinley. If interested in ice, the district about Foraker would keep one busy for several days. While at Peters Glacier, for a change one can go east a short distance to the Clearwater, and there wonderful grayling fishing can be had. And if you should make your trip later in the season and be at Peters Glacier towards the middle of September, take a horse and guide and follow the Muddy down to its junction with the McKinley Fork, and you will be in the midst of the annual caribou migration; countless thousands will pass. Incidentally, it is outside of the Park and you can hunt not only the caribou, but cross the McKinley Fork and in the Kantishna Hills there are bear and moose.

If you go to the Park keep traveling until you reach the bar of the McKinley River. Stop at Shannon's cache and wait until the range clears. You will see one of the most absorbing sights that it has ever been your fortune to behold. There stands McKinley in the midst of his family, glistening in all his brilliancy. To the west, Foraker with several smaller peaks unnamed, and further on, Russell, and still on to the westward the Tonzona hills with Mount Dall standing out above them. And there about McKinley to the east stands Hunter, Brooks and several others. If you ever get there wait until you see the range clear; it should not be a long wait. Then before you leave the country go over to Wonder Lake, visit Polly and John Anderson, and be sure you see the reflection of McKinley and the range. If you happen to be of an inquiring disposition keep right on to the Kantishna, and meet Fanny and Joe Quigley. They are the old residenters of these parts, and are delightful hosts; but I am wandering from the Park.

Of course the Park has other missions. It surrounds the most gigantic and appalling spectacle in America with fitting natural protective lands; it preserves for posterity the greatest herds of large wild animals in America; it preserves a mighty wilderness of varied plant and animal life; it offers the most difficult and interesting feat in mountain climbing in America, which perhaps will become famous throughout the world; and it provides science with an untouched laboratory in which to study many subjects including, importantly, the behavior of glaciers.

The final boundaries of the Park, determined after much discussion and an enlargement made in 1922, are shown in the several maps in this book. The Park contains 2,645 square miles, making it second only to Yellowstone National Park in area. Its southern boundary lies on the crest of the great Alaska Range at its highest altitude, from which the Park lands descend sharply on the north side under vast masses of ice and snow, emerging with the glaciers, on the immense central depression which supports the enormous herds of grass-eating animals, and rise on the north so as to include the southern edge of the Kantishna hills.

It is not so simple as that sounds, however, for almost the entire surface of the Park is tumbled beyond description. Glaciers of prehistoric ages, when the range was higher than it now is, cut the surface of that time into mountains and deep valleys, and disappeared. Glaciers succeeding them "dissected" what they left, as the geologists put it, again and again. The courses of most of these old glaciers will probably never be traced, nor the puzzle of their rock remainders be wholly disentangled. The present stage of this progressive wearing down constitutes the National Park of today. How that of a million years from now will differ cannot be predicted, but it will differ.

Of course, it is not only the glaciers which have produced

the complicated surface of today. From glaciers flow rivers, and from ten thousand mountains, produced by past erosion, flow countless streams to hasten the future. The Mount McKinley country is one of frequent precipitation. Somewhere high up on the range it is nearly always snowing, and probably somewhere in the National Park it is raining. The greater part by far of the present amazing tangle of mountain valley and plain is not the work of glaciers but of streams.

Considering these origins helps us understand the configuration of the country, which otherwise seems planless.

"Here lies a rugged highland area far greater in extent than all Switzerland," wrote Dr. Brooks, "a virgin field for explorers and mountaineers. He who would master unattained summits, explore unknown rivers, or travel untrodden glaciers in a region whose scenic beauties are hardly equalled has not to seek them in South America or Central Asia, for generations will pass before the possibilities of the Alaska Range are exhausted."

A very modest statement this, of the bigness and the grandeur and the difficulty of Mount McKinley Park to those visitors who would go beyond the slender facilities offered by the government service.

No other country is so dominated by its central feature as this. Approaching, one strains his eyes for a long-distance glimpse of the shining summit of Mount McKinley. It is the visitor's first thought in the morning, and his last at night. Whether or not one was fortunate enough to glimpse it is the talk of the evening gathering.

I suppose no other mountain in America has been photo-

Mount McKinley from Wonder Lake

Mount McKinley from Talkeetna

graphed so many times per visitor and yielded so few results. Long-distance views on days of remarkable clearness showing the top of the range with McKinley swelling above it are the most successful photographs.

One of the clearest nearby photographs is that taken by Robert S. Bragaw, Jr., for the Alaska Railroad, from Talkeetna, exhibiting its precipitous south side. One wonders that so many attempted climbing from the south. Scarcely less appalling is its north side, also photographed by Bragaw from Wonder Lake, across the Park. Although I have taken numerous exposures from this point I was never successful in securing such a splendid reflection. Both of the above-mentioned photographs are reproduced in this book.

I quote from the National Park Service information circular:

"No other mountain, even in the far-famed Himalayas, rises so far above its own base. On its north and west sides McKinley rises abruptly from a tundra-covered plateau only 2,500 to 3,000 feet high. For two-thirds of the way down its summit it is enveloped in snow throughout the year. Denali was the name given to this impressive snow-clad mountain by the early Indians. President Harding in describing the impressive peak during his trip to Alaska, said 'above its towering head there is never-ending sunshine in the summer, and in the long winter its unchanging garb of white reflects a sheen of glory no darkness can wholly dim.' Near Mount McKinley, which stands in the center of the vast park area, are Mount Foraker, with an elevation of 17,000 feet, and Mount Russell, rising 11,600 feet above sea level."

Next to the great mountain itself, the park's most wonderful exhibits are its innumerable glaciers, many of them of gigantic size. We have seen that by one of them, the enormous Muldrow Glacier, a river of ice flows from just below the summit. It is by the upper part of this pathway, and this only, that the summit is attained. The upper section of it bears the name of Harper Glacier, but the Muldrow is continuous with it and should not be robbed of the honor of an unbroken descent of the vast mountain.

Swinging northeasterly two or three thousand feet below the summit, it describes a complete semicircle among the broken foothills, and, still within Park limits, becomes the source of the McKinley Fork of the Kantishna River.

The Muldrow Glacier will some day be a household name, but there are many others of great size and importance; west of it, in order, the Peters, Straightaway, Foraker, Herron and Chedotlothna Glaciers are all of the first order of importance. But there are many others of large size which have not yet been either defined or named, and whose snouts only have been mapped as sources of important rivers. Besides these there are scores of lesser glaciers, perhaps hundreds if all the smaller hanging glaciers should be included. It will be many years before all are studied and mapped.

Frozen during the long winters and running freely during the warmer months, all glaciers beget streams which are slender in the mornings and swell as the meltings of the day discharge in the late afternoon. Their broad river beds for some miles are netted with streams forming shining patterns which add to the charm of many a McKinley landscape.

The Park is not without its many square miles of forest, which crowd the slopes and crown the summits of the Kantishna hills on the northern boundary up to 2,800 feet in altitude. The principal trees are black spruce, cottonwood, birch and larch, but none are large. Spruce occasionally reaches two feet in diameter. Willows and aspens are plentiful on the higher levels where the camper finds them useful for fuel. In these rigorous regions they often hide their woody stems underground, thrusting only leaves and catkins above the surface in the short summers. Dwarf birch, cinquefoil, blueberry, labrador tea, bearberry and wild rose are about the only shrubs; but there is a wealth of wild flowers including lupines, sunflowers, asters, gentians, larkspur, fireweed, anemone, shooting stars and many other showy inhabitants of upland wildernesses. Of the white and yellow dryads, the latter are the favorite food of mountain sheep in winter.

There is also an abundance of animal life besides that with which you have become familiar in preceding pages. There are two bears, the black and the grizzly, found in the park area according to my observations. I had been told that the large grizzly, better known as the Alaskan Brown, was an inhabitant of this district. I never came across one nor have I ever met anyone who has; therefore I feel safe in saying that there are no Alaskan Brown bear in these parts. Red fox, which prey on snowshoe rabbits and ptarmigan, are plentiful. All three are plentiful. The marmot is found in the rocks. Ground squirrels are numerous; grizzlies dig them out of their underground retreats for food. There are wolves, coyotes, wolverines, lynx, beaver, land otter, marten and mink.

Bird species are few, but the park is a favorite breeding place for gulls of several kinds, three hundred miles from the sea.

The Alaska willow ptarmigan is abundant. This, the government naturalist explains, is "an Arctic grouse which turns white in winter and brown in summer. In size it is somewhat smaller than the ruffed grouse of the eastern United States. By the time visitors begin to arrive in the park in early June, the male ptarmigan have started to acquire their brown summer dress. At this time, which is the mating season, the brown-backed birds with white wings and underparts, and orange red combs over their eyes may often be seen beside the road leading into the park. When flushed, the males fly up with rapid strokes of their white wings and with hoarse cackles of alarm. This characteristic 'crowing' of the cock ptarmigan often wakens the visitor at night or early morning. The female ptarmigan is smaller and more secretive than the male. Her feathers are neutral colored, so that when she is sitting on her eggs the black and buffy barred feathers of her brown back blend effectively with the brown moss and dead leaves which surround the nest. The nest is placed on the ground, but it is usually well concealed by the overtopping low brush. From six to sixteen large reddish-brown eggs heavily marked with black, fill, even overflow the nest. The female hatches the eggs, but the male usually hides near the nest so as to be ready to sally forth and drive off any thieving short-billed gull or other enemy. Park visitors who make the trip by horseback or by auto up the Savage River to the caribou camp are almost sure to flush one or more coveys."

Again I quote the government naturalist in description of McKinley National Park's most remarkable winged citizen, the surf bird.

"For nearly a hundred and fifty years, since the species was first given its scientific name, *Apriza virgata*, its eggs and nest remained unknown. The surf bird winters in South America as far south as the Straits of Magellan. It breeds among the mountain tops of central Alaska. Twice each year in migration, it traverses the Pacific coasts of North and South America.

"During the past seventeen years Joseph Dixon of the Museum of Vertebrate Zoology of the University of California, has been a member of five expeditions to Alaska. During each of these trips the unknown nest and eggs of the surf bird were diligently sought, but continued search produced only negative results. On May 28, 1926, the first and only nest of this rare bird known to science was discovered and recorded by Mr. Dixon and George Wright. (*The Condor,* Vol. XXIX, pp. 3-16, January, 1927.) The natives of Alaska had a legend that the surf bird lays its eggs 'on the bare mountains in the interior.' This proved to be correct since the nest found was located up on a barren rocky ridge, a thousand feet above timber line near Mount McKinley.

"The surf bird is a shore bird about the size of, but chunkier than, our well-known killdeer plover. It may be recognized in the field in summer as a plump gray bird with a white bar across the wing and a white patch at the base of the tail. These markings show conspicuously when the bird takes wing. When viewed close at hand the triangular black spots on the white lower breast and the rich cinnamon-rufous marks on the back are distinctive characteristics.

"During the major portion of the year the surf bird lives on small salt-water animals which it secures from the wave-washed outlying rocks on the Pacific Coast. During the summer it abandons the seacoast and travels far inland, where it runs about on the high rocky ridges and lives on insects, chiefly flies and beetles.

"It is useless to look for surf birds outside of good mountain sheep country. Because of the small number of these birds, a considerable amount of searching is required to locate them on their breeding grounds. However, for those who are keenly interested in bird life, to catch a glimpse of the elusive surf bird, or better yet, to find its nest, will mark the achievement of the rarest ornithological experience that the park has to offer."

There is but little fishing to be found in McKinley National Park. The streams are too near their birth in the glaciers. But grayling are found in several places, and a few Dolly Varden trout. Splendid lake trout fishing may be had in Wonder Lake, just across the park line on the north, and it gets better as you go farther from the glaciers.

The Park has few historical associations. A few mountains, streams and glaciers bear the names of explorers and geologists who were among the first to enter the area, and lately these old associations are being replaced by new names assigned by the authorities in Washington. Charles Sheldon's stay of nearly a year in the region afterward made a national park has been celebrated in the name of a mountain near his permanent headquarters, which is gradually disappearing, but still goes by the name of "Sheldon's Cabin."

The entrance to Mount McKinley National Park is about a mile and a half from McKinley Park Station, a point on the Alaska Railroad 348 miles from Seward, the seaport terminus, and 123 miles from Fairbanks, the metropolis of interior Alaska. Trains arrive daily from each of these cities. A gasoline motor car, commodious as a Pullman coach, operates between McKinley Park Station and other points along the Alaskan Railroad. This car has a seating capacity of forty passengers and also hauls a trailer with the same capacity.

An old-timer

Jim Boyce with my Alberta ram

CHAPTER IX.

AMERICAN BIG GAME ANIMALS

Mountain Sheep

MANY years ago it seemed to me that the greatest trophy a hunter could secure was a fine specimen of a mountain sheep. I hoped some day one of the many dreams I had had on the subject might in a small way come true. Since those days I have covered many of the sheep ranges of our west, the Canadian Rockies and on through the Cassiar Mountains, the Yukon and Alaska generally. Starting with the Rockies in Wyoming I have hunted and followed many sheep over the high rugged ridges, and learned many of their peculiarities.

I recall one afternoon with Joe Jones as if it were yesterday. We had been hunting steadily and hard for ten days in hopes of locating a large ram. Camp had been moved several times and we were now entrenched on Fall Creek. Joe and I had climbed high and were carefully scrutinizing the crags and crannies on the opposite side of the Shoshone. Needle Mountain towered above us, and, as we followed down its sides with our glasses, familiar spots were picked up. They were sheep, no doubt of it, and the longer we looked the larger they appeared. "Rams," was all Joe said, and I agreed with him. We were even confident that we could see their horns. Early next morning we started our climb up Needle

Mountain and by noon we had reached the level of our rams. Working along until we reached the location where they had been the day before we discovered numerous tracks of ewes and lambs. Following the tracks we located the bunch of nine rams, so we believed, and they turned out to be five big dark ewes and four lambs almost the size of their mothers!

Another time, a year or so later, I was more successful: Again I was with Joe, and we located early one morning five fine rams. One in particular stood out in size and color, as he appeared almost black. A successful stalk was made and the big black ram fell at my shot. The Wyoming sheep are small for *Ovis canadensis* and are generally of the medium dark brown color. This ram that I have mentioned was a very dark brown, and at a distance looked black. His horns also were very dark and curled tight to his head. There seems to be a variation in color in the Wyoming sheep though not as marked as I have observed in the same species in Alberta. A very large Wyoming ram will run fully thirty pounds less in weight than his Alberta brother. I have surmised that the reason for the Wyoming sheep being smaller is largely due to the disease (scab) with which the tame sheep infected them and which all but annihilated them. During the winter the coats of these sheep turn very light for I have seen them in the early spring when they looked as white as goats.

I have also covered some of the sheep ranges in Alberta and it has been my good fortune to have secured several magnificent specimens. The experience that stands out the clearest in my Alberta sheep hunting was one day on Wilcox Pass. Jim Simpson and I were off to shoot some pictures as I had al-

ready secured my rams. On our way up to the top of the pass
Jim spotted a bunch of rams. Pictures were forgotten, the
pack with camera and lunch was cast off, and we began to
climb so as to get above the rams. We succeeded, and there
below us lay six fine rams. The camera was far out of reach
so we just sat down and observed them through our glasses.
One of the younger ones became nervous and looked up. He
must have spotted something suspicious for he started off in
a leisurely manner, then stopped. The largest ram, who was
no doubt the leader, lay directly below us. Something must
have passed between them, for the old fellow rose, looked
up and all over us, was apparently satisfied that we meant
no harm, and turning about like a dog, lay down in his bed
again and fell asleep. The smaller one, with confidence, came
back and lay down with the others. We watched them until
late in the day; then Jim had to drop down to see if they
would move when he crossed their wind. The sheep were
apparently asleep, and Jim kept well out of sight. The instant he had crossed the wind they were up and looking in
his direction, then quietly they turned and climbed to the
top, but in the opposite direction from Jim.

Again there stands out my experience of 1928 in Alberta.
I had but shortly returned from the Sudan where I had been
desperately ill, and I was now trying myself out, and at the
same time trusting that the high altitude and wonderful air
of the Rockies would finish off any of the tropical bugs that
might still remain in my system. We were camped on Ram
Creek, and the day previous Jim Boyce and I started after a
very fine specimen of a black tail buck. The buck was some

distance away, the snow was deep, and my strength not what I had thought. I was completely played out and fizzled on the buck. How I reached the horses I will never know, for I can only remember keeping but one thought in mind, "You will have to make it."

The next morning I said I would try it again. We reached the top of a ridge where we lunched, then climbed still higher. Jim had noticed some fresh ram tracks, but I was only interested in securing a worth while buck. Upon reaching the top and looking over the other side without results, Jim and I started back to examine a draw on the right. Suddenly Jim dropped and whispered, "Ram." We crawled back and then down another ridge and came out on the level with the ram that was across a small draw from us. We lay in the snow for fully fifteen minutes (it seemed like hours) before he lifted his head, and with that he dropped. He turned out to be a very old ram with a magnificent head, the curl measuring 42½ inches, the base 16½, and the spread 24; very heavy even to the points. His teeth were worn down to the gums and loose, every bone in his body stuck out, and his meat was in such poor condition it could not be eaten. It was an act of charity to have put him out of his suffering for he would never have come through the winter.

A little later on the same trip I came across another old-timer, likewise with a magnificent head. This ram was also on his last legs and I am sure could never pass another rugged Canadian winter. I took movies of him and also still pictures, and left him.

The rams in Alberta seem to be divided into two distinct

colors. There are large and apparently old rams, very light in color both as to curl and horns. Besides there are the big black fellows of very dark brown coat and horns of dark color. The difference in color is quite marked; no doubt the blond and brunette exist as in the human race. The Alberta sheep are the finest of the *Ovis canadensis* that I have ever seen. I am sure a ram in prime condition will reach 250 pounds or close to it. Their whole conformation is greater than the Wyoming sheep. This also holds good with the ewes. The color of the ewes seemed to me to be much more uniform and of light brown. I believe the world's record ram was secured in this section, and the curl of its horns rivals that of the sheep of Asia. The horns of both the Wyoming and Alberta rams curl close to their heads.

I also hunted on the sheep ranges above Lillooet, B. C., many years ago. At that time it was generally understood that the sheep on these ranges were gradually blending into the Stone sheep. I saw quantities of sheep on the Lillooet trip, and they were all about the same color; if anything I should say they are lighter than either the Wyoming or Alberta sheep. Most of the horns curled out from the head similar to the Stone and Dall sheep, but we also saw several rams with close curls. The horns of all the rams we secured were much lighter in color than the rams of Wyoming and Alberta. I understand that there are still people who aim to find the line of demarcation between the Canadensis and Stone sheep in the hope of establishing a new species.

Traveling westward you come to the Cassiar Mountains, which are comfortably reached from Telegraph Creek. Traveling south from Telegraph you cross the Klappan River, and on the high rugged ridges beyond you come to the home of the Stone sheep. I believe the Stone sheep were first secured by Jack Stone on the sheep ranges above Sheslay, which is north of Telegraph Creek; but as the Fannin may also be found on these ranges I think that the section to the south of the Klappan is the home of the pure-blooded Stone sheep; seldom are lighter shaded sheep seen on these ranges. Of course I am stating only my own observations and what has been told me by the Indians; also by Mr. Dodd, the Provincial Agent at Telegraph Creek. I saw many Stone sheep, rams, ewes and lambs. They look absolutely black at a distance, but on examination many white hairs are found scattered amongst the mass of black. The white hairs are in greater quantities on the neck and face.

These sheep are considerably smaller in size than any of the sheep that I have previously mentioned, and although I have never weighed one I do not believe a large specimen will dress out at a 150 pounds. I put in several days hunting these sheep with both gun and camera. I secured some fair specimens and shot many feet of film, but it was before the day of the successful long focus lens, so the animals do not stand out very large.

Traveling north from Telegraph Creek over the Teslin trail one first comes to Shesley, beyond which are extensive sheep ranges. We did not stop, but pressed on until Nahline was reached, and from there we branched off to Nakina Summit. On these sheep ranges the grading from the black to the white, resulting in the *Fannini* sheep, is most apparent.

Bunches of sheep may be seen with dark and light animals intermingled. In the description of the Fannin species especial mention is made of the light translucent horns. I saw many of the light specimens with the darker horns, and of the specimens I secured there were two I would have classified as Fannin, one with light and the other with dark horns. The Fannin are also supposed to have more graceful outspreading horns, while the Stone curl closer, but in this I again found great variations. The Indians are satisfied that there is no change in species and that the difference in color is due to local conditions. Both the Stone and Fannin sheep have horns of the outspreading type as a whole, though I have seen exceedingly tight curled horns on both. There is no doubt in my mind that the Fannin is a cross between the Stone and the Dall.

My curiosity having been aroused, I went westward to the headwaters of the McMillan River in the Yukon Territory. This was the spot where I understood the Fannin sheep reached perfection. They were spoken of as "saddle back" or blue sheep. When we came to look them over I was much surprised to find that at a distance, the sheep did appear to have a blue blanket over their backs. Even here there were extremely light and dark specimens in the same bunch. The darker ones were about the color of the light ones we saw at Nakina, while the lighter ones appeared pure white at a distance. I secured a very light and a dark specimen from the same bunch. The lighter one had a pronounced blue blanket when we first located them. Upon close examination of the specimens I found black hairs sprinkled throughout both animals, there being a greater quantity in the dark ram. The head and shoulders of the lighter ram contain very few dark hairs; in fact one must search closely to discover them. As the head stands today, mounted, it would be taken for a Dall sheep. The horns of both these rams were light in color with a tendency towards translucency; their tails were black.

Going still further westward, I hunted the sheep ranges at the headwaters of the White River. These magnificent ranges before the Shushanna Stampede were literally covered with sheep. During the rush they had been ruthlessly slaughtered by some of the stampeders and in many cases just shot to see them fall. Then later they were killed for meat for the Shushanna Camp. When I visited this section the sheep were just beginning to come back, and although we saw numbers of them they were shy and it was very difficult to get within shooting distance of them. These sheep are of the Dall variety but I found many black hairs scattered throughout their bodies though they are not at all noticeable unless searched for. In addition they have the black tails; the horns are of the wide spreading type and light in color, but again I saw a few with closer curls and darker horns.

The next sheep range to the westward that I visited is on the headwaters of the Little Gerstle which empties into the Tanana River. In this particular range I feel somewhat of a proprietary interest. Dr. Arthur W. Elting, of Albany, N. Y., and I were the first to hunt on these ranges; it was virgin country. We found a great number of fat, lazy rams that paid little or no attention to our intrusion. The sheep in this section appeared to me to be the largest of the Dall that I have seen except those of the Rainy Pass section, of which I shall speak later. We secured some very fine specimens on our first trip, and the next year I secured two more; all of these rams had massive heads with curls 40 inches or over. The horns are dark in color, and though they are wide curling they give the impression of being close owing to their massiveness.

These sheep had been enjoying undisturbed ease for years, and showed the effects of it; they were very easy to reach and kill. It is but two days further to the headwaters of the Johnson where quantities of sheep had been taken in the past for meat. The sheep on the Johnson had heads lighter in weight though the weight of the body appeared to be the same. It is my belief that the big heavy heads are in a way exceptional and are only found on old rams that have not been worried to any extent. They are the ones that just lie around and take life easy. When the big heavy-headed rams are killed off it takes many years before they are replaced.

Further to the north, towards the head of Bear Creek and the Robertson River, I found that the sheep had been closely hunted by Indians. They were wild and hard to stalk, especially as they had retired to the rough, high mountain peaks. All the specimens that I examined can safely be called pure white, though in one or two instances I found a few black hairs; the tails were clear white.

We now come to the McKinley Range, and here we find the pure unadulterated Dall sheep. On the eastern sections, such as the headwaters of the Savage, Sanctuary, Igloo and Toklat Rivers, I looked over many sheep. One day on Sable Pass I counted one hundred and twenty-eight in a bunch, and then further on, at Polychrome Pass, over three hundred. These were ewes and lambs. At the head of the Toklat we must have seen as many as five hundred rams when we were taking motion pictures. In all these rams I never saw a really old heavy head; there were many large ones with beautiful curls, but none of those old heavy massive heads. Here again, I surmised that this had been caused by the intensive hunting that had taken place on these ranges in the past. Now that McKinley National Park has been established and there is no longer hunting, the old fellows will begin to appear again. These sheep all seemed to have the light translucent horns.

Traveling along the north side of the Alaskan Range in the shadow of Mount McKinley we leave the Toklat and going over the Highway Pass apparently lose the sheep after we pass Stony River. From Copper Mountain to Mount Foraker it would appear that there are no sheep to be found. But on careful investigation you will find sheep the entire length of the range. The fact is that they were intensely hunted in this section up to the creation of the Park and for two or three years after by prospectors and miners, and took, naturally, to the highest, most inaccessible parts of the mountains.

At the headwaters of the Tonzona River, in the vicinity of Mount Dall, again I found sheep in large quantities and secured some exceptional specimens. The heads were massive and I secured a very large one with close curling horns, dark in color, similar to a *canadensis*.

At Rainy Pass I found sheep of large size with grand heads. They had no fear of men, and their horns were in

Osborn Caribou

From the painting by Carl Rungius

excellent condition; very few had broken points. This was another instance where the sheep had not been disturbed and had plenty of feed. They took life easy, loafing about the high slopes. There was an abundance of fine large heads, and they were comparatively easy to approach.

CARIBOU

Many years ago it was my good fortune to hunt caribou on the marshes at the headwaters of the Humber River, Newfoundland. In those days they were in great numbers, and it was a simple matter to secure the full quota permitted under the hunting license. It was not very sporty, as I went out with my guide to a spot called a lookout. We would wait there until caribou ambled our way, and if there was a sizeable buck in the bunch we crawled to a spot where he could be intercepted, and got an easy shot. It was most inadvisable to tramp over the marshes as our track left behind a scent that for several hours would warn any wandering caribou.

My hunting in Newfoundland was done in the late season so the animals were in heavy coat. They are good-sized animals, very light in color, and all of the bulls we secured were in fine condition and would have weighed somewhere around four hundred pounds. They were possessed with great curiosity, and after one of the bunch had been shot the others would hang around trying to find out what it was all about. The instant they got the scent of man they were off. It was quite plain that these caribou were being intensively hunted, far beyond what was advisable. There were great numbers of them, and a hunting license permitted the taking of three males. Since that time they have become very scarce, and I understand that lately a closed season has been placed on them. The very section hunted by me was covered a few years ago by friends of mine. I believe a total of thirty caribou were seen on the trip, and no large heads, while on my trip a daily average of eighty to a hundred seen is a conservative estimate, with many fine heads.

My next experience with caribou was in New Brunswick at the headwaters of the Nepisiquit River. These were about the same in size as the Newfoundland caribou, but much darker in color. It was also many years ago that I hunted in New Brunswick and at that time there were great numbers of caribou. We hunted in the Newfoundland manner, but in New Brunswick they were found on the so-called barrens, which were large areas of high country that had been burned over many years before. We saw caribou every day we looked for them, and I recall a day when I counted sixty-six. The formation and size of the horns ran about the same as in Newfoundland. Today I understand there are few, if any, caribou left in New Brunswick, at any rate in the sections I hunted in. This, I believe, has been due to migration to other parts, as was the case in Maine. I recall hunting hard in Maine one fall in hope of securing a caribou specimen, but I saw none, though I did find two tracks that I followed for some time without success. The year following, the season was closed in Maine and remains so to this day. I have always thought that when feed becomes scarce, caribou migrate to a more propitious feeding ground. My study of the caribou of Newfoundland and New Brunswick was quite superficial, but

I could not see a very great difference between them beyond color.

I next bring you to the caribou of the Cassiar and Yukon. These magnificent animals of commanding size are the *Rangifer osborni.* They have exceedingly fine heads, very massive and with many points. They are a darkish brown in color, while the older bulls have a very light neck with fine mane. The curiosity of the caribou in this locality appears to be at its peak. We had no difficulty in bringing whole bands over to us by sticking our arms in the air and dancing up and down.

I put in many days in the caribou country both in the Cassiar and still further westward on the headwaters of the McMillan River, Yukon Territory. The *Rangifer osborni* are the largest and finest of any of the various species I have secured. I have made a wide jump from New Brunswick to the Cassiar Mountains and the Yukon, and though I realize there are other species of caribou between, nevertheless I have never been fortunate enough to have secured specimens, very largely due to the fact that I have never really seriously attempted to hunt them there. I secured numerous fine specimens of the Osborn caribou on the several hunts that I have taken into their ranges. Apparently they make a slight migration, as do those of Newfoundland and New Brunswick, but not in any degree resembling the huge migrating bands in the interior of northwestern Alaska. Their characteristics were, generally speaking, very similar to those of their distant relatives which I have already mentioned.

In the Cassiar I spent many days trying to take moving pictures of the caribou, and though our plans were most carefully worked out I had poor results compared with what I wanted. We would carefully stalk a bunch and when we were within filming distance I would suddenly stand up, set up the machine, and start grinding. The startled caribou would bolt out of filming distance before I was able to take any pictures. We then tried to drive the caribou towards the camera. I would set it up, and two of the guides would circle and attempt to start the animals toward it. This plan had been successful with sheep and goat, but again we scored failure, as the caribou would all rush towards the drivers.

Finally I concluded to play on their curiosity, and setting up the camera on the tripod I walked openly towards a bunch of caribou. They would look up in a stolid manner and then come pell-mell towards me. In this way I was able to get some very good pictures, but unfortunately it was before the day of the successful long-focus lens and the motor-driven camera. The camera I had in the Cassiar weighed nearly fifty pounds and the tripod at least thirty-five to forty pounds more. It was no mean job to pack this on your back when trying to get sufficiently close for picture taking.

On the Yukon, below Dawson, I saw numbers of the barren land caribou, while at Beaver I had the opportunity to examine several carcasses that had been brought in by Indians. These caribou were the smallest of any that I had ever seen, and were very dark in color. I was told that the coat turned light later in the season. It was the last part of July when I saw them. I also saw numerous heads at Stewart, Dawson and Fort Yukon. They were much lighter and smaller, and ran more to points without palmation at the top of the rear shaft.

On a trip to the headwaters of the White River I saw several bands of caribou but, as none were sufficiently attractive as specimens, I did not shoot any, and was unable to examine them closely. As I looked them over carefully through my glasses, I believe that they are somewhat larger than the Barren Land animals that I had seen, but much smaller than the Osborn variety. They were very dark in color, the bulls even having dark necks. This latter possibly was due to the fact that all the bulls I saw were young. I believe these were the same caribou of which Mr. Maguire secured species on his trip to the headwaters of the White. I understand they have been classified as a new species and named after Mr. Maguire.

Still further to the westward on the headwaters of the Tanana River we came across caribou that to me seemed to vary from any that I had hunted before. They are quite a small animal, possibly not any larger than the Barren Land species but their markings and horn formation impressed me as being similar to the *osborni*. The horns were large and massive for the size of the animal. We saw great quantities of them, and from what I heard later from John Burnham, who was east of us, we must have been in the vanguard of the migration. These caribou band up somewhere west of Tanana Crossing and come down over the range to the valley of the Delta River. Dr. Elting of Albany was with me on my first trip to this locality, and we secured several fine specimens which I had an excellent opportunity to study. The hair seemed of much finer texture than that of the Osborn caribou. Though the heads seemed very large and massive on the live animals, we soon discovered they were not as large as they appeared. This was due to the small body of the animal which I doubt would dress at two hundred and fifty pounds.

Traveling still further west we come to the McKinley section of the Alaskan Range, on the north side of which great quantities of caribou migrate yearly. During the summer months large bands of bulls may be seen together all through McKinley National Park; and in different sections you will see bands of cows and calves, each sex keeping strictly to itself. I have seen these caribou ranging during the summer months high above the sheep and assumed it was to avoid the flies and bugs that apparently annoy them more than they do sheep or moose. As the summer wanes you will see bands of bulls down in the valleys, all trekking westward, and the same with the cows and calves, but still each keeping to themselves. Somewhere on the western end of the McKinley section of the great range there must be a mutual meeting ground where they come together at the start of the rut. I was confident that the headwaters of the Kuskokwim, where there is a large flat area, was the spot. I betook myself to this section on one of my trips but the caribou were even there still traveling westward.

Suddenly, as if by magic, the caribou disappeared and within ten days they began to be seen again in huge bands traveling east; the beginning of the rut had started. For nearly two weeks we traveled with caribou, as Slim Avery expressed it, "in countless thousands." They were everywhere the eye could see, all moving slowly eastward and feeding as they went. One day at the mouth of Muddy River, Andy Simons and I saw what looked like a shootable bull. We crossed the river and worked our way to the bull, when suddenly we realized that we had stumbled into a bunch of several hundred. They began to appear from everywhere. We stood perfectly still while they trekked by us. They sounded like an army on the march, and in addition they were making a peculiar grunting noise. Some passed close enough for us to have touched them. Apparently they had lost their sense of smell, for we were amongst them, and, although a few looked us over in a more or less suspicious manner, they passed on. Another time our outfit passed through a bunch of possibly seventy-five and, though some of us were walking, they paid no attention, and followed along for quite a distance.

Do not think from this it was an easy matter to secure a good head. The fine specimens were almost always in the midst of the bunch, and great patience was necessary before a clear shot could be secured. You can imagine my surprise one day when I saw the companions of a particularly fine specimen which I wanted (possibly seventy to eighty) stampede wildly when my shot rang out. They didn't stop to look back, or circle to see what had happened to their lordly master as most caribou do, but just ran until they were out of sight.

These caribou are fine heavy-bodied animals, somewhat lighter in color than the Osborn caribou, and smaller in size. The horn formation varies considerably from others I have hunted. We killed some exceptionally heavy fine heads, but they were not as large or heavy as Osborn heads that I had previously secured. The caribou migrate as far to the eastward as Fairbanks in the fall, and from all I can gather the migration is becoming larger every year. This is no doubt due to the fact that the Indians are gradually disappearing and with them their annual decimating slaughter.

I drifted still further westward, and at Rainy Pass found caribou that appeared to differ from those I have just described. These apparently do not migrate but remain in the general locality of the headwaters of the Kuskokwim. I was fortunate in reaching this country with the United States Geological Survey party in charge of Stephen R. Capps. Our trip did not follow the route taken by Captain J. R. Hubback, an English explorer of several years before, but nevertheless I covered much of the ground he had gone over. Captain Hubback secured specimens of these caribou which he sent to Dr. Nelson, then Director of the United States Biological Survey at Washington, who, I understand, has classified them as *Rangifer stonei*, the caribou that once were to be found on the Kenai Peninsula and disappeared almost over night. I secured two fairly good specimens of this caribou. The horns of these animals were much longer on the rear shaft and stood up straighter than any that I saw among McKinley Range caribou. We left the Rainy Pass section early in September, but I am sure that even larger bulls could have been found when the rut was on. The entire horn structure seemed much heavier and rangier than that of their neighbors a short distance east.

In 1930 I returned to Rainy Pass again, and remained there until towards the latter part of September. The caribou were daily coming out in larger numbers, and a great many large bulls were looked over. Finally, towards the head of

Rocky Mountain Moose

From the painting by Carl Rungius

Moose Creek, not far from the mouth of the stream that heads up in Simpson's Pass, I secured a splendid specimen. Near high noon on September 10th we located two bull caribou, and after a simple stalk I killed the larger one. The head had forty-five points, a truly grand head.

I had an opportunity to observe the caribou on the Alaskan Peninsula when I was there on a bear hunt. These are *Rangifer granti*, the Barren Land species. They were almost white at the time I saw them (May), though before we left their coats had started to turn and a strong sprinkling of black had appeared. I studied these caribou many times at close range through my glasses, and also photographed them, but none were killed so that an examination was impossible. The bulls had just started to grow their horns, so my only idea as to what they might develop in general formation was through shed antlers and several heads that I saw. Some of these heads were very large and massive and did not differ materially from heads I have seen on other species.

Caribou as a whole have similar characteristics, their curiosity being the most conspicuous. To me they are one of the most interesting of the various animals that I have hunted. My regret is that I am not sufficient of a naturalist, and have not accumulated the necessary data for a scientific study of the various species and their peculiarities.

Moose

It seems only yesterday that I was looking forward with feverish excitement and enthusiasm toward my first hunt for moose, but sad to relate it was many, many years ago. With keenness and expectancy, my heart beating like a trip hammer, I crawled slowly after my guide until we reached the proper distance, then trembling I raised my rifle and let off the shot. The moose rose and shambled off, to be followed with several more shots. They were taking effect, and finally the grand old monarch came to earth.

This was my first moose, and I was so excited that I could hardly speak as I came up to the fallen animal. Every little detail stands out on that hunt, and many times I have gone over it in my mind. It was a great moment in my life.

My last moose was on the Kenai a few years ago. We had stalked him for some time and finally it came for me to decide whether I would shoot or not. I was all calm and calculating, and when I decided in the affirmative I left my guide and made the last part of the stalk alone. Coming as close as I deemed wise I carefully looked over the old bull with my glasses, and located the exact spot at which to shoot. Carefully taking aim I killed him with the first and only shot. There was no excitement; it was cold, deliberate slaughter. I turned to Andy Simons in disgust and remarked, "I will never kill another," which to date is true; but at times comes the thought, "I wonder."

Many trips after moose have taken place between that first moose in Canada and the last one in Alaska. For several years I hunted moose in New Brunswick with varying success as to the quality of specimens, but with the exception of one year, when an unholy jinx seemed to follow me, I was always fortunate in bringing home my trophy. Quebec and New Brunswick lacked the class of head I was looking for, or they were too scarce for me to stumble over, so I wandered west and north. In Quebec and New Brunswick the moose were apparently identical, which was to be expected.

On my trend towards the north I hunted in the Rockies for a few years and saw many moose which I looked over as closely as possible through my glasses. At that time the season was closed so I was not able to examine them closely, but found them fine big animals very dark in color. As moose had been protected for many years in Wyoming they had no fear of man or his evil smell. I had several most interesting experiences. We met a fine big bull with a goodly-sized head one day on the trail near Butte Creek, and as he kept right along coming we stopped for a few seconds. We were sure he would depart as we drew near, so we started on our way again. The old fellow wasn't accustomed to getting off that trail for anything or anyone. He stopped when quite near and looked us over, but never did he budge. We decided it was better judgment to let him have his way, so we pulled off the trail and passed right alongside of him.

One evening when camped near Hidden Basin on the Thorofare River, I tried a couple of calls and was immediately answered. In a few minutes an old bull walked through camp, stopped at a bush near one of the tents and proceeded to strike his horns against it; at the same time he kept up a goodly assortment of grunts. I think he would have wandered off but "Jonesy," our cook, poured water from the kettle. This nearly started a riot and it took sometime before the old fellow quieted down. I always felt that he was never quite satisfied that we did not have that cow in one of the tents.

Another day, off to secure a blacktail buck, we saw from a steep side hill, below on the river flat, an old bull with a cow. The old fellow was making amorous advances to his companion when three small bulls suddenly appeared and began an annoying competition. The old bull held his ground, driving them off, but not without a tussle. This occurred about nine o'clock in the morning; at two in the afternoon one of our men who was packing in an elk killed the night before, saw the fight still in progress. The next morning I was curious enough to look over the battleground. The moose had all left but the snow was pretty well stained with blood. This ends the tale as we never again ran across the party. I would have known the old bull, but the others were not sufficiently distinctive to have been recognized.

I have many times come face to face with a bull moose and stood quietly watching. Invariably the bull would look at me in a rather surprised manner and then go on quietly as if he had not noticed anything suspicious. Gradually he would drift towards cover, and the instant he was out of sight was off at express speed. I have always felt that, because an old bull was monarch of all he surveyed, even in front of man he would not show the white feather though realizing his danger. As soon as he was out of sight, however, it was too much; he just had to run. In every instance of this sort the wind was towards me. When a moose gets the odor of man he throws all valor to the winds.

I have always felt that calling was one of the meanest advantages that could be taken of a poor unsuspecting amorous bull. At the same time it is the only way they can be

hunted at certain times of the year, and to bring out an old
bull requires patience, experience and science. Though many
people are skeptical about the calling of moose I am positive
it can be done as I have seen many bulls called successfully
into close shooting distances; in fact I have done it myself.
Calling is a most difficult feat where the moose have been
intensively hunted and fooled many times by fake cows.
Where the bulls are not so wise it is a simple matter. In the
Yukon, on Lake Creek, I called both evening and early morning, but though I secured several answers I was unable to
bring out any of the bulls. It was rather late in the rut and I
took it for granted that the 'loves at hand were more fascinating than the possible lure of the uncertain. I am glad to
say that I have never killed a moose that had been called, but
am sorry to admit that this was because no large head ever
came to my call. This happened to be my luck; great numbers
of fine specimens have been secured in this way by others.

In Alberta some years ago I was hunting *Ovis canadensis*
and, though I was told there were a few moose to be found
in that section, none were seen on the entire trip, not even
tracks. In 1928, again in Alberta, I saw many moose, in fact
several every day I was in the hills. These moose appeared
to have about the same characteristics as their Canadian
brethren of Quebec and New Brunswick. These heads varied
somewhat, being of slightly different formation, generally
smaller and with narrower palms. I did see two very fine
heads with wide massive palms and heavy points, not varying greatly from the moose of the Cassiar and the Yukon.
The moose of the Cassiar and the Yukon are grand animals

with heavy heads and wide palms with numerous points. Even the smaller spreading heads are well developed, and a greater number of larger heads, say in the 50-inch class, will be found in these neighborhoods.

In the Cassiar the license formerly permitted two moose, generally resulting in the first head secured being inferior. I made up my mind to secure two fine specimens on my first trip, so when I killed my first head with a 58-inch spread and a goodly number of points I was satisfied that I had made a good beginning. I worked for days to secure a specimen up in the sixties. Dennis and I had siwashed for four days; during this time we fought out a blizzard with no tent, and above timber line. I looked over bull after bull, always with the remark within shooting distance, "something bigger." Finally I wandered back to our main camp where Bill Morden was tearing to go, and well fed up on the snow.

On our way back to Telegraph Creek Dennis spotted a fine big bull which promised to measure up to what I was after; I could see two heavy brow palms with five points on one and six on the other. The right main palm stood out high and massive with twelve points. As I raised my rifle Dennis said, "Wait, I no see left horn."

"That head is good enough for me," was my reply, and with that the old battler pitched over dead. You can imagine my feelings as I came up to the dead moose and saw that the right horn was broken off close to that fine brow palm. The head was useless, and I did not even bring it out. I realized that I had been too hasty, but I had carefully looked over the head through my glasses several times during the stalk. As

Sketch of a Moose, by Carl Rungius

I looked at the fallen moose I realized that I had never seen him on the left side. Dennis just detected something wrong as I was starting to shoot, but it was too late.

The following year I was again with Dennis at the head of the Iskut and we were after what we thought was a grizzly bear. It was nearly half-past nine at night but still quite light, and, as we looked diligently for that bear, there, across a valley, stood the largest moose I had ever had the fortune to cast my eye upon up to that time. Suddenly things got rather busy with Mr. Bear, and after dispatching him I heard Dennis whistle. Across the valley still stood the moose quite unconcerned at the shots. "Big head just like Cook Inlet moose," Dennis whispered.

Things were coming my way that day, for earlier I had secured a monster goat with record horns, and just now a large brown bear. With this behind me I couldn't help but kill the fine old bull though he was quite a distance away. He turned out to be the largest specimen that had ever fallen to my lot—well over sixty inches in spread with grand palms and thirty points.

I recall an experience on the headwaters of the McMillan River in the Yukon. We had been working hard for two weeks endeavoring to locate large rams, traveling with back packs and dogs packed to the limit of their capacity. We stopped for lunch and in the midst of its preparation one of our Indians brought us to life with, "Me see long way off ten big buck sheep." Great excitement ensued and it was not until we had quieted down that our head guide, Ira Van Bibber, discovered that our rams were actually the freshly cleaned horns of five large bull moose. They were high above timber line, and those white horns did stand out like a bunch of Fannin sheep.

That night we had two sides of a fat bull moose roasting in front of a roaring fire. The Indians put on a wonderful feed, keeping at it all night, with songs between each rib. There were some fine heads in that bunch and I often have the experience brought back to me as I glance at the mounted head of an old bull with thirty-three points hanging on the wall of my trophy room. That day was the turning point of our McMillan hunt as sheep, grizzly, caribou and additional moose just piled in on us until our licenses were exhausted.

It was several years after that hunt before I killed another moose. I looked over many moose in different sections of the Alaskan Range, and recall one afternoon when Slim Avery and I sat on a hillside above a willow patch at the head of the Tonzona River. The willows gradually began to take shape, and shortly, in ones and twos, there were eleven moose before our eyes; how many more that willow patch contained we were never able to discover.

Another day in the Tonzona Basin, Andy Simons and I saw nineteen moose and though there were many good heads the 70-inch one I was looking for was not to be found. In Rainy Pass, Andy Simons and I saw many bulls, and it was at this spot that the moose appeared to have grown in size. The general characteristics seemed the same, but there is no doubt in my mind that these moose must be an off-shoot from the Kenai, or possibly some of the *Alces gigas* had strayed into these parts. As Andy and I had framed up a siwash trip

to the Kenai after our return from Rainy Pass, I did not attempt to hunt moose, and those that I saw were what we
stumbled over in our various travels.

Since my trip to Rainy Pass I understand that two different
hunting parties have been there. Just think! It had taken us
sixteen days to reach Ptarmigan Valley, while those that have
followed landed there in an airship in somewhat over two
hours after taking off from Anchorage. Both these parties
secured superb moose, well over 70 inches in spread, but at
that they didn't get the kick out of the trip I did, lining up
the Skwentna River.

On our return from Rainy Pass, Andy Simons, Jack Lean
and I left for the Kenai. The moose of the Kenai are magnificent specimens in size, much greater than any I had ever seen
before excepting at Rainy Pass. I saw so many moose in the
Kenai, though I only hunted four days, that my mind was
just one great confused moose. The specimen I secured was
a very large animal with a magnificent set of horns with very
wide palms, thirty-one long points, and a spread of 62½
inches. The points all turn up, and so cut down the spread,
but it makes a fine basket-shaped head. This is the last moose
that I have killed, and I have already described his down-
fall.

Among all the moose that I have seen in the various sections in which I have hunted, extending in the east from New
Brunswick on through the west and northwest to the far
reached Kenai Peninsula, I count but few variations in general
characteristics that are not accounted for by feed and freedom
from hunting. I realize that there are several classified spe-

cies, and I am not keen to start an argument with the scientists, but it has been my observation that the color variation occurs in all sections. There are dark, jet-black moose with dark tan markings, and likewise light tawny ones that look almost dirty yellow at a distance. The large moose I secured in the Cassiar was, in size and color, a typical Kenai bull, which was noticed by my Indian guide, Dennis, who was familiar with the moose of the Kenai.

Deer and Elk

My first experience in hunting was in the Adirondacks after deer. For many years I would work hard in the fall months for periods of two to three weeks in the hope that I might kill a fine white-tail buck. I have secured a variegated bunch of buck heads but none is really fine. After the Adirondacks I drifted to Maine and Canada, but uncertain results followed me. I can honestly say that, next to sheep, I have put more time and effort in hunting white-tail deer than any other animal, without having been successful in securing one fine specimen. I have killed many bucks, but their heads as trophies do not come under the class to feel proud about. The best head I have ever secured is an eight pointer, four on each side. I killed two or three in Maine with ten points but their heads are smaller than the eight pointer just mentioned.

In those early days I was not very keen in observing, nor very particular in reference to the head as long as it was a buck and fat, as the meat was an important factor. I had many distressing disappointments in those days of inexperience; in fact I recall one instance quite clearly. My guide and I came into a clearing and there stood a fine big-bodied deer. My guide told me to shoot as it was a fine buck. On the shot the buck dropped, and walking towards the fallen deer I placed my rifle alongside a tree. As my guide and I stood alongside the buck, sharpening our knives before starting to butcher, I remarked that he had a rotten head, and asked why he said it was a fine big buck. My guide started to answer when suddenly there was a lively scramble and the next we knew the deer was off for a swamp wherein he disappeared before I could reach my rifle. We never saw him again though we searched through that swamp for hours.

One day in Maine I was traveling through a rather dense woods with my guide when I heard a shot followed by a peculiar singing noise. My guide dropped flat behind a tree and called for me to do likewise. We were under fire, and after what seemed hours, but was probably seconds, a wounded deer appeared traveling slowly and finally laid down a short distance off. The shots and singing noise stopped, and we expected every minute to see the hunters, but none appeared. After waiting a reasonable length of time I went over and put the deer out of its misery; it was a small three point buck. Twice after this I had a similar experience as to the shooting, but no deer appeared. Then one day I happened to meet several men spread out in line ready for anything to jump. I stopped to talk with them for a few seconds and in that time one seemed proud that he had killed nine deer; at least he claimed he had.

This was many years ago, and after the experience I decided to give Maine a wide berth in the future, and to this day I have never returned. On this same trip I remember running across two small bull moose late one afternoon on my return to camp. My guide was most anxious and insistent that I kill either one or both if I so wished, but I had no desire to do so. Upon my return to camp I told my experience to guides of a nearby hunter, and they hustled out early next morning to the marsh and killed both bulls. They then hauled in the entire carcasses and had them on exhibition and for sale.

In Canada, New Brunswick and Quebec, I have wasted much energy and brain matter hunting deer, to say nothing of time and money, without startling success. I came to the conclusion that fine large buck heads were too scarce to waste further time on, and so I drifted into hunting farther west. In Lillooet, British Columbia, and Wyoming, I tried out my luck on the black tail, but here again I have been unable to secure a really fine specimen. I have seen many fine heads, but always luck was against me. One time on the Lillooet hunt I had just started to climb the ridge opposite our camp. I was carrying my rifle without a cartridge in the chamber as the gun had gone off on half cock the day before while I was carrying it on my back. A fine buck walked straight towards us and when within about fifty yards he stopped and started feeding, standing broadside. I threw a shell into the chamber, but instead two jumped up from the magazine and jambed tight. Before I got things straightened out the buck was on the run and about two hundred yards off, and for all I know is still going. After that experience I changed to a bolt action and have used it exclusively ever since.

One day in Wyoming, with snow on the ground nearly a

foot deep, Joe Jones and I followed a bunch of deer which included a large buck. We tracked them into heavy timber, and circled in the hopes of cutting them off. Suddenly we bumped into the bunch, which stampeded, the buck whirling off by himself. "There he goes; bust him," called Joe. Seeing a buck that looked to have a large head I held on a clearing and fired as he passed through. When we came up to the buck we found I had killed the smaller of the two, with four points on each side.

It was not until 1928, after my return from the Sudan, that I secured a fine black tail of ten points, five on either side, on a hunt in Alberta. We had just made camp after a fair day's trip and I was fixing my bag in the tent. Jim Boyce, my head guide, came to me and said he could see a large buck deer, and asked me whether I cared to go for it. Of course I went, and after a good tramp and then a short stalk I pushed my rifle over the top of the ridge, and though the first shot was a fatal one I sent two more to quiet the struggling animal.

I recall another experience with Joe Jones in Wyoming. We had been up Cabin Creek targeting a new rifle and on our return startled a buck deer which ran up the mountain-side. Joe had a 303 Savage and at once opened up. After four shots with a few pertinent remarks from me, he turned and said, "Shoot him yourself." I took the rifle and holding on the shoulder followed the deer until the report rang out and the deer dropped dead. Feeling rather puffed I turned to Joe and said, "Got him right through the heart." Joe went up to the deer and turned him over to butcher. He suddenly stopped and yelled down to me, "Say Bill, where did you say you hit this buck?" I might have been suspicious but I was so cocksure of where that shot had hit I replied, "through the heart." "Well, who in hell hit him in the head?" came back to me. Sure enough, my cocksure shot had gone wide of the mark, but we had meat to start our trip with just the same.

Then there was a buck which we needed badly for meat, and as we couldn't get near I had to try a long shot. Joe Jones was with me on this occasion also, and I had a 405 Winchester. I had to shoot at over two hundred yards, and on the third shot the deer dropped. We were congratulating ourselves when the deer jumped up and started rapidly up that mountain-side. He disappeared over the top of the highest ridge, with daylight showing through a hole in one of his ears and lead spitting about him on every side. We were without meat that night and for several days to come.

I could go on telling experiences of deer hunting for an indefinite time but these details become tiresome, so I will give you my last. I have just returned from Scotland (1929) where I had some marvelous grouse shooting, and secured two stags. I leased a deer forest, which, let me explain, is about the barest, rockiest, most mountainous country you will ever experience. Rossdhu consists of eighteen thousand acres, and is as rough as any Rocky Mountain sheep country I have ever traveled in. It is true we started from about sea level every morning, but we climbed from 2,500 to 4,000 feet before we reached the place from which we could locate the deer.

My first day started in a most auspicious manner as we

Left to right: The pony boy, the head stalker,
assistant stalker and lunch boy

The head stalker, Campbell, locating beasts

located four stags early in the day, two of which had fine shootable heads. After a strenuous stalk that took till two o'clock in the afternoon, we finally were close to the point of getting a shot. Suddenly the stags rose and disappeared; they had been warned by tame sheep that had seen us. For four days I worked hard, following the old Scotch stalker, but the stags all were too wise for us. When at last after a most discouraging time in the fog, we started for home a stag was located below us, and my chance had finally arrived. I had to shoot directly downhill, and was fortunate to bring the stag to ground. It was a good nine pointer, five on one side and four on the other. The stag was dressed out and the horns tied to a long staff which the head stalker had been carrying. With a man holding each end of the staff, they started down hill dragging the stag. Bringing up the rear was the third man, who kept the stag straight with a rope fastened to the two hind feet. In this way it was dragged downhill where a pony and another man were waiting. The stag was then tied on the saddle of the pony and packed to the stalker's cabin.

The hunting party consisted of a head stalker, an assistant stalker, a lunch boy and a pony boy and pony. The stalker, his assistant and the lunch boy all came along with me to the hills, and the pony and pony boy traveled along the valley to be in readiness in case a stag should be killed. A telescope is used to locate and look over the stags. After a stag is located and the stalker decides he is shootable, the entire party starts forward. There being no cover, it is quite a tricky performance to come within shooting distance. As the distance shortens the assistant stalker and lunch boy lag behind, while the stalker and I would crawl and squirm along the ground, much of which was wet; but that made no difference.

When we had worked up to five or six hundred yards, even though the wind was favorable and we had never shown ourselves, the stags would become restless, sensing danger. Finally the point would be reached for the shot, and, provided the stag had not been frightened off by sheep or flushing grouse or ptarmigan, I would raise up to fire. A quick shot was all that I would be able to get. If we had not had to contend with the tame sheep we would have had much more pleasure on those bare deer forests.

It nevertheless was a most interesting experience and I thoroughly enjoyed watching the stalker. I had heard fabulous tales as to the prowess of the Scotch stalkers. I have been out with several guides on the sheep ranges in the west and northwest who, I am confident, could take care of themselves with the Scotch stalkers, if not show them a thing or two.

My last day on the hills brought me another chance. We were on the top of Ben Vorlich, about 4,000 feet, and far below was a stag that my stalker remarked was "a verra fine beast." To reach him seemed to me a cinch, as high, pinnacled rocks gave us an excellent cover, and a strong wind was blowing across Loch Sloy directly below us and coming straight up that hillside. We crawled and scrambled down those rocks and never once showed ourselves, finally reaching a large boulder. The stalker whispered that the stag was just on the other side, and to get ready to shoot. I raised above the rock quietly and carefully, expecting to get a chance to look over the head. The stag was just starting to run, and not having more than a few seconds time I swung over on his shoulder as the gun went off. The stag went down the hillside like an express train.

I was sure I had hit but possibly it was low. Suddenly we noticed him falter, and then turn several somersaults and disappear. When we reached him he was lodged against a rock overhanging a steep drop. The head was a fairly heavy eight pointer, that of an old stag whose head had gone more into size than points. There is one more thing I want to impress upon anyone who intends to stalk stags in Scotland. Be sure and have a bottle of Scotch in your kit at all times, for when a stag is killed custom demands that it shall be wet —that is, that the bottle of Scotch shall be passed and everyone invited to take a "wee drop." Not over a half glass is permissible. It is hard work, good sport, and well worth the trip to be out with an old Scotch stalker; they are a great lot.

In reading over this last chapter I find I have completely ignored our grand elk. Many of the best times I have had out in the hills have been in Wyoming after elk with my old friend, Joe Jones. (Poor old Joe, with whom I have had many exciting experiences on those wonderful Rockies of Wyoming, has gone to the happy hunting ground.) Joe had his shortcomings, but, as a man in the hills in those days long ago when we rambled together, he had no peer. May he find the rest where he has gone that he never had here, and may he find hills he loved so well to ramble in.

One day Joe and I were looking for a real old buster bull, and we were skirting along the boundary of the Game Preserve in the hope that some of the old fellows might have wandered beyond that imaginary but sacred line. There, below us, in a small open park, stood a fine seven point bull. He was very much excited and was stamping the ground, and every few minutes he would throw back his head and send forth a deep bugle. It was quite a temptation but, before we were really seriously tempted, an answering bugle sounded a short distance from us. Fortunately this bull was on the right side of the line, and was aiding and abetting us. The young bull must have called that old fellow some very insulting name for he came up the hill on a run and never stopped until he was within thirty yards of us, and across the line.

He really had no intention of stopping when he did, but as he came on our side a 220-grain 30 bullet hit him square on the point of the shoulder. With the discharge of the rifle our horses stampeded and for a few seconds it looked as if they would not stop this side of Cody. The bull was down, and, as I thought, giving his last dying struggles. Joe started off on a run to head off the horses if possible, and yelled to me to get over on the other side to help him. We chased those horses hard but finally one of them, mine, tangled his leg in the reins and so Joe caught him, and then riding, succeeded in overtaking his own horse.

We went back to my fallen elk to find that he had disappeared. Picking up his track we followed him down the hillside and across the park where we had first seen him. We here entered a jumbled mass of down timber, in which we knew the bull must be, but search as we did we found no further trace of him, though we were sure we heard him breathing his last. We gave up finally and returned to the horses that had been left on the top. I was thoroughly disgusted at not having made certain of the elk by putting another shot into him for good measure, but I was sure it was all over. We started for camp, which was a long distance off, both quite dejected, as a seven pointer is not to be picked up every day.

When we were within two miles of camp a deep guttural bugle rang out on the cool air of that late afternoon.

"That's an old fellow," said Joe. "Listen so we can locate where he is."

Again rang out that old challenge, and then again, and again.

"Come," said Joe, "here's the old bull you're looking for; he's larger than the one you wounded."

There stood the bull with his harem; a goodly one he was, and he was sending out challenge after challenge to all nearby bulls to come and try to take them away. Joe looked him over carefully through his glasses and turning said, "That's a bigger head, Bill, than the other; there are six points on one side and seven on the other; better bust him." I hesitated for a few seconds as I had sort of a jinx on me that day.

"Come on," said Joe, "bust him; he's not going to stay there forever."

I took a slow careful aim, holding on the shoulder, and with the crack of the rifle the elk dropped. This time I immediately ran up to the fallen animal and was going to shoot again but Joe stopped me, as the bull was dead. It was a very fine head, in fact the best I ever secured, and in these days it is difficult to better it. By the time he had butchered the elk it was dark, so we left it until the following day before bringing it to camp.

Another time Joe and I had been watching a bunch of elk in Hidden Basin and discussing a bull whose head we could not quite make out. We crawled closer, and then a further discussion ensued as I did not think the head was large enough; I could only make out one horn. From whispers our conversation became louder. and suddenly the bull rose and started off through the trees. "Bust him, he's a walloper," beseeched Joe. Well, he did look big, and so I hurriedly threw a cartridge into the chamber and let go at the disappearing animal. I plainly saw him flinch and go down on his left leg, but he was up and away again.

"You made a mistake Bill, you should have killed that elk when you had the chance," was Joe's comment. We traveled then to the head of the Basin and towards late afternoon picked up the tracks of a bunch of elk. Suddenly we found ourselves in the middle of the bunch. Coming over a slight rise in the ground we saw the bull stampeding, and at the snap glance I had of him he looked good. Joe was yelling, "Bust him Bill, bust him."

Well, I did, with two shots in the shoulder; the first one stopped him, and with the second he rose up and went over backward. As the elk fell Joe bawled out, "You shot him in the horn, Bill." When we came up to the bull we found that one royal had been broken off close to the shaft.

As I looked at the fallen elk he seemed familiar and I turned to Joe and said, "That's the elk I shot at this morn-

Alaskan Brown Bear

From the painting by Carl Rungius

ing." "Like hell it is; that one had two good horns," was Joe's reply. Saying nothing further I proceeded to investigate and found a bullet hole in the left rump. The next day when we packed the meat to camp I cut out the bullet and found it was a split 220 grain 30/06. It was one and the same bull, and my bullet must have hit a branch of a tree and split.

I could go on telling many experiences with elk. Like goat they are too easy, but their meat is fine eating and none was ever wasted in our camps. This is more than I can say of the goat.

BEAR

For many years bears were to me a mysterious, elusive, vicious species of mammal that I had hunted intensively without success, throughout the greater portion of the northwest. I had seen a few small black bears in Quebec and New Brunswick, but had never secured a specimen.

It was in the Cassiar country, near Nakina Summit, on a beautiful, clear day, that luck first came to me. I had separated from my guide and was looking over the side of a high ridge when suddenly I located what looked to me to be a huge grizzly. Not wanting to risk messing up the stalk, I signaled Dennis, my guide. We worked up to close quarters and I secured Mr. Bear. He turned out to be a brown phase of the black bear and not the vicious grizzly I had hoped.

For the balance of the trip I did much talking about the large brown bear I had killed, being greatly pleased and proud of my performance. You can imagine my disappointment when Mr. Dodd, the Provincial Agent at Telegraph Creek, after measuring our trophies for his official records, handed me the slip. At the end of the list I read, "One small brown bear cub." To say I was indignant and hurt is putting it mildly, and I ventured a few remarks. The result was that we returned to measure the skin. It was simply outrageous how that skin had shrunk. I maintain to this day that it must have been an unusually large bear.

Other bears were secured on different trips, but all of the black family. It seemed that the grizzly would actually depart from the sections I hunted. I was becoming thoroughly accustomed to my fate and was about satisfied that it would never fall to me to secure a grizzly. Suddenly my luck turned. It all came to pass one morning while hunting in the McMillan country in the Yukon.

We were on our way to the sheep mountains. A black object appeared over the top of a high ridge. As it drew near we saw a fine silvertip of goodly proportions, and, as luck would have it, he came close to where we were waiting. It took five shots from the 30/06 to bring him down. He turned out to be a splendid specimen, but showed no signs of the vicious man-eater I had expected in the grizzly.

In removing the hide I noticed a tumor on the side of the neck. Upon opening the sack, I removed a broken tusk from another bear, no doubt left there in one of the many fights my old battler had participated in. My Indian guide became visibly excited when he saw the piece of tooth and told me this was "great good luck. Many times more you see grizzled bear. You carry him alway."

And so my luck turned, for never since have bears failed me on a hunting trip. Take the omen for what it is worth; no doubt it is just a coincidence, but nevertheless it made an impression on me and that broken tooth travels with me "alway."

On an exploring trip toward the headwaters of the Little Gerstle River, a tributary of the Tanana, we met the first grizzly for that year. Instead of making tracks for another country he started on a brisk trot toward us, and it was not until he was within possibly fifty yards that he decided to turn and depart. Our guns were packed; so we would have been at a disadvantage if the bear had really meant business.

It did not take us long to discover that nearly all the bears in this section would come toward us as in a charge, but when they got our wind they departed. Our head guide, John Hajdukovich, said this was usual, as they had never been hunted; but he told us not to take too much for granted, as some of them would not turn and depart.

One morning, as we were on our way toward the headwaters of the Robertson River, my hunting companion, Art, had wandered considerably ahead of the outfit. There were six men in our party and six pack horses. As the traveling was uncertain, each man was leading a pack horse. We had no saddle horses. I happened to look up toward the top of the grade we were climbing. Just then a grizzly appeared at a gallop, heading directly for Art.

My first impulse was to yell and at the same time to extricate my gun from the pack of the horse I was leading. The guides joined in the yelling and general excitement while I attempted to run uphill to get between Art and the bear. He seemed to be the only cool one in the bunch, for he stood quietly watching the bear coming toward him, in spite of the fact that his gun was securely fastened on the pack of another horse.

Between the grade, which was steep, and my yelling, which was reinforced by that of the men, the bear was stopped. She rose on her hind legs and began sniffing, then turned and disappeared over the ridge. I followed, to find that she had circled and was again in the act of reconnoitering. Just as she turned, a 30/06 bullet broke her back, and it was not long before her hide was on the top of a pack. Art remarked that curiosity was a bad trait, even in a bear. He has always claimed that if my wind had held he would have been forced to send in my name for a Carnegie medal for saving his life.

There were several other bears encountered on that trip. One came within twenty-five yards of Art, who sat covering it with his rifle and waiting to see just what would happen. Luckily for one or the other, the bear decided to depart and, from all indications, continued to travel for many miles in the opposite direction.

The next season, while camped on the headwaters of the Little Gerstle, where I intended to hunt sheep, I was requested one morning by Johnny Healy, an Indian who was along with us, to come with him and kill a couple of grizzlies that were just above camp. We went up the bed of the stream on which we were camped, for a quarter of a mile, when we came to a bend. There, above us, about three hundred yards off, were the two grizzlies. We ducked down beside a cut bank, but not before one of the bears had seen us.

This bear started immediately in our direction and, without any stops, came directly to the spot where we were trying to hide. When he was within thirty yards, I decided to shoot. And although I put five shots in what ordinarily are vulnerable spots, he still kept coming. The bear was upon me, but, fortunately, badly wounded. Rising on his hind legs, he stood looking at me for a second and then made a final lunge. A bullet between the eyes dropped him within a few feet of where I was standing. The other grizzly ran off. My Indian had long since disappeared. Thus ended this episode.

In the spring of 1927, I was on the Bering Sea side of the Alaskan Peninsula and had considerable opportunity to observe the Alaskan Brownie in his home haunts. I never realized the humanness of these bears, nor the fact that they not only are affectionate to their young but also have a sense of humor. Many sows and cubs have I watched through the glasses, some far away and others quite near.

One morning we saw a large sow with two good-sized cubs come down over a steep snowslide. The old sow found a soft snow bank and lay down. The cubs started to play and then decided to explore thereabout. They finally wandered to the edge of a steep canyon wall with a sheer drop of several hundred feet to the valley floor. Rising on their hind legs, they came up to the edge, where they stopped.

Finally one leaned away forward and looked down, pulling himself back quickly when he realized the drop. He then turned to the other cub, who couldn't make up his mind to take a look. After reassurances from brother the timid cub also leaned over and looked down. All this time they were standing on their hind legs. When they had broken the ice and their nerves were restored, they would alternately lean over, take a look, and pull back. No doubt it was a game they were playing. After some time at this game they tired and started to rough-house one another, rolling over and over in the snow. All this time the mother appeared to be asleep.

On another occasion we saw a sow with two cubs following, every one apparently serene and happy. Suddenly the sow made a quick wheel and cuffed the nearest cub, rolling it over and over. Then she turned and went on her way as if nothing had happened. No doubt the cub had made some facetious remark to mother.

One day we saw a sow with three cubs. As we were attempting to reach a boar that was some distance off, we paid practically no attention to them. We were unsuccessful in getting anywhere near the boar, and upon our return we wondered what had become of the sow and cubs. Suddenly we came upon them, lying asleep on a snow patch. We had noticed the black spots on the snow, but thought they were rocks until within a few yards.

Not wanting to shoot and having used up all the film I had with me, we drew back and circled them. When we crossed their wind, we thought they would surely detect us, but such was not the case. They slumbered on.

High up on one of the steepest peaks of the Pinnacles we saw a sow with four very large cubs. Mother was lying on a flat rock while the "kiddies" were enjoying a few winter sports. The cubs would climb high on the slide, then sit on their rumps and come shooting down to a level bench below. They did this several times until one started a rough-house, and then the four went at it. It must have got a little too warm, for mother came down and separated them, sending each one off in a different direction.

One morning toward the end of our stay we saw a sow break through the snow out of her den. After a short time she put her head back in the hole and succeeded in bringing out a wee cub. The cub came but a short distance and dove back again. We watched this sow for several days and saw her bring out two cubs and gradually get them accustomed to their surroundings. The last day I hunted up this valley I saw that same sow with her two cubs down quite low and an easy mark for the rifle. Somehow both Andy and I seemed to have a proprietary right in those cubs, and I no more could have shot that sow than I could a personal friend.

Several times I have watched cubs playing. Getting a little tired of romping alone, they would start after the mother to join in. At first the sow would invariably try to cuff them off, but in all cases would end by joining in and playing like a human mother with her offspring.

In closing let me say that I consider the bear the most human and inoffensive of the wild animals. They are keen, and many times will see you first and depart without your having had a glance at them. There are bad bears and, by the same token, good ones. I believe the latter are by far in the greater numbers. To say that the bear is not a dangerous animal, especially the Alaskan brown, is foolish, for there are too many cases on record to disprove such a statement. It is my impression, nevertheless, that if you do not bother them they will not bother you, though there are exceptions even to this.

Grizzlies are rapidly disappearing, for their friends are few and far between. Give them a show, for they are a great experience in a hunting trip, even if you only see one, with no chance for a shot. After a man has killed a few bears, what happens? Their hides are either packed in camphor or given away as presents.

You who have killed a big grizzly for the first time realize the thrill and sensation. Why not try to protect that thrill for others? After the first two or three there is no more excitement in killing a bear than in slaughtering a cow.

It seems too bad that the laws of Alaska cannot be construed to permit the Alaskans to protect their property without declaring the Alaskan brown bear an outlaw and removing it from the protected list. The time is not far distant when the authorities will realize the error that has been made, and the Brownie will be put back again among the protected. But why the poor, simple, harmless black bear should be opened up for the slaughterers is more than I can understand. He seems to have been entirely overlooked. His only condemnation has been due to petty thieving from a poorly designed cache. Give him a chance and put him back where he belongs!

GOAT

For several years in my early days of hunting it was my ambition to secure a Rocky Mountain goat, and finally my desire was accomplished. I was following the tracks of a ram one day while hunting in the Lillooet, B. C., district, when I suddenly spotted a goat. All ambition for the ram disappeared, and nothing would do but that I go after that goat.

Three old Billys

My guide, an Indian, was greatly disgusted, and it is needless to say that I never came within shooting distance of that goat. I became obsessed with the desire to secure a goat and I was confident that I never would be successful; but finally, while traveling with the pack train, a goat was located on a far distant mountain. The day was dull and cloudy, with snow in the air. Our head guide, Bill Manson, and I went off for the goat after having given explicit instructions where the outfit was to camp.

After a long tramp and a good stiff climb we came up to the level of the goat, and I despatched it without much difficulty. Coming down that ice-clad peak was not such a simple matter, especially as I was wearing a new idea in shoes with rubber soles. We finally made the valley and forded the creek, and then came our climb to a high basin where we hoped to find camp. The wind was now a gale and the swirling snow heavier. Of course we were bucking the wind and snow, as that seems to be the regular thing. At last the basin was reached, and also the spot where we hoped to find camp. The storm had become a blizzard and we could hardly see more than a few feet ahead. We wandered about, Bill in one direction and I in another, trying to locate camp but without success. I was sure I could hear the horse bell, but Bill seemed to think I was going nutty. We had about given up the idea of locating camp when off in the distance on the skyline stood the kitchen horse. It took but a short time to locate camp after that and I can assure you it looked good to me.

Later on the same trip, my friend Pop and I got into a bunch of goat. A battle ensued, and it was not until we had five down before we came to our senses. It was within our license as we were entitled to three each.

In the Cassiar I had more time to study the goat in his environment, and at the same time began to realize that he was pretty tame sport. All one needs is good legs and wind to climb to his haunts. The actual stalking is easy, and likewise the shooting, as I found very little difficulty in coming within fifty to seventy-five yards for the shot.

I had one strikingly different experience in the Cassiar. Having secured my rams on that trip, consisting of one Stone and two Fannin, in three shots, I had reason for feeling quite elated especially as two of the rams were running when I shot them. We saw an old Billy Goat away up a fine valley, with wind coming down strongly towards us. It was a cinch, as he was lying in an easy position to approach with plenty of cover.

But the well laid plans of mice and men often go astray, and so it was in this case. When we were within three to four hundred yards of that goat the wind changed and there was nothing to do but start shooting. The first shot was very low, the second slightly high, but the third found a spot directly behind the shoulder. If I had stopped at that I think the goat would shortly have laid down, and the rest would have been easy. Not satisfied I let go another that hit amidships and electrified the goat. He started off and I continued to shoot until he dodged behind some rocks. The day was young, and it had all seemed so easy that I could not realize how I had put myself in such a jackpot. Well, I started to run across the rocks, and whenever I saw the goat I would shoot. Such methods are not conducive to good shooting, but I did get one home every now and again, and though the goat had slowed perceptibly, he nevertheless continued to climb, with me after him. Just as he reached the top and was trying to pull himself over I placed another shot that should have finished him. He hung for a few seconds, almost toppled, but with an extreme effort pulled himself over the top. I used twenty-one shots, all the cartridges I had with me, on that goat. There were many in him, but none despatched him. Dennis finally succeeded by sticking him in the neck.

It was nearly eleven o'clock before we reached camp that night. It was some mush we had to make, and through a section that was supposed to be thickly infested with grizzly bear. My cartridges were all gone but we never saw a sign of Mr. Bear, so all was well. It was a fine Billy, with horns nearly eleven inches long, but with all of that I sheepishly recounted my experience even unto the twenty-first cartridge. I soon discovered that to stalk a goat was quite a simple proposition and required purely patience and endurance.

I secured other goats on my trips to the Cassiar, and one especially comes to my mind. We broke camp one morning and Dennis and I left the outfit intending to hunt and catch up in time to help make camp. I had already secured one goat on the trip through the insistence of Dennis that I must have at least one. The head was fair, over ten inches, but not unusual. The day we started for the head of the Iskut it was our hope that possibly I might have the good fortune to see a grizzly bear. We were thoroughly scouring all the hillsides with our glasses as we traveled on. It turned out to be the banner day of any and all of my hunting days. We located sheep, ewes, lambs, and many goats, but no bear. Suddenly Dennis broke in with "I see big goat, more big than I see before." I looked over the white speck which was quite some distance off, and was not able to make out much but that the goat was pretty large. "I don't want him Dennis," was my reply. Dennis looked more intently and then came, "Mr. Beach, he kill record goat; I never see such big goat."

To satisfy Dennis I drifted over nearer the Billy and at last my glasses were able to pick up the head. At once I came to life as I realized even at that distance I had never seen anything like it before. The stalk did not even become interesting; we were on top of the ridge and it was simply walking possibly two miles until I came within shooting distance. The old Billy was on a ledge across a canyon from where we were, and standing broadside, sublime in his belief that he was safe from all intruders. As I stepped out in the open he looked stupidly at me, and just then a shot to the heart finished his mountain climbing for evermore. He sank slowly to the ledge with hardly a tremor, while Dennis and I were trying to discover how we would be able to reach him. We were optimistic for with the last kick he succeeded in throwing himself off the ledge. I saw him strike on a rock several hundred feet below, then bounce off that and land on a slide down which he rolled until he came to another drop, over which he went, and then all sight of him was lost. I looked down that canyon with my glasses and decided it was useless to climb down as I was sure his head would be completely demolished. We ate our lunch, I bemoaning the fate of losing that great goat head.

Suddenly Dennis got up and said, "Me go down and see, mebbe head not broke." I was skeptical, and laughed at Dennis; but nevertheless he started down the steep side of the canyon. Time lengthened, the afternoon began to wane, but no Dennis until at last I feared something had happened to him. I went to the edge and bellowed at the top of my lungs, "Oh, Dennis, you all right?" and then listened. An answer came, and not far distant, "Me come." Even after that it was sometime before I spotted Dennis, carefully climbing up with the head on his back. As soon as he came closer he yelled up, "Him all right, wait you see." At last making the final climb he dropped the head at my feet saying, "Where your measure?" I already had my tape in hand and stretched it over the horns to find that they measured 11⅞ inches and 6⅝ inches in circumference at the base. The head was hardly damaged, a little scratched, and the fine points gone possibly less than a quarter of an inch. I realized it was somewhere near a world's record. Dennis said the body was badly crushed but it was the largest goat he had ever seen and thought it would weigh over three hundred pounds, but I fear this was optimistic.

We picked up the tracks of the pack train and caught up with them in time to finish making camp. Off again before supper, and that very evening I secured the large brown bear and my 63½-inch moose that I have already described. We were back in camp for supper shortly before eleven o'clock, and had great comfort in relating the capture of the bear and moose. As Mrs. Beach was along with me I thought I would string it out and so only told of the bear. Ned Brooks and

Sammy, the Indians, listened intently and then Ned said, "We see you kill bear but what you kill with other two shot?" The whole truth then came out and we had a great party that night. As I have said before it was my "Banner Day."

The year I was in Alberta with Jim Simpson, after having secured my specimen of *Ovis canadensis*, I was traveling the high ridges hoping to locate an elusive grizzly when suddenly we bumped into three Billy Goats about a hundred yards below us. Jim wanted me to shoot, but no, I didn't want one. They were all looking up at us, and first one rose and jumped out of sight, and then the second. Jim was making rather insulting remarks about my fearing that I couldn't hit him. The third and last one was up and about to go, but just at that second Jim rubbed me too far. As he jumped I let him have it, and I was sure the shot had gone true. We found the Billy about thirty yards below, stone dead. The goat, though a good-sized one, was small in comparison to the Cassiar goats; I doubt if he would weigh over a hundred and fifty pounds. The horns were 9¾ inches long and had a fair base. I would grade them about the same as the goats secured in the Lillooet district.

The year I went into the head of the White River, Alaska, I promised Dr. Nelson that I would secure a specimen of goat for him from Pyramid Mountain which rises up in about the center of the Nizina Glacier. Our experience in securing this specimen was one of the most miserable I have ever had. We made camp on the edge of the glacier on silt, and packed in tent poles and firewood. The weather was perfect the first day and we were able to secure a fine specimen of Billy Goat.

It was one of the largest-bodied goats I ever examined; I estimated him at three hundred pounds. Whether it was larger than my big Cassiar goat I cannot say as I did not see the carcass of that goat. From my observation of the Cassiar goat before I shot I would say the Nizina Billy was as large, if not larger, in body. The head was nothing remarkable, for, as I recall, it did not go over 9½ inches but was very stubby and heavy at the base. I looked over a number on Pyramid Mountain but none seemed to have large horns though they were very heavy in body. We went up again the second day as I wanted to secure a Nanny and kid, but the rain started and for four days I don't think I have ever seen rain come down harder. Our camp became untenable, the silt was a quagmire and worked up through the ground cloths of our tents and made everyone most uncomfortable. We gave out of firewood so Andy Taylor and Bill Graham went up the Nizina Glacier where there was an abandoned roadhouse on the ice which had been a hustling hostelry during the Shushanna stampede. They pulled down some of the logs from the house and hauled them into camp tied with a lasso to the horn of their saddle. My patience was exhausted at the end of the fourth day, and though the storm had not yet finished we pulled across the Nizina, never to return.

The hunting of goats did not appeal to me after I had gained some experience in it. They are a simple, foolish animal, and when they reach a high, rough, rocky spot they feel safe in their fastness. They are tough and sometimes hard to kill. In several cases I have had to shoot seven to eight times before they reached the end; it seemed as if they had no feeling after the first shot and could continue to travel even though hit several times in vital spots. I have also had goats throw themselves off high cliffs after they had been hit. One instance in the Cassiar when I had mortally wounded a Billy over a canyon on the Nahalin River, he attempted to drag himself to the canyon edge and even though I got between him and the canyon and poured lead into him, he kept dragging along and forced me to step to one side as he made his final lunge and went over the cliff. The goats of the north are greater in body and in horns than in any of the other districts, and I think the finest of all can be secured in the Cassiar.

CHAPTER X.

ON CONSERVATION OF BIG GAME

As a lad I found game aplenty. Then, it was kill anything in sight and as much as one could or cared to. The word conservation to the best of my knowledge was not used to cover game. I recall as a boy hearing that the buffalo herds were being depleted, but no one gave it serious consideration until too late. In later life, as I saw game disappearing, I began to realize that something must be done. By this time conservation had become a most important activity amongst sportsmen and others interested in the continuation of wild life. So I joined actively in the ranks of conservation where I have worked earnestly since.

My thoughts on conservation all have been along the lines that game should be conserved so that those who follow may go out into the wilds and ramble over the snow-bound peaks in quest of game as successfully as I have. Because I have reached the stage where killing no longer thrills is no reason why I should oppose others having my experiences.

From my viewpoint game animals were created for other wild animals to feed upon. Very few, if any, ever die a natural death even before the advent of man and the high-powered rifle. Conservation! I wonder if that covers what we are really trying to attain. I realize there are many so-called conservationists who would prefer to have the sheep, caribou, moose and deer killed off by wolves and mountain lions than to have them hunted and killed by man.

At times I have visited places which ten to twelve years before had been alive with game, only to find them almost bare of wild life. Many conservation laws passed with careful consideration have failed after years of operating to stop the reduction of the game herds. I have traveled to parts of Alaska that could be reached only after many days of hard, tiresome labor and discovered wonderful garden spots teeming with game. These same places are now reached in two or three hours by airships without discomfort. Is this fair to our fast disappearing game? Men who would never consider toiling up a swift, treacherous river for days on end would jump at the chance of a short air trip to reach virgin game country.

Why is it that in this country of ours, with its vast ranges and every opportunity for increasing its game the supply is slipping—with the time not far distant when our game will be a thing of the past? In the first place, we pass many and complicated laws, and then forget to furnish the means of enforcing them. We trust to the good faith of the man with the rifle. I wonder if it is wise. In this country where laws are openly defied and broken, how are we to expect that one class only, the sportsmen, will strictly adhere to the statutes? At that I believe they come nearer to it than any other class. We know what has happened in Wyoming with the antelope. Could anything be more vicious than rounding up these poor animals with automobiles and then slaughtering them? Does this come under the head of sport? Are we on the right track? Aren't we aiming for an ideal that is impossible?

In 1929 I visited a friend in Scotland who had leased a grouse moor. This was an old moor that had been shot over for hundreds of years. In three weeks' shooting we killed over 2,500 birds. "Slaughterers" I can hear our died-in-the-wool conservationists proclaim. But think! This has been going on annually for several hundreds of years. The adjoining moor is one of the oldest in Scotland and belonged to the Royal Stuarts. The new part of the castle was built in the fifteenth century, and there has been shooting there every year with the day bag the equivalent of today's.

I had several talks with the gamekeeper during which I questioned him as to how he decided the number of grouse which should be killed each season. He impressed upon me the necessity of killing down the grouse so that too many would not be left over for the breeding season. They know by experience that if too many birds are left over the net of the next year's crop will be small, as disease is likely to break out; and this also holds good with rabbits. In our country we strive to build up great quantities of a species, say ptarmigan and rabbits, only to have them almost wiped out by disease.

In Scotland vermin of all kinds is annihilated, and all hawks are considered dangerous and ruthlessly destroyed. The Scotch gamekeeper works and worries to find ways and means of increasing the quantity of his game. The hunting license in Scotland is a simple piece of paper stating that you are entitled to shoot. There is no limit on any species. Game of all kinds may be purchased at every butcher shop in London or any town outside when in season. Bear in mind that shooting in England and Scotland has been going on for centuries and there is still quantities of it. There is one big difference on the other side, and that is that law is strictly obeyed. Of course there are poachers but they do not get very far and are quickly found out.

Why don't we in this country go into the business of increasing the quantities of game for the purpose of hunting and shooting them? If we imported a few of those old Scotch gamekeepers and put them in charge of the Wyoming antelope herd with the power they have in Scotland, there would be shooting for all the rest of time.

After the grouse shooting I went further north to stalk stags, as it is called there. I found that the same conditions prevailed. Those deer were watched, and the herds kept at the proper breeding strength. All old stags were killed, and likewise dry does and any small or deformed specimens. Here again I found that a scientific study was made to increase the deer herds to the maximum for the feeding grounds. I have been told that you can't do the same in this country, for on the other side the game is all on private preserves, while we have open hunting country. It will come to the same thing here unless the people wake up and make efforts to increase the game supply in proportion to the increase of hunters.

Very nearly every type of bird has been raised in captivity. The Bob White quail is now being successfully raised. The Wild Turkey is another species that patience and science has saved from extinction. Many species of wild ducks have also been hatched and reared in captivity. The states and the government have fish hatcheries, and young trout and salmon are put out in various streams.

Why should not a united effort be made throughout the country to raise in captivity for restocking purposes the various species of our game birds? Let us stop harping about reducing the bag limits and all put our shoulders to the wheel in the endeavor to raise sufficient money, first for enforcement of the game laws, and second for establishment of game farms throughout the country to produce necessary birds for restocking. Create greater game reservations for the protection of our quadrupeds. Let us take as our platform, "We want more shooting," and then get busy, and with brains and science accomplish it. There has not been a solitary species that has faced extinction that could not have been saved if we had only gone about it with brains and the expenditure of money. Look at the Buffalo! Play the game fairly, and exert our energies towards more game and more shooting. Import a few Scotch gamekeepers!